GEMS AND GEM MATERIALS

PLATE I

First row: 1, sapphire, Burma; 2, 3, sapphire, Ceylon; 4, sapphire, Australia.
Second row: 1, star sapphire, Ceylon; 2, 3, yellow sapphire, Ceylon; 4, star ruby,. Ceylon.
Third row: 1, 3, rubies, Ceylon; 2, ruby, Burma; 4, chrysoberyl cat's-eye (cymophane), Brazil.
Fourth row: 1, chrysoberyl, Ceylon; 2, chrysoberyl, Brazil; 3, 4, alexandrite, Ural Mountains, in daylight and in artificial light, respectively.
Fifth row: 1, red spinel, Burma; 2, red spinel, Ceylon; 3, garnet, (almandite), India; 4, garnet (pyrope), Africa.

GEMS AND
GEM MATERIALS

By EDWARD HENRY KRAUS
Professor Emeritus of Crystallography and Mineralogy and
Dean Emeritus of the College of Literature, Science, and
the Arts, University of Michigan

And CHESTER BAKER SLAWSON
Professor of Mineralogy, University of Michigan

FIFTH EDITION

McGRAW-HILL BOOK COMPANY, INC.
NEW YORK AND LONDON
1947

GEMS AND GEM MATERIALS

XIII
35361

PREFACE TO THE FIFTH EDITION

During the last three decades the general public has become increasingly gem conscious. There has also been a distinct trend toward the use of gems in industry—a trend which may be aptly expressed as from "luxury to utility." This trend was accelerated by the demands of production during the Second World War, requiring a great increase in the use of industrial diamonds, synthetic rubies and sapphires, and the rock crystal variety of quartz. Although dealers in gems and prospective purchasers are today generally much better informed than formerly concerning the properties, identification, and uses of gems, the need for authoritative information persists. The reception accorded the book since it first appeared in 1925 has been very gratifying.

As it was necessary to introduce many changes and additions, the book has been entirely reset. In Part I, the chapters on crystal forms, physical properties, optical properties, the cutting and polishing of gems, and manufactured gems have been expanded. There is a new, concise, and fully illustrated chapter on crystal structure and X-ray methods. In Part II, all of the descriptions of the minerals have been revised, and five new ones added. The optical constants of the transparent minerals and substances are given in greater detail. In Part III, some of the tables have been expanded. A selected bibliography has been added.

In the preparation of the various editions, helpful suggestions, information, and permission to use illustrations have been received from various sources, especially from Messrs. Henri Polak, Sal Asscher, and Asscher and Company, Amsterdam, Holland; Messrs. E. G. Sandmeier, Locarno, and J. Telecki, Biel, Switzerland; Professor F. Slavik, Praha, Czechoslovakia; Professor Reinhard Brauns, Bonn, Dr. W. Fr. Eppler and Mr. Herman Wild, Idar-Oberstein, and Dr. C. Plonait, Königsberg, Germany; Mr. P. Grodzinski, London, England; Messrs. Fera and Kadison, Dr. Sydney H. Ball, Messrs. Lazare, Leo, and George Kaplan, A. F. Seemann of the Linde Air Products Company, Inc., Stephen

Varni, Andries Meyer, L. H. Stern, and Miss Gwynne Richards, New York City; Mr. August Rassweiler, Chicago; Mr. B. W. St. Clair, West Lynn, Massachusetts; Messrs. Jack Levy and M. E. Vedder, Detroit; Mr. R. M. Shipley and the Gemological Institute of America, Los Angeles; the American Museum of Natural History; the *National Geographic* magazine.

For assistance in preparing photographs our thanks are due Mr. Marion V. Denny, Curator of Mineralogy, University of Michigan. The authors are also indebted to many friends and colleagues for their kindly interest in the book.

EDWARD HENRY KRAUS
CHESTER BAKER SLAWSON

ANN ARBOR, MICH.,
   August, 1947.

EXTRACT FROM THE
PREFACE TO THE FIRST EDITION

Man has always been keenly interested in minerals suitable
for personal adornment and ornamentation, but mineralogists
generally have made few attempts to give systematic instruction
in this phase of their science at our institutions of higher learn-
ing. The need for reliable information on the part of the lover
of and the dealer in gems and gem materials has increased greatly
in modern times. This is the result of: first, a more general use
of natural gems and, second, the introduction upon the market
of large quantities of manufactured material of pleasing qualities.
To meet to some extent this demand for more knowledge of
precious stones, a regular course of lectures dealing with this
extremely fascinating branch of mineralogy was organized a dec-
ade ago at the University of Michigan. The course has annually
attracted a sizable group of students. The aim of the course is
to give information about some of those things in the admiration
and esteem of which credulity and sentiment, rather than accurate
knowledge, are generally the dominant factors. To make the
content of these lectures available to a wider circle, especially to
those engaged in the sale of gem materials, this text has been
prepared.

LIST OF COLOR PLATES

PLATE I   Frontispiece
PLATE II   Facing page 140
PLATE III   Facing page 206
PLATE IV   Facing page 218

CONTENTS

PAGE

PREFACE TO THE FIFTH EDITION v

EXTRACT FROM THE PREFACE TO THE FIRST EDITION vii

CHAPTER
    I. INTRODUCTION 1

PART I

    II. CRYSTAL FORMS 11
    III. PHYSICAL PROPERTIES 25
    IV. OPTICAL PROPERTIES 52
    V. CRYSTAL STRUCTURE AND X-RAY METHODS 81
    VI. CHEMICAL PROPERTIES. 89
    VII. FORMATION AND OCCURRENCE OF GEM MINERALS 91
    VIII. CUTTING AND POLISHING OF GEMS 99
    IX. THE NAMING OF GEMS 138
    X. MANUFACTURED GEMS 140
    XI. METALS USED FOR GEM MOUNTINGS 174

PART II

DESCRIPTION OF INDIVIDUAL GEMS 179

PART III

CLASSIFICATION OF GEM MATERIALS, ACCORDING TO VARIOUS PROPERTIES 287

TABLE
    I. CRYSTAL SYSTEM 287
    II. HARDNESS 288
    III. SPECIFIC GRAVITY. 289
    IV. COLOR. 290
    V. MISCELLANEOUS PHYSICAL PROPERTIES 292
    VI. OPTICAL CHARACTER 292
    VII. INDICES OF REFRACTION, OPTICAL CHARACTER, AND BIREFRINGENCE 293
    VIII. DISPERSION 295
    IX. PLEOCHROISM 295
    X. COMPOSITION 296
    XI. SUMMARY OF THE PROPERTIES OF THE GEM MATERIALS DESCRIBED
        IN THE TEXT, ARRANGED ALPHABETICALLY FOR READY REFERENCE 298

SELECTED BIBLIOGRAPHY 317

INDEX 321

Chapter I

INTRODUCTION

Man and Minerals.—From the earliest times down to the present, minerals have played an exceedingly important part in the development and progress of the human race. Primitive man made his first rude weapons and utensils from stone, such as flint and other compact varieties of quartz which were easily chipped into rough shape. These artifacts are largely the material upon which the archaeologist builds his concept of humankind in the early paleolithic age, called the old or rough-stone age. As man became more adept in the art of working stones into a required shape, he was able to smooth them and sometimes to give them a crude polish. With this knowledge he emerged into the neolithic age, that is, the new or smooth-stone age.

With the development of the art of recovering metals from their ores, man passed successively through the copper, bronze, and iron ages, in which minerals were even more important than in the stone age. Then came the discovery that coal would burn, and the coal age was inaugurated. As the result of the many significant developments and discoveries that have been made in science and technology during the last fifty years, which involve the greatly increased use of minerals and mineral products, we have passed through periods designated as the machine and motor ages.

Although at present we are emerging into a period of electronics, plastics, and sulfa drugs, the widespread use of piezo-electric oscillating quartz plates in industry and technology has led to the prediction that the world may soon become crystal-controlled. Some of these advances have been possible because of the many applications of such gem minerals as the diamond, ruby, sapphire, and quartz. The war has caused a notable shift in the use of these gems from luxury to utility, or from "tool to jewel." Man's dependency upon minerals is today greater than ever before.

1

When the study of the substances upon the earth was first begun, they were divided into three kingdoms: the animal, the vegetable, and the mineral kingdoms. All animal life of the land, sea, and air was referred to the first kingdom. With a more intensive study of that group of organisms, zoology was developed, and with it such allied sciences as anatomy, physiology, animal breeding, and paleozoology. The vegetable kingdom included all the plants, from fungi and lichens to trees and flowers. Botany and such related sciences as agriculture, forestry, and paleobotany are the outgrowth of study of the vegetable kingdom. The early naturalists assigned to the mineral kingdom the entire residue of naturally occurring substances: minerals, rocks, soils, air, seas, lakes, and rivers. From the investigation of this kingdom a large number of modern sciences have developed, including mineralogy, geology, chemistry, physics, meteorology, and oceanography.

Gems and Precious Stones.—The role that minerals and metals have played in the progress of civilization has just been briefly discussed. Besides their employment in the manufacture of articles essential to the comfort and welfare of man, minerals have long been used, on account of their beauty, for personal adornment. Minerals especially suited to that purpose are known as *gems* or *precious stones*. The cutting and carving of gems was probably first carried on in Babylonia, several thousand years before the birth of Christ. In those times and until quite recently engraved gems were much used as seals. The medicinal and magical powers which were generally ascribed to gems in former days added to their popularity.[1] Now gems are worn primarily because of their beauty.

Although minerals which are used for gem purposes must be appropriately fashioned by the gem cutter, their various inherent properties are generally unchanged. For example, the diamond which is cut and sold as a gem has not been altered in any respect, except as to shape. This is in marked contrast to most of the materials in common use. Thus, metallic iron, lead, and tin are obtained by means of various metallurgical processes from ores which bear little or no resemblance to these metals.

[1] See Kunz, G. F., "The Curious Lore of Precious Stones" and "Magic of Jewels and Charms."

Definition of a Mineral.—Since gems are minerals, it is well to state the meaning of the term *mineral*. A mineral may be defined as *a substance occurring in nature with a characteristic chemical composition, and usually possessing a definite crystalline structure, which is sometimes expressed in external geometrical forms or outlines.* Many of the artificially prepared compounds of the laboratory correspond to naturally occurring minerals. For example, aluminum oxide, Al_2O_3, occurs in nature as the mineral corundum of which the ruby and sapphire are gem varieties. It is now produced in the laboratory in large quantities and is used in place of natural rubies and sapphires. Such artificial products are called *synthetic minerals*. Some varieties of synthetic minerals are well adapted for gem purposes and are termed *synthetic gems* (p. 146).

The composition of a mineral is nearly constant so that a specific chemical formula may be assigned to it, for example, SiO_2, silicon dioxide, for quartz. Owing to the presence of impurities variations in the chemical composition are often observed. The replacement of an element by another closely related to it also causes variation in the chemical composition; see the garnet group (p. 208).

The phrase "usually possessing a definite crystalline structure" means that the structural units of a mineral, which are atoms or groups of atoms, are generally arranged in an orderly and definite way, characteristic of the particular mineral. Most gem minerals as found in nature exhibit external geometrical forms or outlines. These forms are known as crystals, and they are more fully discussed in Chapter II. The diamond, ruby, sapphire, and emerald usually occur as crystals (Fig. 1). Opal and amber are gem minerals which do not possess a crystalline structure and hence are not found as crystals but rather as compact, amorphous masses (Fig. 2).

In some definitions of a mineral the term *inorganic* is incorporated, in order to restrict the use of the term *mineral* to substances which are not the result of organic processes. Such definitions would exclude from consideration as true minerals pearls, amber, coral, and jet, which are discussed in this text.

Qualifications of Gem Minerals.—Minerals, in order to be suitable for use as gems, must possess as many as possible of the following qualifications: (1) *beauty*, (2) *durability*, (3) *rarity*, (4) *fashion*, and (5) *portability*.   Rarely are all these qualifications possessed by a single gem.   The diamond, however, has each of these properties to a marked degree and, accordingly, is the most generally esteemed gem.

1. *Beauty.*—To be used as a gem, a mineral must possess to a large degree this primary qualification.   Beauty in a gem depends upon its transparency, brilliancy, luster, fire, and color.   These

Fig. 1.   Fig. 2.

Fig. 1.—Diamond crystals, enlarged.   (*Courtesy of Cranbrook Institute of Science.*)

Fig. 2.—Opal.   (*Photograph by H. C. Dake.*)

properties are defined and discussed in Chapter III.   A colored diamond is unique among gems in having all these desirable qualities.   Colorless diamonds fall short only because they lack color. Rubies and emeralds have very desirable colors, but their brilliancy and fire are not exceptional.   The opal is attractive mainly because of its play of colors.   Turquois makes its appeal by color alone, for it is opaque.   Many other illustrations might be given. Although many of the foregoing properties are possessed to some degree by gem minerals as they are found in nature, these properties are greatly improved by cutting and polishing.   The beauty of gems and, therefore, the value are much enhanced by the gem cutter (p. 99) and by special methods of treatment (p. 140).

2. *Durability.*—Some beautiful minerals are so soft that they can be easily scratched, and hence quickly lose their attractiveness.

That is, they lack durability. Such minerals can, however, be used to advantage in brooches or pins, where they are not so much exposed to abrasion as when mounted in rings. The satin spar variety of the mineral gypsum, which has an attractive sheen and silky luster, is a good example of a mineral of this kind (p. 257). In order to wear well and retain its attractiveness a gem stone should be harder than the dust particles in the air. For this reason the most valuable stones are those which are decidedly harder than quartz: diamond, ruby, sapphire, and emerald. Aside from hardness, the tenacity of a mineral is an important factor in the durability of a gem. Thus some relatively soft minerals which are tenacious or "tough" possess durability to a marked degree. Jade is an excellent example of a mineral which is not very hard but extremely tough. Jade, therefore, wears well as a gem. The durability of a gem is determined by its various physical properties. These are discussed on pages 26 to 33.

3. *Rarity.*—This is a valued attribute in gems. It is natural to esteem most highly things which are scarce, even though they may not be superior in their intrinsic qualities to many commoner substances. On this account some gems which are beautiful and durable but not rare make little appeal. Garnets are an illustration. Though often very attractive, they are generally worth little more than the cost of cutting. The common mineral beryl occurs in many colors—blue-green, golden-yellow, pink, and emerald-green. The green variety known as emerald is the rarest and most valuable, even though it is scarcely more beautiful than some of the others.

4. *Fashion.*—Another factor in determining the use of a mineral for gem purposes is fashion or vogue. The effect of fashion upon the value of gems is enormous. Some rather unimportant mineral may become popular temporarily as a gem because it is worn by royalty or leaders of fashion. Color greatly influences popularity; thus, red, blue, and green stones have always possessed greater popular appeal than yellow gems. Certain gems are invariably fashionable. This is especially true of the diamond, ruby, sapphire, and emerald. Then, too, a number of gems are popular locally in the district in which they occur. This constitutes another phase of the influence of fashion on the wearing of gems. Examples of these locally used gems are chlorastrolite, thomsonite,

and datolite in northern Michigan; tourmaline and apatite in Maine; malachite in Russia.

5. *Portability.*—Because gemstones are usually small in size, they can be easily transported or carried from place to place, even in considerable quantities. This is especially true of such valuable gems as the diamond, ruby, sapphire, and emerald. During the Second World War many persons living in countries which were overrun by the Nazis were obliged to emigrate. Because of the easy portability of gems, these persons frequently were able to carry stones of considerable value with them and by selling them to support themselves for a period as well as to supply markets which had become depleted. Although this easy portability is generally of very material advantage to the owner or dealer, it naturally requires that great caution be exercised to guard against loss and theft, especially in the case of the very precious stones.

Since small quantities of gems commonly represent large sums of money and because they are easily transported, gemstones have for centuries been considered a desirable form of investment. This has been especially true in periods of economic and political instability.

The interrelationship of these five qualities—*beauty, durability, rarity, fashion,* and *portability*—is extremely important with respect to the use of gemstones, to demand and supply and, consequently, in determining the price at which gemstones are sold. Thus, demand is largely dependent upon current fashion, while supply is controlled by rarity.

Number of Gem Minerals.—During the last half century the number of minerals used for gem purposes has increased considerably. The newer stones include beautiful but previously unknown or rare varieties of well-known minerals as well as some newly discovered ones. A good example of the first group is kunzite, the rose-colored, transparent variety of spodumene, a mineral which is usually white and opaque (p. 265). The beautiful blue zircon, the result of heat treatment (p. 143), which has become very popular, is a good example of the increased use of a previously uncommon variety. Among the minerals discovered during the last fifty years, the sapphire-blue benitoite has found a rather limited use as a gem. Summary descriptions of the gem minerals described in this book are given on pages 298 to 315.

Mineralogy and Gems.—That branch of mineralogy which deals with the properties, occurrence, and adaptation of those minerals which are used for personal adornment or ornamentation is called *gemmology*. On account of the remarkable advances which have been made in the manufacture of artificial and imitation gems, gemmology should include a discussion of such material. There is a tendency at present to use the simpler spelling of this term, *gemology*.

A knowledge of the science of mineralogy is necessary for the fullest appreciation and understanding of gems and their properties. For example, mineralogy teaches that both the ruby and the sapphire are varieties of one mineral, corundum; that the emerald differs from aquamarine only in color; and, further, that the trade names applied to gems are often not unintentionally deceptive. Moreover, some knowledge of mineralogy and chemistry is necessary for the understanding of the processes by which artificial gems are manufactured. Since the various physical and optical properties are extremely important in gemstones, especially in their identification, a mastery of the fundamentals of physics is also essential.

In recent years the general public and the dealer have been eager to obtain authoritative information concerning gems and gem materials, that is, to become versed in the scientific phases of gemmology. The various gemmological and mineralogical societies in this country and abroad have been very influential in stimulating this interest.

The first part of this text consists of an elementary presentation of those portions of mineralogy cognate to the study of gems and gem materials. It is designed to furnish the reader with the general scientific background necessary to a full understanding of the second part of the text, in which the individual gem minerals are described. The third part consists of tables which classify gems according to their various properties.

PART I

Chapter II

CRYSTAL FORMS

Crystals.—When a mineral, or a chemical substance prepared by man, is bounded by regularly arranged natural plane surfaces, resulting in a definite geometrical form or outline, the substance is said to be a *crystal*. Gem minerals occur almost universally in well-formed crystals. For that reason an elementary study of crystallography is of value to those interested in gems, especially since a knowledge of the more common crystal forms is often of marked assistance in the identification of uncut material. Moreover, the efficient cutting of gems is possible only if their crystallographic properties are well understood.

Owing to the great advance in our knowledge of crystals and the crystalline state during the last half century, there has been a marked change in the conception of a crystal. It is now well established that the form and the natural plane surfaces of a crystal are the outward or external expression of a definite internal orderly arrangement of the atoms which make up the crystal. In non-crystalline solids, such as glass and opal, the internal arrangement is not orderly. These solids are devoid of natural plane surfaces. They occur in irregular masses and are called *amorphous*. In crystallized substances the various properties generally vary with direction, while in amorphous solids the individual properties are the same in all directions. In the study of crystal structure, that is, of the internal arrangement of the atoms, X-ray methods are of the utmost importance.

While the general public may continue to consider a *crystal as a solid bounded by natural plane surfaces*, the scientist now defines a crystal as a *solid whose component atoms are arranged in a definite three-dimensional pattern*. See Chapter V for a discussion of crystal structure and X-ray methods.

Constancy of Crystal Angles.—Practically every mineral is found in crystals of a definite and unique type. Measured at the same temperature, similar angles on crystals of the same substance remain constant regardless of the size or shape of the crystal. That is, while the sizes and shapes of the faces of a crystal may have been distorted by irregular growth, the angles between given faces are constant for all crystals of the same substance. Distorted crystals are discussed on page 21.

Size of Crystals.—Crystals vary in size from those of microscopic dimensions to those weighing many tons. Crystals of spodumene

FIG. 3.—Gigantic crystals of spodumene, Etta mine, near Keystone, South Dakota. (*Photograph by South Dakota School of Mines.*)

have been found at the Etta mine, near Keystone, South Dakota, 36 to 47 feet long, and weighing about 37 tons (Fig. 3). Beryl crystals have been obtained from Acworth and Grafton, New Hampshire, which weighed several tons.

Crystal Systems.—According to the internal arrangement of the component atoms, that is, in terms of the fundamental space-lattices, as determined by X-ray analysis, all crystals are readily classified into six groups, called *crystal systems*. This classification can also be made in terms of the lengths and angular relationships of imaginary lines, passed through the center of a crystal, called the *crystal axes*. The elementary study of crystals is based upon the crystal axes, rather than upon space-lattices (p. 81).

1. *Cubic System.*—Crystals in this system have three equal and perpendicular axes. Figure 4 represents a crystal, with it axes, of

the cubic system.   Diamond, spinel, and garnet belong to this system.

2. *Hexagonal System.*—Hexagonal crystals have four axes. Three of these are equal, horizontal, and intersect at 60 degrees (Fig. 5).   The fourth axis is perpendicular to these and therefore

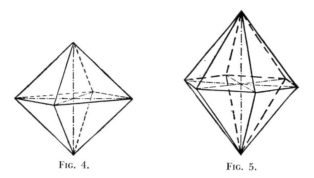

FIG. 4.   FIG. 5.

vertical.   It is longer or shorter than the horizontal axes.   Beryl, corundum, quartz, and tourmaline are all representatives of the hexagonal system.   Emerald and aquamarine are gem varieties of beryl; ruby and sapphire, of corundum.

3. *Tetragonal System.*—Crystals of this system have three axes, which intersect at right angles.   The vertical axis is longer or

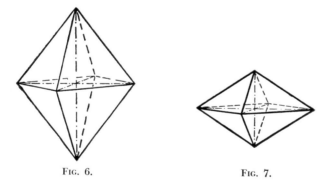

FIG. 6.   FIG. 7.

shorter than the two equal horizontal axes (Fig. 6).   Zircon and vesuvianite are tetragonal gem minerals.

4. *Orthorhombic System.*—This system is characterized by three perpendicular and unequal axes (Fig. 7).   To this system belong topaz and olivine.

5. *Monoclinic System.*—The three axes of this system are un-equal. Two intersect at an oblique angle, and the third is per-pendicular to them (Fig. 8). Epidote, spodumene, and titanite crystallize in the monoclinic system.

6. *Triclinic System.*—Triclinic crystals have three axes, all un-equal, and all inclined to each other (Fig. 9). To this system belong labradorite and some moonstones.

The classification of crystals into systems may also be made in terms of the elements of symmetry, that is, planes, axes, and

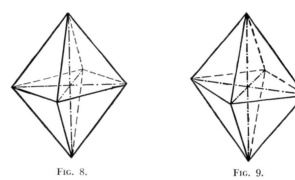

FIG. 8.   FIG. 9.

center of symmetry. Based upon symmetry the six crystal systems are subdivided into thirty-two classes of symmetry. Crystals with the highest type of symmetry, that is, those most symmetrically developed, are representative of the cubic system. Crystals with the lowest type of symmetry belong to the triclinic system.

Certain relationships between the systems may now be pointed out. The morphological classification of crystals into systems is by no means artificial. The optical properties form another natural basis for the classification. Both the crystal form and the optical characteristics depend upon the arrangement of the atoms which make up a crystal. The optical properties will be discussed later in more detail (p. 52), but it may be indicated here that by them, crystals may be divided into three groups: (1) cubic crystals; (2) hexagonal and tetragonal crystals; and (3) orthorhombic, mon-oclinic, and triclinic crystals.

Light passes through crystals of the cubic system without being resolved into two rays; that is, such substances are *singly refractive* (Fig. 10). They are also called optically *isotropic* because light travels through them with the same velocity in all directions. Amorphous substances, those which do not crystallize, are also singly refractive and isotropic.

All other substances are, in general, *doubly refractive;* that is, a ray of light, in passing through them, is resolved into two rays (Fig. 11). These crystals are optically *anisotropic,* for light travels through them with different velocities in different directions.

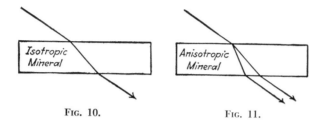

FIG. 10.   FIG. 11.

Hexagonal and tetragonal substances show, however, single refraction in one direction, parallel to the vertical axis. This isotropic direction is called the *optic axis.* Since crystals of these systems have only one such direction, they are called *uniaxial.*

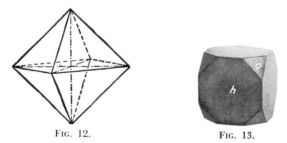

FIG. 12.   FIG. 13.

Substances crystallizing in the orthorhombic, monoclinic, and triclinic systems have two isotropic directions or optic axes, and are therefore called *biaxial.* Other distinctions serve to differentiate the systems within these groups. A tabular presentation of the classification of substances with respect to their optical properties may be found on page 64.

Crystal Forms.—All those faces of a crystal which intersect the several axes in the same way belong to a single *form,* which is an assemblage of corresponding faces. For instance, each face of an octahedron (Fig. 12) cuts all three crystal axes at the same distances from the center of the crystal. A crystal may consist of one form only or of two or more forms. The latter case is termed a *combination* of forms (Fig. 13): *h,* cube; *o,* octahedron (see cubic system below). The forms and combinations of forms which occur most frequently on gem minerals will now be considered.

Cubic System.—In the cubic system the following are the more common forms:

Cube or Hexahedron.—The cube has six square faces and is exactly like the geometrical cube (Fig. 14).[1]

Octahedron.—This form has eight faces, which are triangular when the octahedron is uncombined with other forms (Fig. 15).

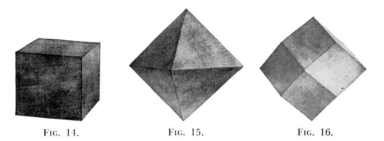

FIG. 14.   FIG. 15.   FIG. 16.

Dodecahedron.—This form has twelve diamond-shaped or rhombic faces (Fig. 16).

Tetragonal Trisoctahedron.—The apparently unwieldy name of this form is in reality an abbreviated definition of its character. The term *tetragonal,* from a Greek word meaning four-angled, indicates that the faces are four-sided, whereas the word *trisoctahedron* means that the form has three times eight or twenty-four faces (Fig. 17).

Tetrahedron.—This is a form with but four triangular faces. It is identical with the regular tetrahedron of geometry, which is the solid with the smallest possible number of faces (Fig. 18).

As indicated above, these forms may occur simultaneously upon a single crystal, which is then called a combination of forms. Figures 19, 20, and 21 illustrate combinations of the cubic forms: *h,* hexahedron; *o,* octahedron; *d,* dodecahedron; and *i,* tetragonal trisoctahedron. The combination illustrated by Fig. 19 is fre-

---

[1] The illustrations in this chapter are principally photographs of idealized wooden models of natural crystals.

quently observed on the diamond and spinel; that by Fig. 20, on the diamond, and by Fig. 21, on garnet.

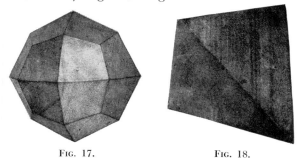

FIG. 17.   FIG. 18.

Hexagonal System.—The forms in the hexagonal system generally have faces in numbers which are multiples of six.

Hexagonal Prisms.—The prisms of this system may have either six or twelve faces arranged parallel to the vertical axis (Figs. 22

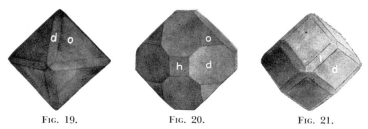

FIG. 19.   FIG. 20.   FIG. 21.

and 23). A prism alone cannot enclose space, but resembles an open tube. For this reason a prism is called an *open form.* Other forms must be present in combination with a prism.

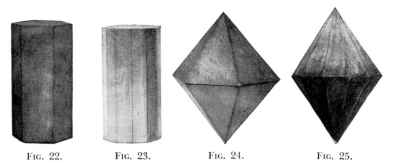

FIG. 22.   FIG. 23.   FIG. 24.   FIG. 25.

Hexagonal Bipyramids.—As the name indicates, these are forms which resemble two pyramids placed base to base. The complete forms have twelve or twenty-four faces (Figs. 24 and 25). Bipyramids enclose space, and are called *closed forms*.

Basal Pinacoid.—This is an open form, consisting of two parallel faces which are perpendicular to the vertical axis. In Figs. 22 and 23 the top and bottom faces constitute the basal pinacoid.

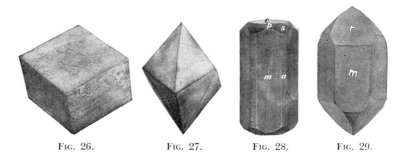

FIG. 26.   FIG. 27.   FIG. 28.   FIG. 29.

Rhombohedron.—The rhombohedron has six rhombic or diamond-shaped faces. It resembles a cube that has been compressed or elongated along an axis passing diagonally through its center (Fig. 26).

Scalenohedron.—This form is bounded by twelve faces which are scalene triangles—hence the name (Fig. 27). Both the rhombohedron and the scalenohedron are characterized by having equatorial edges which run alternately up and down.

Combinations of prisms (*a* and *m*), bipyramids (*p* and *s*), and the basal pinacoid (*c*) are frequently observed on beryl, as illustrated by Fig. 28. A combination of the rhombohedron (*r*) and prism (*m*) as it occurs on quartz is illustrated by Fig. 29.

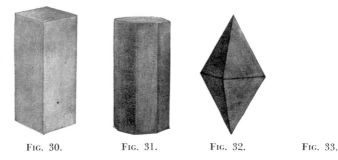

FIG. 30.   FIG. 31.   FIG. 32.   FIG. 33.

Tetragonal System.—The forms of this system are closely related to those of the hexagonal system.

Tetragonal Prisms.—The prisms have four or eight faces, and are parallel to the vertical axis (Figs. 30 and 31).

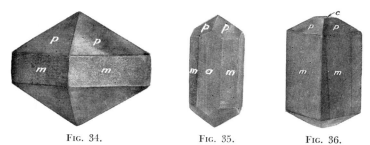

FIG. 34.   FIG. 35.   FIG. 36.

Tetragonal Bipyramids.—These forms are like hexagonal bipyramids, but have eight or sixteen faces, instead of twelve or twenty-four (Figs. 32 and 33).

Basal Pinacoid.—This form is similar to the pinacoid of the hexagonal system (top and bottom faces, Figs. 30 and 31).

Combinations of the foregoing forms are observed on crystals of zircon (Figs. 34 and 35) and vesuvianite (Fig. 36): prisms, *a* and *m;* bipyramid, *p;* basal pinacoid, *c*.

Orthorhombic, Monoclinic, and Triclinic Systems.—The crystal forms of these three systems are so much alike that they may be readily discussed together. The corresponding forms in these systems can perhaps be most easily distinguished by the number of faces they possess.

Prisms.—These are forms with faces parallel to the vertical axis but which intersect the other axes (Fig. 37).

FIG. 37.   FIG. 38.

Domes.—Domes are often called *horizontal prisms*. These forms are like prisms in shape, but are parallel to a horizontal rather than to a vertical axis (Fig. 38).

Bipyramids.—These forms are similar to the bipyramids previously described (Fig. 39), but may have fewer faces.

FIG. 39.   FIG. 40.

Pinacoids.—In these three systems a crystal may have as many as three sets of pinacoids, each set consisting of two parallel faces. Each face cuts one of the axes and is parallel to the other two. Figure 40 is a combination of the three pinacoid forms.

The following table shows the variations in the number of faces of the forms, as they occur in these three systems:

Form	Orthorhombic system	Monoclinic system	Triclinic system
Prism...............	4	4	2
Dome...............	4	2 or 4	2
Bipyramid...........	8	4	2
Pinacoid.............	2	2	2

In the triclinic system, owing to distinctive conditions, no form can have more than two similar and parallel faces.

FIG. 41.   FIG. 42.   FIG. 43.

Some combinations of forms in these systems are: Fig. 41, topaz, orthorhombic; Fig. 42, orthoclase, monoclinic; Fig. 43, albite, triclinic. Prisms are designated by the letters m, M, and l; domes, by y; bipyramids, by i, o, and u; pinacoids, by b and c.

Distorted Crystals.—Misshapen or distorted crystals are common. An ideally developed octahedron, as observed on the diamond, is illustrated by Fig. 44. The heavy outline in Fig. 45 shows a distorted octahedron, two parallel faces being very large. It is obvious that the interfacial angles have not been changed. Crystals of the diamond are frequently distorted in this manner (Fig. 46) and are known as *flats*. Figures 47 and 48 illustrate an-

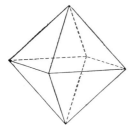

FIG. 44.—Ideal octahedron.   FIG. 45.—Octahedron distorted as a "flat."   FIG. 46.—Diamond "flat." (*Courtesy of Walter Schwartz.*)

other type of distorted octahedron. Large crystals are more apt to be distorted than small ones; compare Figs. 293, 310, and 317.

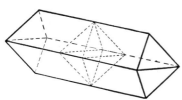

FIG. 47.—Elongated distorted octahedron.   FIG. 48.—Distorted octahedron of the diamond. (*Courtesy of M. L. Van Moppes and H. B. Wallace.*)

Compound Crystals.—Thus far crystals have been described as single individuals. Crystals consisting of several individuals may also occur. These are known as *compound crystals,* which may be of two types: *parallel groups* and *twin crystals*. In the diamond industry twin crystals are called *macles*. In a parallel group two or more crystals of the same substance have so intergrown that the crystallographic axes of one individual are parallel to those of the others (Fig. 49). Occasionally crystals of different substances may be grouped in this way.

FIG. 49.—Parallel group of quartz crystals.

In twin crystals the individuals have intergrown in a definite manner or, as it is termed, according to a definite law. Parallelism of the separate individuals is not essential. There are two types of twins: *contact twins* and *penetration twins*. As the name implies, contact twins are those in which two crystals are in contact one with another. The two parts of such a twin have grown side by side, and are so related that one part may be considered as having been rotated through 180 degrees about an axis known as the *twinning axis*. Figure 50 illustrates a contact twin commonly observed on spinel and the diamond. Penetration twins are those in which two individual crystals are so intergrown that they penetrate one another. The mineral staurolite well illustrates this type of twin (Fig. 51). Its twins often resemble crosses and are

FIG. 50.

FIG. 51.

sometimes called *fairy stones*. Reentrant angles are characteristic of twinned crystals.

In crystallography the word *twin* is used in a broad sense. A twin may consist of more than two individuals. This is the result of repeated twinning. *Cyclic* and *polysynthetic twins* are formed in this way (Figs. 52 and 53, respectively). Polysynthetic twinning frequently gives rise to characteristic fine, parallel lines, called *twinning striations,* on the surface of the specimen. These represent the boundaries between individual crystals. Twinning stria-

FIG. 52.—Cyclic twin of rutile.

FIG. 53.—Polysynthetic twin of albite.

tions can often be easily seen along the edges of some diamond crystals. In some instances, however, this type of twinning can be observed only in polarized light under the microscope. When pressure is applied to a crystal in a definite direction, *gliding* may be produced, causing a twinned structure.

Twinning in diamond crystals often causes great difficulty in cutting, because of the non-parallelism of the various portions of the crystal. Such diamond crystals are said to have *knots;* see page 29.

Pseudomorphs.—The term *pseudomorph* has the meaning "false form." When one mineral alters to another in such a way that

FIG. 54.—Petrified wood (one-third natural size). Clover Creek, Idaho.

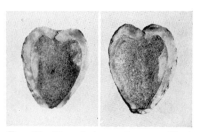

FIG. 55.—Two halves of an opalized shell. White Cliffs, Australia.

the crystal form of the original mineral is retained, the specimen is called a pseudomorph. A typical example is the alteration by oxidation and hydration of pyrite (FeS_2), cubic, to limonite

($Fe_2O_3.nH_2O$), amorphous. The limonite then has the external form of the pyrite crystals, but the inner crystalline structure of pyrite is entirely lacking. Thus limonite has assumed a false form. The variety of quartz known as *tiger's-eye*, a pseudomorph after crocidolite, is a common gem mineral (p. 223). Other cases of pseudomorphs are petrified wood in which the wood fiber has been replaced by quartz or opal (Fig. 54) and also silicified and opalized shells and fossils (Fig. 55). Some pseudomorphs are used as gem and decorative material.

Chapter III

PHYSICAL PROPERTIES

In this chapter those physical properties which are generally easily recognized will be defined and discussed. Optical properties, the determination of which involves the use of the polarizing microscope or other optical instruments, will be treated in the next chapter.

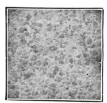

Fig. 56.—Marble.

Structure.—With respect to structure, minerals may be classified as follows:

Amorphous Minerals.—These have no definite structure or regular internal arrangement of atoms. Opal is the most important amorphous gem. Glass is another typical amorphous solid. The substances known as *colloids* and *gels* are amorphous. Opal is a gel.

Fig. 57.—Calcite (scalenohedron). Joplin, Missouri.

Cryptocrystalline.—Masses which appear to the unaided eye to be amorphous, but which are revealed by the microscope or by X-ray analysis to be crystalline, are called *cryptocrystalline.* Some forms of quartz, such as agate and flint, possess this structure.

Crystalline Aggregates.—These are solids which are composed of grains, each of which is readily visible and has a definite internal structure. The whole mass of a crystalline aggregate, however, shows no natural regular external form. Coarse marble illustrates this type of structure (Fig. 56).

Crystals and Crystal Aggregates.—In crystals the definite internal structure finds expression in the presence of natural plane surfaces which bound the substance (Fig. 57). A crystal aggregate is

25

a group of distinct crystals, partly intergrown (Fig. 58). When substances occur in well-developed crystals, their growth has been slower than that of crystalline aggregates. Crystals are therefore likely to be purer, more transparent, and of better color than crystalline aggregates. For this reason they are of greater value for use as gems than minerals with other structures.

FIG. 58.—Calcite.   Cumberland, England.

Cryptocrystalline substances, crystalline aggregates, crystals, and crystal aggregates are collectively known as *crystalloids*.

Many more or less self-explanatory terms are often used in describing the various types of aggregates and amorphous masses. These are of little importance here, since the minerals serviceable as gems usually occur in distinct crystals.

Hardness.—Hardness is defined as the resistance which a mineral offers to abrasion or scratching. The Mohs scale is commonly used as a measure of the hardness of minerals. It consists of ten minerals arranged in order of increasing hardness, as follows:

1. Talc.	6. Orthoclase (feldspar).
2. Gypsum.	7. Quartz.
3. Calcite.	8. Topaz.
4. Fluorite.	9. Corundum.
5. Apatite.	10. Diamond.

Frequently beryl, with a hardness of $7\frac{1}{2}$ to 8, is substituted for topaz, because of its greater abundance. The values assigned to the members of this scale show simply the *relative* and not the actual hardness. For example, the assigning of the hardness 8 to topaz and 4 to fluorite does not mean that topaz is merely twice as hard as fluorite. In fact, topaz is many times harder; see the table on page 30.

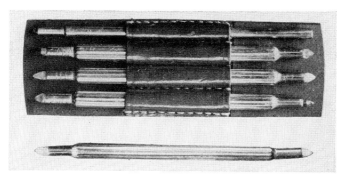

FIG. 59.—Hardness pencils or points.

To supplement the Mohs scale, the fingernail, a copper coin, a knife blade, a piece of glass, or a steel file may be used. They have the following values:

	HARDNESS
Fingernail	Up to $2\frac{1}{2}$
Copper coin	Up to 3
Knife blade	Up to $5\frac{1}{2}$
Window glass	$5\frac{1}{2}$
Steel file	6 to 7

The hardness of a substance is determined by finding which mineral in the Mohs scale will just scratch the material in question. If a mineral is scratched by quartz (7) and not by orthoclase (6), it is said to have a hardness of $6\frac{1}{2}$. Two substances with the same hardness will scratch each other equally well. Care should be taken to distinguish between an actual scratch and a chalk mark. The latter is the mark left on the harder mineral and consists of the powder of the mineral which is the softer. This powder is easily removed by rubbing the specimen with the finger.

The hardness of rough or cut gems is best determined by using *hardness pencils* or *points,* that is, holders with conical-shaped fragments of the test minerals mounted in the ends (Fig. 59). A set of four pencils in a leather case is shown in the figure. The seven test minerals used in this set are as follows: orthoclase, 6; quartz, 7; zircon, 7½; topaz, 8; chrysoberyl, 8½; corundum, 9; diamond, 10. Another convenient arrangement of hardness points is the *hardness wheel* (Fig. 60) with the following six test minerals: olivine, 6¾; quartz, 7; zircon, 7½; topaz, 8; chrysoberyl, 8½; corundum, 9. As is obvious, the pencil and the wheel permit of very easy manipulation.

In the determination of the approximate hardness considerable reliance can be placed upon the ease or difficulty with which a

Fig. 60.—Hardness wheel.

specimen is scratched, that is, whether the scratch is obtained readily or only with the exertion of considerable pressure. Moreover, the sharpness of the hardness point and the smoothness of the surface being tested are important factors.

Instead of using a set of hardness points some jewelers attempt to determine the approximate hardness by means of a very fine steel file. If the file "bites" the tested material, its hardness is below 7. The file will not bite stones harder than 7 but will slide over the edge being tested, often leaving a steel streak. Since many imitations, especially glass ones, have a hardness less than 7, while the really precious gems are much harder, the file can generally be used to distinguish between them.

Hardness is of the utmost importance, for durability, a cardinal virtue in gem minerals, is largely dependent upon it. It is also of great assistance in the identification of minerals. In determining the hardness of a gem the scratch should be as short as possible, perhaps ¹⁄₃₂ inch. On cut gems the scratch should never be made on the table or other prominently exposed facet, but rather near the equatorial edge of the stone, known as the *girdle* (p. 101). A small hand lens is frequently of service in detecting whether or not a gem has been scratched. A slight scratch on the girdle can be easily concealed by the setting of the stone.

Although the determination of hardness may be made rather easily, the careless use of hardness points on gems has often resulted in much damage to the stones. Hardness determinations should therefore be made with caution. In fact, cut gems may be very accurately and rapidly determined by means of other properties which can in no wise injure the stones, for example, specific gravity (p. 33), index of refraction, double refraction, and pleochroism (p. 56).

It might be inferred that the hardness of a substance is a constant quantity. This, however, is not correct, for the hardness varies with the crystallographic direction. Ordinarily the variation is so slight as not to be readily detected by the usual methods. But in some minerals this variation is quite marked. Cyanite, which occurs in elongated crystals, has a hardness of 4 to 5 parallel to the length of the crystals, whereas the value at right angles to the elongation is much higher—6 to 7.

The variation of hardness with direction is of the utmost importance in the cutting of the diamond. Failure fully to recognize this variation has led to many erroneous statements that diamonds from different localities show marked differences in hardness. The presence or absence of twinning in the crystal, that is, of knots (pp. 23 and 110), also greatly influences the ease or difficulty of cutting and hence the conclusions drawn as to hardness. It is well established that the hardness of the diamond is greater on surfaces parallel to the octahedron than on those parallel to faces of the cube or the rhombic dodecahedron (p. 119). Moreover, in the case of the diamond the hardness on the same surface varies with direction and the sense of direction. The apparent hardness of minerals is influenced by their brittleness and by the presence or absence of fractures or cleavages. These factors must be taken into consideration in fashioning them as gems.

The hardness of a mineral determines to a great extent its durability. One of the ever-present substances which tend to abrade gems and to dull the polish materially, and consequently the brilliancy and beauty of the stone, is dust, which may contain finely divided particles of feldspar and quartz. For this reason, in order to wear well and remain beautiful for any considerable length of time, a gem should have a hardness greater than that of quartz. The *precious* stones, diamond, ruby, sapphire, and emerald, are all decidedly harder than quartz. The softer stones are sometimes regarded as *semi-precious* (p. 179).

The hardness of metals and alloys is generally regarded as resistance to deformation and is determined by various indenting methods. These indenting methods cannot be used satisfactorily with minerals, since they are not easily deformed under pressure without rupturing.

Many attempts have been made to determine the hardness of minerals on a quantitative basis, using scratching, abrasion, grinding, and indenting methods. Because of the many factors involved, such as: (1) brittleness, (2) presence or absence of cleavages, fractures, or twinning, (3) variation of hardness with direction, which in most instances has been neglected, (4) differences in crystal structure, and (5) the use of non-comparable material by the various investigators, the results vary greatly. The following table clearly shows this lack of concordant results.

TABLE OF COMPARATIVE HARDNESS VALUES

	Mohs *	Pfaff †	Jaggar ‡	Rosiwal §	Knoop ¶ Peters Emerson
Corundum.............	9	1,000	1,000	1,000	1,000 ‖
Topaz.................	8	459	152	139	764.5
Quartz...............	7	254	40	117	486.2
Orthoclase............	6	191	25	32	342.4
Apatite...............	5	53.5	1.23	7.15	269
Fluorite..............	4	37.3	0.75	4.66	100
Calcite...............	3	15.3	0.26	4.49	82.6
Gypsum...............	2	12.03	0.04	2.42 **	19.6
Talc.................	1	—	—	1.1 ††	—

*†‡§¶ Scratching, abrasion, boring, grinding, indenting method, respectively.
‖ Alundum, synthetic corundum.
** Halite, rock salt.
†† Steatite.

The marked differences in results are further shown by the divergent determinations obtained by Rosiwal (grinding) and by Knoop, Peters, and Emerson (indenting) for the average hardness of the diamond as compared with that of corundum. According to Rosiwal the diamond is 90 times, while according to Knoop et al. it is 5 times, harder than corundum.

In the table given on page 288 gem minerals are arranged according to their hardness.

Cleavage.—Many minerals readily split or separate along definite planes. This property is called *cleavage*. It is frequently conspicuous and highly characteristic. A mineral can be cleaved either by striking it a properly directed blow or by pressing upon it in a definite direction with the edge of a knife blade. Cleavage takes place more readily parallel to planes with densely packed atoms, which consequently are more widely separated from one another. The cohesion forces between these widely spaced planes are weaker than in other directions. Figure 61 illustrates the distribution of the carbon atoms in the diamond; *A* and *B* are two of the four possible directions in which cleavage readily takes place.

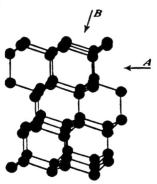

FIG. 61.—Model showing arrangement of carbon atoms in the diamond.

Cleavage is described by (1) indicating the crystal face parallel to which it takes place, (2) the ease with which it is obtained, and (3) the character of the surface which results. The planes along which the separation takes place are called *cleavage planes,* and the resultant surfaces are known as *cleavage faces.* These planes are parallel to possible crystal faces, for which they are named. For instance, the diamond and fluorite have cleavages parallel to the faces of an octahedron, and accordingly are said to possess *octahedral* cleavage (Fig. 62). Topaz cleaves easily parallel to the basal pinacoid, and its cleavage is called *basal.* Other important cleavages are the *cubical* and *rhombohedral.* The ease with which cleavages are obtained is indicated as *easy* and *difficult.* The character of the cleavage faces is described by such terms as *perfect, imperfect, distinct,* and *indistinct.*

The presence of cleavage is frequently to be recognized by cleavage cracks within a crystal or by the irregular character of the surfaces, which may be made up of a number of small, parallel, step-like cleavage planes.

Cleavage is a property of great importance in the cutting of gemstones. It is constantly employed, especially in the case of the diamond, to give the uncut material the proper form for efficient cutting and to remove flaws (see p. 111 for further reference to cleaving in the cutting of the diamond). In some instances a considerable blow is necessary to cleave a mineral; in others a sudden shock or even dropping it to the floor may be enough to cause cleavage cracks. Gemstones possessing easy cleavage must accordingly be handled cautiously when being cut or polished in order to avoid the development of cleavage cracks. Also in the setting of gems with easy cleavages great care must be exercised; for if the

FIG. 62.—Famous Cullinan diamond after being cleaved
parallel to face of octahedron (see Fig. 282).

pressure of the prongs is too great or unequally distributed, cracks are apt to be formed. Moreover, even if such stones are properly set they may be cracked when worn, especially in rings, when accidentally hit against a solid object.

Cleavage may sometimes be recognized by examining with a lens the gemstone near the prongs. If very minute portions have been broken off along the girdle by the pressure of the prongs, the resulting surface is very likely to show whatever type of cleavage the stone may possess. In this way one may distinguish between diamond, with its perfect octahedral cleavage, and glass imitations, which have no cleavage, but instead show a shell-like fracture.

Cleavage is independent of hardness and is possessed alike by minerals which are extremely soft and by those which are very hard. An easy cleavage may, however, influence the apparent hardness of a mineral by giving the impression that the mineral is softer than it actually is. As cleavage depends upon the internal structure, it may be observed only on those substances which occur in crystals or crystalline masses. Amorphous substances do not possess cleavage.

Gem minerals recovered from sands and gravels (p. 94) are often of superior quality; for, during the process of transportation by streams or by waves along the shore or the coast, stones with even small cleavage cracks or inclusions will tend to break along these lines of weakness. The fragments thus formed are generally quite free from structure flaws.

Parting.—Parting is a separation somewhat similar to cleavage and is sometimes called *false cleavage*. It is observed on crystals which are twinned, and is a separation along juncture planes of the twinned parts. The twinning may be simple or polysynthetic. Twinning and parting may also be the result of the application of pressure upon a crystal, causing *gliding*. A twinned diamond possesses both octahedral cleavage and octahedral parting. Corundum has basal, rhombohedral, and prismatic partings.

Fracture.—The fracture of a solid refers to the character of the surface obtained when it is broken in a direction parallel to which there is no cleavage or parting. Since amorphous substances have no cleavage or parting, they always show a fractured surface when broken. When the fractured surfaces are curved and shell-like, the substance is said to have *conchoidal* fracture. This type of fracture is quite common among gems. Quartz, opal, and glass are good examples of conchoidal fracture. In minerals with an *even* fracture the surfaces are smooth and even; with *uneven* fracture they are rougher. Minerals which are more or less fibrous break with a *splintery* fracture. Splintery fracture is well illustrated in jadeite.

Tenacity.—This property is defined as the resistance which a substance offers to being broken or crushed. Substances are said to be *tough* or *brittle* depending upon whether they possess a high or low degree of tenacity. Tenacity depends upon the ease with which cleaving, parting, or fracturing takes place when the gemstone is subjected to a blow or to pressure. Jade is a very tenacious mineral.

Specific Gravity.—The relationship between the weight of a substance and the weight of an equal volume of water is called its *specific gravity*,[1] commonly abbreviated *sp. gr.* Since the value of

[1] The terms *specific gravity* and *density* are commonly considered as being synonymous.

the specific gravity can be obtained without in any way injuring the stone, its determination is a valuable aid in the identification of gems. Thus quartz may be readily distinguished from the diamond, for the former has a specific gravity of 2.65; the latter, of 3.52. That is, quartz is 2.65 and the diamond 3.52 times heavier than water.

When a solid is suspended in a liquid, its weight is decreased by an amount exactly equal to the weight of the displaced liquid.

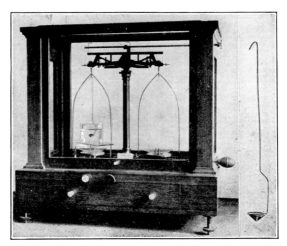

Fig. 63.—Chemical balance arranged for specific gravity determination. Platinum wire basket at the right.

The majority of methods for determining the specific gravity of solids are based upon this fact. The solid is weighed first in air, then in water. Its loss of weight in water is equal to the weight of the volume of water displaced by the solid. Therefore, the specific gravity of the solid is equal to its weight in air divided by the loss of weight in water.

$$\text{Specific gravity} = \frac{\text{weight in air}}{\text{loss of weight in water}}.$$

There are several methods for the determination of the specific gravity of solids. These involve the use of:

1. The chemical balance.
2. The pycnometer.

3. Heavy liquids and the Westphal balance.

4. The Jolly balance.

5. The Krätschmar direct-reading balance.

1. In using the *chemical balance* for the determination of the specific gravity of a gem, the stone is suspended by a fine thread or wire or in a wire basket (Fig. 63). It is weighed, first in air, and again when suspended in a beaker of water. The beaker is supported over the scale pan in such a way that it will not interfere with the weighing. If

$$W = \text{weight of the gem in air,}$$

and $\qquad W' = \text{weight of gem in water,}$

then $\quad W - W' = \text{loss of weight of gem when in water.}$

The *specific gravity* of the gem therefore $= \dfrac{W}{W - W'}.$

While this method, sometimes called the *hydrostatic method,* is very accurate, it is time-consuming. It is applicable to fairly large specimens.

2. The method which makes use of the *pycnometer* or *specific gravity flask* is accurate but slow and may well be used with powdered material, very small fragments, or small cut stones. An appreciable amount of the material should always be used. The pycnometer in its simplest form consists of a small glass flask (Fig. 64) fitted with a ground-glass stopper, which is pierced lengthwise by a capillary opening. The flask is first weighed empty (A). The specimen is then placed in the flask and the whole weighed (B). The flask containing the specimen is now filled with water and weighed (C). After removing the water and the specimen, the flask is filled with water and again weighed (D). The specific gravity can now be calculated from the following formula:

Fig. 64.—Pycnometer.

$$\text{Specific gravity} = \frac{B - A}{D + B - A - C}.$$

Care must be exercised to remove all air bubbles. This can usually be done by boiling the water and allowing it to cool. This process may be simplified by recording the weights of the flask when empty (*A*) and when filled with water (*D*), for use in the foregoing formula.

3. The *Westphal balance* is an instrument for determining the specific gravity of liquids. For use with this balance there are available heavy liquids which may be diluted to give solutions of

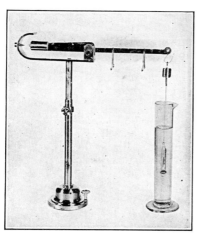

FIG. 65.—Westphal balance.

any given specific gravity, within certain wide limits. From the end of a graduated beam (Fig. 65) a thermometer body or sinker is suspended in a cylindrical vessel containing the liquid. Weights are placed along the beam until the sinker neither rises nor falls in the liquid. The specific gravity of the liquid can then be read directly from the position of the various weights on the beam.

To determine the specific gravity of a gem by means of the Westphal balance, one of the heavy liquids is suitably diluted until the immersed gem remains suspended midway, without movement up or down. For this reason this method is sometimes called the *suspension method*. The specific gravity of the liquid and the gem having thus been matched, it is a simple matter to determine the specific gravity of the liquid, with the Westphal balance. The value determined for the liquid is obviously also the specific gravity of the gem. This method combines accuracy with reasonable rapidity. It is used principally with small stones having specific gravities which do not exceed the maximum specific gravity of the liquid used.

The heavy liquids listed in the table on page 37 are suitable for use with this method. Their maximum specific gravity is given, which of course may be lowered by dilution.

At ordinary temperatures the last compound is a solid, but it melts to a liquid at 70°C. and may then be used. Methylene iodide is easily diluted with benzol; the others, with water.

	Specific Gravity
Methylene iodide	3.31
Potassium mercuric iodide (Thoulet's solution)	3.196
Cadmium borotungstate (Klein's solution)	3.284
Barium mercuric iodide (Rohrbach's solution)	3.58
Thallium formate ⎫ (Clerici solution) Thallium malonate ⎭	4.65
Thallium silver nitrate (Penfield's or Rector's solution)	5.0

A set of standardized specific gravity liquids with fixed intervals may be made for ready use by properly diluting any one of the first five liquids. Such a set may be made without the use of the Westphal balance by matching liquids with a series of stones with known specific gravities. The availability of a standardized set of heavy liquids permits determinations to be made quickly.

Fig. 66.—Amber and copal (natural resins) float on a solution of salt; bakelite sinks to the bottom.

A solution of common salt, consisting of at least four heaping teaspoonfuls in a tumbler of water, is very serviceable in distinguishing the artificial substance bakelite from the natural resins, such as amber. Bakelite has a specific gravity of 1.26, whereas that of amber and the natural resins is about 1.1. As the specific gravity of the salt solution is intermediate between these values, bakelite, being heavier, sinks to the bottom, and the lighter natural resins float on the solution (Fig. 66; see also pp. 277 and 282). This method can also be used to distinguish such plastic gem materials as leucite, ameroid, plexiglass, and vinylite from amber and other light natural resins (p. 170).

4. A rapid determination of the specific gravity of a gem can be made with the *Jolly balance* or *spiral spring balance*. While this method is not quite so accurate as the first three described, it permits satisfactory determinations to be made. It can be used to best advantage with larger stones.

This balance (Fig. 67) consists of an outer upright tube to which the inner fixed vernier and the movable doubly graduated scale are attached above the milled-head. This tube contains an inner tube which can be moved by the large milled-head. To the

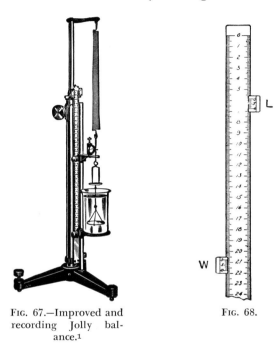

FIG. 67.—Improved and recording Jolly balance.[1]

FIG. 68.

second tube the outer movable vernier is attached. A movement of the inner tube upward carries the second vernier and the graduated scale with it. Within the inner tube there is a rod of adjustable length, which carries the spiral spring, disk index, and scale pans. With this form of balance only two readings and a simple division are necessary to determine the specific gravity.

In using the balance it is necessary that the graduated scale, the two verniers, and the index, which is attached to the spiral spring, all be at zero, the lower scale pan being immersed in water. This is accomplished by adjusting approximately, by hand, the length

[1] This balance is manufactured by the Eberbach and Son Company, Ann Arbor, Michigan.

of the rod carrying the spring, so that the disk index is approximately opposite the horizontal line on the mirror. By sighting across the index, and making the necessary corrections with the micrometer screw directly below the spring, the index, its image, and the line on the mirror may be brought into the same plane. This position is called the zero position. The gemstone is then placed on the upper scale pan, and by turning the large milled-head the inner tube, graduated scale, and outer vernier are all carried upward until the index on the spring is again at zero. The fixed inner vernier W (Fig. 68) now records the elongation of the spring due to the weight of the gem in air. The scale is then clamped by means of the screw at its lower end (Fig. 67). The stone is now transferred to the lower scale pan, which is immersed in water, and the inner tube lowered by the large milled-head until the index is again in zero position. During this operation the outer vernier moves downward on the graduated scale, and its position may now be indicated by L (Fig. 68). This is obviously the decrease in the elongation of the spring due to the immersion of the stone in water. The readings at W and L are all the data necessary for the calculation of the specific gravity. For

$$\text{Specific gravity} = \frac{\text{weight in air}}{\text{loss of weight in water}} = \frac{W}{L}.$$

It is also obvious that these readings are recorded so that they may be checked, if necessary, after the operations and calculation are completed. A determination can be made with this instrument in about two minutes. As already indicated, this method gives best results with fairly large specimens.

5. With the *direct-reading specific gravity balance* described by Krätschmar,[1] calculations are not necessary. The specific gravity is read directly from the scale regardless of the weight of the specimen. It is an adaptation of the pendulum or bent-lever balance first devised by Leonardo da Vinci.

When the scale pans A and B (Fig. 69) are both empty, the pendulum hangs vertically. The pendulum swings to the left when the specimen is weighed in air in pan A, and comes to rest

[1] *Centralblatt für Mineralogie, Geologie, und Palaentologie*, Abt. A, pp. 221-224, 1932.

at a point which depends upon the weight of the specimen; the greater the weight, the greater the deflection. The deflection of the pendulum is obviously less when the specimen is placed in scale pan *B,* immersed in water. The first deflection is due to the weight of the specimen in air, the second to the weight in

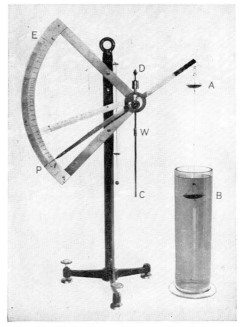

FIG. 69.—Krätschmar direct-reading balance.

water, and the difference between the two to the loss of weight in water.

The pendulum can be counterpoised with the weight of the specimen when in scale pan *A* by moving the counterbalancing weight *W* along the pendulum bar *CD* so that the pointer *P* comes to rest at *E.* Thus, the deflection after such counterbalancing is always the same, regardless of the weight of the specimen in pan *A.* The circular scale *EP* is so graduated that when the specimen is placed in pan *B* the reading on the scale gives the specific gravity directly.

The operation of the balance is very simple: The specimen is first placed in scale pan *A,* and then the counterbalancing weight

W is moved along the pendulum bar CD until the pointer P remains opposite E on the circular scale. The specimen is then transferred to pan B and the system allowed to swing freely until it comes to rest. The position of the pointer P on the graduated scale gives the specific gravity directly.

In order to overcome surface tension a small amount of a wetting agent should be added to the water used in methods 1, 2, 4, and 5. This will prevent the adherence of small air bubbles to the specimen due to incomplete wetting. It will also prevent water creeping up on the wire suspending the immersed scale pan. When specimens are porous or have been pierced with a hole, as in the case of beads, care must be taken that the air in the pores and the holes is entirely displaced by the liquid.

Table III (p. 289) gives a list of the gem minerals arranged according to their specific gravity.

Color.—The beauty of gems depends to a large extent upon their color. Indeed, some gems depend solely on color for their charm and appeal. Turquois might be cited as an example.

With respect to color, minerals are divided into two classes, *idiochromatic* and *allochromatic*. The color is an inherent property in idiochromatic minerals, some essential constituent of the mineral being the pigmenting agent. The gems containing copper as an important constituent belong to this group. These include the green minerals malachite, dioptase, and chrysocolla and the blue azurite. Gem minerals with a metallic luster, such as pyrite and hematite, are also idiochromatic. In idiochromatic minerals the color is constant and therefore is a property which is of assistance in their identification.

Allochromatic minerals are perfectly colorless or white when pure. Because of the presence of a pigment they are often colored. The pigmenting agent may be a closely related element which enters into the chemical constitution of the substance, or it may be present in disseminated submicroscopic particles or as inclusions of other minerals. It is evident that allochromatic minerals may therefore show a variety of colors. Commonly a distinct name is given to each variety. Thus, colorless quartz is called rock crystal, whereas some of the varieties of colored quartz are the purple amethyst, the brown to black smoky quartz, the pink

rose quartz, and the golden citrine.   The majority of gem minerals are allochromatic.

It frequently happens that the pigment of allochromatic minerals is unevenly distributed.   The color may then occur in irregular patches or blotches, as is often the case with amethyst and
sapphire.   Figure 70 shows an irregularly colored sapphire so cut

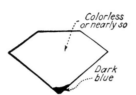

FIG. 70.—Irregularly
colored sapphire cut so
as to appear blue.

FIG. 71.—Tourmaline show-
ing zonal distribution of color
and spherical triangular outline.   San Diego County, California.

that the dark-blue portion forms the culet.   This orientation
causes the whole stone to appear blue when viewed from above.

On the other hand, the color may be distributed in regular and
sharply bounded zones or bands.   For example, tourmaline often
exhibits a zonal arrangement of colors.   Crystals of that mineral
are usually long, with a spherical triangular outline in cross sec-

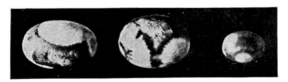

FIG. 72.—Thomsonite.   Isle   Royale,   Lake   Superior.
Natural   size.

tion.   The crystals may be banded in horizontal layers across the
length or in concentric zones parallel to the spherical triangular
outline (Fig. 71).   These zonings are very striking and attractive,
combinations in pink and green being especially common.   The
variety of quartz known as agate also is banded with different
colors.   The coloring may, moreover, be so distributed as to pro-

duce most interesting and attractive markings, as on thomsonite (Fig. 72) and chlorastrolite (Fig. 363).

Coloring by inclusions is illustrated by moss agate, which contains tree-like or *dendritic* inclusions of manganese oxide (Fig. 331). In other stones inclusions may be arranged in a definite manner, as is the case of chiastolite, which is a variety of andalusite containing cross-shaped groups of inclusions of a black, carbonaceous material (Fig. 73). Rutilated quartz, also called Thetis or Venus hairstone, is attractive because of long and slender inclusions of rutile (Fig. 319). The beauty of sunstone is due to golden inclusions of iron oxide.

FIG. 73.—Andalusite: variety, chiastolite. Lancaster, Massachusetts.

In many of the stones illustrated, the color may be most attractively distributed. A list of gem minerals grouped according to their color is given on page 290.

Color Description.—It is difficult to arrive at a satisfactory color classification of gem stones because there are no accepted standards of comparison. This may be well shown if one attempts to describe the difference between the blue color of aquamarine and that of sapphire or the difference between the blue of turquois and that of lapis lazuli or azurite. One of the inherent difficulties in arriving at a standard of color description is the wide difference in the ability of different individuals to perceive the minute and subtle distinctions in color variations. The totally color-blind individual who sees no colors but only shades of white, gray, and black represents one extreme, and the artist or designer who can make delicate distinctions in color values represents the other. Many so-called normal individuals, who are between these extremes in their ability to distinguish colors, can recognize slight color differences between two gems when placed side by side, but they are unable to distinguish between these same gems when they are viewed separately. Color classification depends, then, not only upon the ability to perceive differences in colors but also upon color memory or the ability to carry in mind the mental impression of a color.

Color, moreover, is not entirely dependent upon the substance that is viewed, for a colored substance absorbs part of the light that falls upon it and reflects the unabsorbed part to the eye. What the eye actually perceives is controlled in part by the inherent physical properties of the stone and in part by the character and source of the light in which the stone is seen. Before the introduction of modern methods of illumination, there was a wide variation between daylight and artificial light and consequently in the appearance of a colored stone. Although modern lighting has overcome this difficulty to a considerable extent, it is nevertheless desirable in determining the color of a stone to view it either in daylight or under one of the special lamps which simulates daylight very closely. Moreover, it should be emphasized that daylight varies considerably depending upon the clearness or cloudiness of the sky and, if the stone is viewed indoors, upon the color scheme of the room. The determination of color is most dependable when made under controlled conditions as, for example, with the diamolite (Fig. 221).

In describing the color distinctions between gems the following factors are important: (1) *size,* (2) *transparency,* and (3) *glossiness.* For example, if two stones, five and ten carats in weight, are cut from a single uniformly colored crystal of aquamarine, the five-carat stone will appear lighter in color because it is not as thick as the ten-carat stone. The lack of transparency of turquois gives to it some characteristics of color not present in aquamarine. The third factor, glossiness, although it may be observed in transparent gems, is more important in material that is opaque or nearly so. The lapidary should be able to detect at a glance whether or not uncut material, for example, turquois, will when cut and polished exhibit the desired glossiness.

In color description, three basic elements or color attributes are recognized. These are: (1) *hue,* (2) *tone,* and (3) *intensity.* The recognition and use of these attributes greatly facilitate the more accurate description of color.

1. *Hue.*—This may be defined as color in terms of the spectrum. Thus, the hue of color may be red, orange, yellow, yellow-green,

green, green-blue, blue, or violet. Purple, which is a mixture of red and blue, may be added to this list. In colored gems, the hue is generally dependent upon the pigment present.

2. *Tone.*—The relative brightness in a scale running from dark to light is the tone of the color. The effect of the size of the specimen upon the color illustrates best what is meant by the tone. If several stones varying in size are cut from a large uniformly dark blue crystal of aquamarine, the spectrum characteristics of the pigment, that is, the hue, producing the color in the crystal and in all of the stones cut from it would be identical. The color of the cut stones would, however, vary from dark blue to light blue depending upon their size and thickness. That is, there would be a marked change in the tone. The variation in the tone is conveniently described as *dark* (deep), *medium,* or *light* (pale). The expressions *deep* and *pale* are to be avoided, since they are often used to indicate intensity of color. The terms *tint, color value,* or *saturation* are frequently employed for tone.

3. *Intensity.*—The vividness or intensity of color as applied to gems is not to be confused with the physicist's definition of the intensity of light, by which the amount of light or light energy is meant. As applied to gems the intensity of color is expressed in terms of its appearance, as being *high* (vivid), *average,* or *low* (dull or drab). A color of high intensity possesses a distinctness and definiteness which readily distinguishes it from one of low intensity. But the intensity of a color must not be confused with the tone of color, for a light-blue turquois may, because of its vivid character, have a high intensity. Moreover, because of its porous character, turquois may readily absorb oil or grease, which tends to dull or deaden the vividness of the color without in any way changing the spectrum color characteristics, that is, the hue of the gem. The terms *magnitude* and *shade* are sometimes used for intensity of color.

The distinction between tone and intensity of color may be illustrated by placing upon a cut and polished specimen of turquois pieces of slightly frosted and smoked glass. When the turquois is viewed through the frosted glass, the tone of the blue color will be lightened; that is, it will become paler; but when seen through the smoked glass, the intensity will become lowered; that is, it will become dull or drab. By increasing the amount of frosting on the surface of the glass the tone of the turquois will steadily become lighter until it finally merges into the white of the frosted glass. Similarly, if the dark film upon the smoked glass is increased in thickness, the intensity of the blue will steadily become lowered until it finally merges into black.

Certain of the color hues in gems, such as red, green, and blue, have always been more popular than others. In general, the darker tones of these hues are the more valuable. The attractiveness and popularity of colored gem stones are due in a large measure to the high intensity of their colors.

Streak.—The streak of a mineral is the color of its powder, as determined by rubbing the specimen over a piece of white unglazed porcelain. Only a few of the minerals used as gems have colored streaks, for example, malachite (green), hematite (reddish brown), and pyrite (black).

Play of Colors.—Many opals exhibit a great variety of internal hues, forming a brilliant and beautiful patchwork of color. As the stone is turned, or as it is observed from another direction, the color of each individual patch changes. This phenomenon is known as *play of colors.* Labradorite shows the same effect, except that the patches of uniform color are larger than in the opal. The beauty of these minerals is almost entirely due to their play of color. The cause of the phenomenon is the interference offered to light by minute cracks or inclusions within the mineral. This is quite similar to the color effect observed in thin oil films and in soap bubbles. Play of color must not be confused with fire (p. 55).

Chatoyancy.—The changeable, wavy, silky sheen shown by fibrous minerals, such as satin spar (Fig. 375), tiger's-eye (Fig. 323), or cat's-eye, is known as *chatoyancy.* Chatoyant gems are usually cut cabochon (p. 99).

Opalescence.—This consists of milky or pearly reflections from the interior of a substance. It is usually observed to best advantage on gems cut with rounded surfaces, that is, on cabochon cuts. Opal and moonstone have this property.

Asterism.—Minerals show asterism if they exhibit a star-like light effect when viewed in a strong beam of reflected or transmitted light. In many cases this is due to regularly arranged inclusions of minute size. Rubies and sapphires, particularly those from Ceylon, may show asterism in strong reflected light, when cut with a rounded convex surface (Fig. 74). They are then known as *star rubies* and *star sapphires* and are highly prized. Rose quartz and mica often show asterism in transmitted light (Fig. 75). Asterism is also observed on some cut stones of garnet, spinel, and chrysoberyl.

When the minute inclusions are arranged in a hexagonal or trigonal pattern, as in ruby, sapphire, and quartz, stars with six

Fig. 74.—As-
terism shown by
star sapphire.

Fig. 75.—Asterism
shown by phlogopite from
South Burgess, Canada.

rays are observed. If the pattern is rectangular, as in garnet, the stars may have four or eight rays.

Asterism can be produced artificially by ruling fine parallel lines in an appropriate pattern on the flat back of transparent gem material having a cabochon cut.

Luster.—The appearance of the surface of a mineral in reflected light is its luster. Luster is a function of the transparency, re-fractivity, and structure of a mineral. It is in no way related to hardness. There are two principal types of luster, *metallic* and *non-metallic*.

Metallic luster is that of metals and minerals of a metallic appearance. All substances with metallic luster are opaque. Only a few gemstones possess this luster. Pyrite and hematite are examples.

All other types of luster are collectively referred to as non-metallic. Some of the kinds of non-metallic luster observed on gem minerals are:

Adamantine.—The splendent luster typical of the diamond and possessed only by substances with high indices of refraction.

Vitreous.--The luster of glass or quartz.

Resinous.—The luster of resin.

Greasy.—The appearance of an oiled surface.

Pearly.—This is the luster of mother-of-pearl, usually shown by minerals with a platy structure.

Silky.—The luster of fibrous minerals, such as the satin spar variety of gypsum.

Dull.—As the name indicates, the surfaces of minerals with this luster are not at all bright or shiny.

When the luster is intermediate between metallic and non-metallic, it may be called *sub-metallic.*

FIG. 76.—Transparent quartz from Dauphiné, France.

Luster may be used advantageously in the identification of uncut material.

Transparency or Diaphaneity.—Transparency is the ability of a substance to transmit light. Light passes freely through a *transparent* mineral, and objects can be easily and distinctly seen through such a substance. Rock crystal is an example of a transparent substance (Fig. 76). Light is feebly transmitted through a *translucent* mineral, and no objects can be distinguished on looking through it. In thin layers jade is translucent. No light can pass through *opaque* objects, which include all metallic minerals. *Sub-* or *semi-transparent* and *sub-* or *semi-translucent* are terms used to indicate intermediate stages of diaphaneity. The majority of gem minerals are transparent. This is especially true of the more precious stones.

It may be noted that diamonds are transparent to X-rays, whereas imitations made of lead glass are opaque to the same radiations. An X-ray photograph will serve to distinguish the genuine diamond from glass imitations (Fig. 276).

Luminescence.—When some gemstones are exposed to direct sunlight or to any other source of ultraviolet rays, they glow or become luminescent. Such luminescence may also be produced by exposure to X-rays, cathode rays, and radiations from radioactive substances. Luminescence is generally best observed in the dark. Luminescent colors are frequently markedly different from those of the unexcited minerals. The display of these colors is not only interesting but may be even quite spectacular.

A substance is said to *fluoresce* if it is luminescent during the period of excitation and to *phosphoresce* if the luminescence continues after the cause of excitation has been removed. The diamond, kunzite, ruby, opal, and amber may show luminescence to a marked extent.

Fluorescence and phosphorescence in ultraviolet light can be readily induced by the use of mercury-vapor and argon lamps or by an iron-arc apparatus, all of which are available in convenient forms.[1] Luminescence phenomena may in some instances be useful in determining gemstones.

Luminescence may also be observed when some minerals are scratched, rubbed, or pounded, and is then termed *triboluminescence* or, when heated, *thermoluminescence*. Triboluminescence is sometimes observed on diamonds when accidentally rubbed in the dark.

Heat Conduction.—A gemstone which is a good conductor of heat feels cold to the touch, whereas one which is a poor conductor feels warm. This is due to the fact that the temperature of the body is considerably higher than ordinary room temperatures. Accordingly, a gemstone which is at room temperature will absorb heat when placed in contact with the skin. If the stone is a good conductor, it will remove heat rapidly from the skin and thereby lower its temperature at the point of contact and give a feeling of coldness. Obviously, a poor conductor removes heat more slowly and will feel warmer to the touch than a good conductor. Inasmuch as quartz is a good conductor, it feels cold to the touch, but a glass imitation is a poor conductor and feels much warmer.

[1] See SLAWSON, C. B., "The Fluorescence of Minerals," *Bulletin* 5, Cranbrook Institute of Science, Bloomfield Hills, Michigan.

Electrical Properties.—Some gem minerals may possess the following interesting electrical properties: (1) *frictional electricity,* (2) *pyroelectricity,* and (3) *piezoelectricity.* These types of electrical properties will be discussed briefly.

1. *Frictional Electricity.*—Vigorous rubbing with a cloth or piece of fur will cause some minerals to become electrified. They will then attract bits of paper. Diamond, tourmaline, and topaz may be positively electrified by friction with a cloth. On the other hand, amber becomes negatively charged.

2. *Pyroelectricity.*—Minerals which possess polar axes of symmetry may become electrified when subjected to a marked change in temperature. They are then said to exhibit *pyroelectricity.* Tourmaline is an excellent example of a pyroelectric mineral; for if a light-colored crystal is heated, positive and negative charges develop on the opposite ends. As can be seen from Fig. 77, crystals of tourmaline are usually elongated along the c axis, which is polar in character. On account of the polar character of its horizontal axes, quartz also exhibits pyroelectricity.

FIG. 77.

Pyroelectricity can be easily detected by *Kundt's method.* After the crystal to be tested has been gently heated, it is momentarily brought in contact with a conducting medium to discharge the electricity which has been developed during heating. It is then allowed to cool on an insulated support. The distribution of the electric charges may be determined by dusting the cooled crystal with a finely powdered mixture of red lead and sulfur, the particles of which are electrified by friction in their passage through a fine sieve in the nozzle of the bellows containing the powder. The red lead, having been positively electrified, collects at the negative end of the crystal, and the negatively charged sulfur is attracted to the positive end. That is, the negative end of the crystal becomes red in color; the positive end, yellow. Pyroelectricity is closely related to piezoelectricity.

3. *Piezoelectricity.*—By means of pressure electric charges may be developed in crystals with polar axes. This electrification is called *piezoelectricity.* Quartz and tourmaline are gem minerals which exhibit both pyro- and piezoelectricity.

When pressure is applied to a piezoelectric crystal, the charges of electricity at opposite ends of the polar axis are not the same. At one end, the charge is positive; at the other, negative. When the pressure is released, the character of the electric charges is reversed, and what was positive becomes negative, and vice versa. By placing a piezoelectric crystal, for example, quartz, in an electric field the crystal can be made to expand and contract. Moreover, very thin sections or plates of quartz can be made to vibrate or oscillate at very high speeds. Because of the great constancy of the frequency of oscillation such crystal plates are used in enormous quantities in electric and radio apparatus. The war has emphasized and extended the value and use of piezoelectric oscillating quartz plates. Large quantities of high-grade quartz are used in their production. Because of their greater accuracy, clocks controlled by oscillating quartz plates have replaced the pendulum clocks in some important astronomical observatories.

Chapter IV

OPTICAL PROPERTIES

Many of the attractive characteristics of gemstones depend upon their optical properties. In the preceding chapter those optical properties have been considered which may be readily determined without the use of specially designed instruments, such as the refractometer, polarizing microscope, dichroscope, and so forth. The properties which can be determined with these instruments are very important in the accurate identification of gemstones. Some of the essential properties of light will be re-

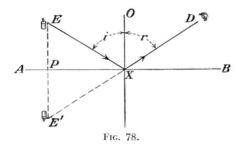

FIG. 78.

viewed before these optical instruments and their uses are described.

Reflection of Light.—When a ray of light falls upon a mirror or other polished surface, it is reflected in such a way that *the angle of reflection is equal to the angle of incidence, and the reflected and incident rays lie in the same plane.* This is illustrated by Fig. 78. A ray of light EX from the candle at E strikes the reflecting surface AB at X, with the angle of incidence EXO or i. It is reflected to the eye at D, and DXO or r is the angle of reflection. To the eye the object E appears to be at E'. The angle r is equal to the angle i, as the law of reflection states.

Refraction of Light.—When light impinges upon the surface of a transparent substance, some of the light is reflected and some enters the substance, that is, it is refracted. In the case of cut gemstones, refracted light is more important than that which is reflected.

When light passes obliquely from one medium to another, as from air into water, the path of the ray is not straight, but bent. That is, the ray is *refracted*. The bent appearance of a stick thrust into a pool is due to this fact. Figure 79 illustrates the refraction of light. A ray of light *Dx*, in air, strikes the surface of the water *AB* at *x*. Instead of continuing in the same direction after entering the water, the ray is refracted in the direction *xE*, that is, toward *OM*, the normal to the surface of contact. Whenever light passes from a rarer to a denser medium, as in this case, the ray is bent toward the normal. The reverse takes place when light passes from a denser to a rare medium. It is then bent away from the normal. In Fig. 79 the angle of incidence *DxO* may be designated as *i* and the angle of refraction *MxE* as *r*. The law of

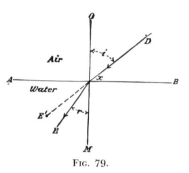

Fig. 79.

refraction then is: *The incident and refracted rays lie in the same plane, and the ratio between the velocities of light in the two media, V and V', and the ratio between the sines of the angles of incidence and refraction, i and r, are equal and constant for the media concerned.* In the case of air and water,

$$n \text{ (index of refraction)} = \frac{V \text{ (air)}}{V' \text{ (water)}} = \frac{\sin i}{\sin r} = 1.333.$$

The constant *n* is the *index of refraction,* the velocity of light in air being taken as unity. For water, *n* is 1.333; for the diamond, 2.42. The velocity of light in a substance is proportional to the reciprocal of its index of refraction. Consequently, light is bent or refracted more in substances with high indices than in those with low indices. A gemstone may usually be identified by the determination of the index of refraction *n*. Methods for the determination of this important constant are given later (p. 56).

Dispersion.—A common experiment in elementary physics is the resolution of white light into its component colors, by passing sunlight through a glass prism (Fig. 80). Of the component colors

which together make up white light, red is refracted least and
violet most, while the other colors—orange, yellow, green, and
blue—occupy intermediate positions in the band of colors, known
as the *spectrum*.   In other words, the velocity of red light is the
greatest and that of violet light the least.   That is, *dispersion* of
light has taken place.   For this reason indices of refraction can

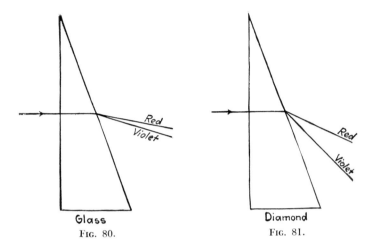

Glass   Diamond
FIG. 80.   FIG. 81.

be accurately determined only with light of a definite color (*monochromatic light*).

The difference in the velocities of red and violet light in passing
through a substance indicates the strength of the dispersion of that
substance.   This is numerically expressed by the difference in the
indices of refraction for violet and red lights.   The diamond is
characterized by a very high dispersion, about three times that of
common glass, as shown by the data on page 55 giving the values
of *n* for various colors of light.

The high dispersion of the diamond is the important factor in
producing the *fire* so characteristic of that gem.   This highly
prized attribute is due to the fact that the component colors of
white light in passing through the diamond are widely dispersed
(Fig. 81); and on emergence under favorable conditions, practically pure colors may be observed.   That is, when a diamond is
viewed in one direction, a flash of yellow may appear, while slight
turns of the stone may produce red or blue flashes.   Substances

like quartz or glass, which have low dispersion (Fig. 80), show little or no fire.

		DIAMOND	GLASS
n, red light, extreme.........(wave-length) 763 mμ [1]		2.402	1.512
red.................................. 670		2.408	1.514
yellow............................. 589		2.417	1.517
green............................. 527		2.427	1.522
violet, extreme....................... 397		2.465	1.532

Dispersion:

$$\text{Diamond} = 2.465 - 2.402 = 0.063$$

$$\text{Glass} \quad = 1.532 - 1.512 = 0.020$$

Total Reflection and the Critical Angle.—If light passes from a denser to a rarer medium, the ray is bent away from the normal (Fig. 82). The angle of incidence I in the denser medium is

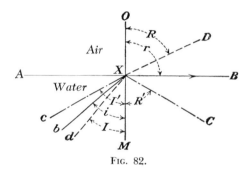

FIG. 82.

smaller than the angle of refraction R in the rarer medium. For a definite angle of incidence i in the denser medium, the angle of refraction r in the rarer medium will equal 90 degrees, and the ray of light will just graze the surface between the media. If the angle of incidence be further increased, as in the case of I', the light ray cannot emerge, but is reflected back into the denser medium according to the law of reflection, making R' equal to I'. This is the phenomenon of *total reflection*. All light in the denser medium impinging at the surface AB with angles of incidence greater than i will suffer total reflection.

[1] μ equals one-thousandth of a millimeter and is called a *micron;* mμ is a *millimicron,* that is, a one-thousandth of a micron or a millionth of a millimeter. The present tendency is to express the wave-lengths of light and of X-rays in angstrom units, Å. (ten-millionths of a millimeter). Thus, the values above would be 7,630 Å., 6,700 Å., and so forth.

The value of the critical angle may be expressed by

$$\sin i = \frac{1}{n},$$

in which n represents the index of refraction and i is the critical angle. Light is totally reflected if it impinges at the surface with a greater angle than i. From this formula it follows that, the higher the value of n, the smaller will be the critical angle i, and that more light may be totally reflected within the substance. In the diamond, for an intermediate color, n is 2.42, and i, 24° 26′ (Fig. 83); for water, n is 1.333, i, 48° 36′ (Fig. 84). The low value of the critical angle in the diamond permits total reflection to take

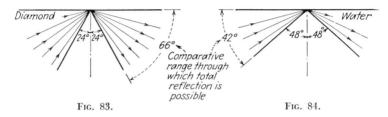

FIG. 83.   FIG. 84.

place through a wider angular distance; that is, the light exterior to a small cone, the surface of which makes an angle of 24 degrees with its axis, can be totally reflected in the diamond. Because of repeated total reflections in cut stones, the brilliancy is very much enhanced. On the other hand, because the critical angle is much larger, total reflection of light does not take place so readily in water (Fig. 84), and in other substances with relatively low indices of refraction, as it does in the diamond. Accordingly, gemstones with low refractivity, for example, quartz ($n = 1.55$, $i = 40°\ 10′$), are not very brilliant. Moreover, repeated total reflections in cut stones with high dispersion tend to improve the fire.

Determination of Indices of Refraction.—The determination of the index of refraction is one of the most accurate and readily applied means of identifying precious stones. There are three methods which are commonly used:

1. Approximate immersion method.
2. Becke's method.
3. Refractometer method.

It is highly desirable to use the refractometer method because of its accuracy, ease of operation, and applicability to unmounted and mounted stones.

As indicated previously, monochromatic light should be used for the accurate determination of the index of refraction of a substance. Monochromatic light may be readily produced by volatilizing salts of the following elements in a non-luminous gas flame:

Lithium (gives a red flame of wave-length 670 mμ).

Sodium (gives a yellow flame of wave-length 589 mμ).

Thallium (gives a green flame of wave-length 535 mμ).

Color filters may also be employed to furnish monochromatic light. In the identification of gemstones by means of the indices of refraction, sufficiently accurate results may be obtained by using ordinary light.

Approximate Immersion Method.—This method depends upon the fact that a transparent solid becomes practically invisible when placed in a liquid with the same color and the same index of refraction. The solid and the liquid form a continuous medium for the passage of light so that the boundaries of the solid tend to disappear. By using a series of liquids with different indices of refraction, the approximate

Fig. 85.—Diamond (*left*) and glass (*right*) immersed in cinnamon oil.

index of most minerals may be found. The stone is immersed in one liquid after another, until that liquid is found in which it most completely disappears. The stone then has approximately the index of that liquid. Figure 85 shows the appearance of a glass imitation immersed in a liquid with approximately the same index. The greater the difference in refractivity between the liquid and the solid, the greater will be the *relief* of the solid, that is, the more plainly will it be visible. This method may be applied to colored as well as colorless stones. With colored stones it is more difficult to tell when the relief is least, for the color of the stone tends to indicate its outline.

The following liquids may profitably be used in the approximate immersion method:

Water...$n = 1.33$
Ethyl alcohol....................................... 1.36
Glycerine... 1.47
Petroleum oil (mineral oil)......................... 1.48
Cinnamon oil...................................... 1.60
α-Monochlornaphthalene............................ 1.63
α-Monobromnaphthalene............................ 1.65
Methylene iodide.................................. 1.74
Sulfur in methylene iodide......................... 1.79

By mixing these liquids in the proper proportions, solutions with intermediate indices of refraction are easily obtained.

It is common practice to prepare with these liquids a series of standardized index liquids, the individual members of which have indices of refraction varying by one unit in the second decimal place. The indices of the various liquids in the series may be rapidly and accurately determined with the refractometer (p. 59). There is no liquid with an index so high as that of zircon (1.92) or of the diamond (2.42), but the range of the liquids given above includes the indices of refraction of nearly all other gems, as well as those of the usual gem imitations. Figure 85 shows the diamond (n 2.42) and glass immersed in cinnamon oil (n 1.60). It is quite obvious that the index of refraction of the glass imitation, as indicated by the low relief, is approximately the same as that of the cinnamon oil.

Becke's Method.—This method was devised by Becke and makes use of the polarizing microscope (p. 65). It is an application of the immersion method to small fragments and gives a high degree of accuracy. The method depends upon the total reflection of light.

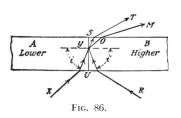

FIG. 86.

Let A and B (Fig. 86) be two substances in contact, B having a higher index than A. If the microscope be focused upon the contact, a band of light will be observed at SO which will move toward B when the tube of the microscope is raised; on lowering the tube it moves toward A. This band is caused by the concentration of light on one side of the contact, for all rays of light in A which strike on the contact will pass into B irrespective of the angle of incidence i. Thus, the ray X will emerge as OM. But when light passing through B impinges upon the contact, the size of the angle of incidence is of great importance, for now the passage is from a denser to a rarer medium. In all such cases total reflection will take place if the angle of incidence *i* is larger than the critical angle. For instance, the ray *R* will emerge as *ST*. As before mentioned, the raising of the microscope tube will displace the band of light, as a result of this concentration of rays, toward the substance with the higher index. The intensity of this line of light is often accentuated by lowering the substage

 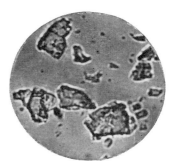

FIG. 87.—Crystals have higher index. FIG. 88.—Crystals have lower index.

FIGS. 87 and 88.—Crystals in index liquids showing Becke lines.

or by partly closing the substage diaphragm. Whether or not the index of the gem or mineral being investigated is higher or lower than that of a known substance can thus be easily determined (Figs. 87 and 88).

The indices of refraction of fragments, and even of fine powder, of gem materials can be determined by placing them on a microscope slide and then covering them with a liquid with known index (p. 58) and noting the movement of the band of light. The operation is repeated until a liquid is found whose index matches that of the fragments. In this case the fragment is invisible or the edges show colors. When the difference between the index of the fragment and that of the liquid is slight, the fragment appears smooth and thin and is said to have *low relief*. If this difference is quite large, then the fragment has a dark border, appears rough and thick, and is said to have *high relief*.

Refractometer Method.—For this method four hand-size instruments are at present available which may be used for the rapid

and accurate determination of the indices of refraction of gemstones.   These are known as the *Tully, Smith, Rayner,* and *Erb
and Gray refractometers.*   They make use of the principle of total
reflection.

Figure 89 illustrates the Tully refractometer.   The most essential part of the instrument is a polished hemisphere of glass *B*
with a very high index of refraction.   The exposed portion of
the hemisphere is a flat polished surface.   The mounted or un-

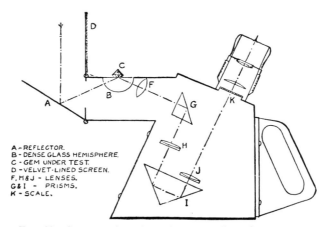

A - REFLECTOR.
B - DENSE GLASS HEMISPHERE.
C - GEM UNDER TEST.
D - VELVET-LINED SCREEN.
F, H & J - LENSES.
G & I - PRISMS.
K - SCALE.

Fig. 89.—Cross section through the Tully refractometer.

mounted stone *C* to be tested is placed upon the glass hemisphere.
However, a drop of liquid of high index, such as methylene iodide,
must be first placed upon the hemisphere in order to displace the
film of air which would otherwise be present between the stone
and the hemisphere.   A broad beam of light from the reflector *A*
enters the instrument through the opening at the left and passes
up to the lower surface of the stone, which should be flat and well
polished.   The instrument is so designed that the hemisphere of
glass and the mounted stone may be rotated in the horizontal
plane.   Such rotation is desirable with substances having strong
double refraction.

The light thus passes from a dense to a rarer medium, that is,
from the hemisphere to the stone.   Part of this light impinges
upon the stone at an angle less than the critical angle and continues through the stone and into the air.   But some of the light
impinges upon the stone at an angle which exceeds the critical

angle. This light is therefore totally reflected back into the hemisphere, and, after passing through it and several prisms and lenses, falls upon a graduated scale *K,* which is viewed through the eyepiece at the right. It is obvious that this light, which has been totally reflected from the stone *C,* will illuminate part of the graduated scale, while the rest of the scale will be somewhat darker. The position of the boundary between the lighter and darker portions of the scale is a function of the critical angle of the stone with reference to the glass hemisphere. This angle, of course, depends upon the relative indices of refraction of the

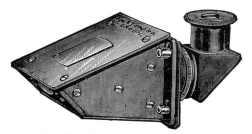

FIG. 90.—The Smith refractometer.

gem and the glass. Since the index for the glass is known, the scale may be so graduated that the position of the boundary of the illuminated area will indicate the index of refraction of the stone. Thus, the index of the gem may be read directly from the scale. The divisions of the scale correspond to 0.01, but the index may be estimated to 0.001. The range of the instrument is limited by the index of refraction of the glass used, which may be as high as 1.88.

In using the refractometer the liquid for the film between the stone and the hemisphere must have an index of refraction higher than that of the stone to be tested. Thus, methylene iodide can be used for stones with indices up to 1.74, whereas a solution of sulfur in methylene iodide permits indices up to 1.79 to be determined. It should be pointed out that, because light is reflected from both the liquid film and the stone, ordinarily two readings may be made on the scale, one caused by the liquid, the other by the stone. The band caused by the liquid film is easily recognized, since the index of the liquid is known. If the stone has a strong double refraction two index readings may be made. In case the stone has indices higher than that of the liquid, only one reading, namely, that of the liquid, is possible.

The refractometer method is rapid, and determinations which are usually sufficiently accurate can be made with ordinary light, that is, white light or sunlight. When greater accuracy is desired, monochromatic light should be used (p. 57). It is common practice to make determinations with ordinary light, in which case one observes a fringe of colors, instead of a sharp boundary to the illuminated area. Readings should then be made in terms of

FIG. 91.—The Rayner refractometer.

FIG. 92.—The Erb and Gray refractometer. (*Courtesy of Gemological Institute of America.*)

the middle of the colored band. If the stone has more than one index of refraction (p. 64), two boundaries may be observed, each for a different index.

The Smith (Fig. 90) and the Rayner (Fig. 91) refractometers are simpler but very useful instruments. The Erb and Gray refractometer (Fig. 92) is so constructed that the position of the eyepiece can be adjusted and the glass hemisphere rotated.

The index of refraction of a gem, in connection with the color and other easily noted properties, is usually sufficient for identification. Because of its accuracy and ease of operation, the refractometer method is well adapted for use with cut stones, either mounted or unmounted. On page 293 the indices of refraction of the more common gem minerals are listed.

Double Refraction.—When a ray of light passes into a cubic or amorphous mineral, it continues in the mineral as a single, refracted ray. This is designated as *single refraction.* In general, light passing obliquely through minerals of the other five crystal systems is not only refracted, but also resolved into two rays which travel with different velocities. This is called *double refraction*. It is illustrated by Fig. 93, which represents a section of calcite. Calcite is a mineral with exceedingly strong double refraction, so strong indeed as to be readily detected by the eye. Figure 94 shows the apparent doubling of print as seen through a cleavage piece of calcite.

In Fig. 93 the ray *DX* strikes the section of calcite at *X*, and is resolved into two rays, *o* and *e*. The velocity of the *o* ray is the

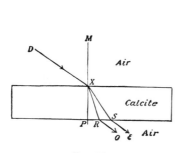

FIG. 93.

FIG. 94.—Calcite: variety, Iceland spar, showing double refraction. Big Timber, Montana.

same in all directions through the crystal, and this ray is called the *ordinary ray*. But since the velocity of the *e* ray varies according to the direction in which it passes through the crystal, it is called the *extraordinary ray*. In calcite *o* is the slower ray, and it is refracted more than the faster ray *e*. However, in other substances this relationship may be reversed.

Optical Groups.—As indicated on page 14 the crystal systems may be classified into optical groups. Cubic and amorphous minerals are termed *singly refractive* or *isotropic*. Light travels through such minerals with the same velocity in all directions. These substances have but one index of refraction, usually designated as n. Examples of this group are: diamond (cubic), $n = 2.42$; spinel (cubic), $n = 1.72$; opal (amorphous), $n = 1.45$.

All substances belonging to the other crystal systems are *anisotropic;* that is, the velocity of light varies with the direction in which it passes through them. However, these substances may have either one or two isotropic directions, known as the directions of the *optic axes.* Those substances with one isotropic direction are called *uniaxial;* those with two, *biaxial.*

Hexagonal and tetragonal crystals have one isotropic direction which is parallel to the vertical crystal axis, and they are therefore *uniaxial.* Substances of this group are subdivided into two classes according to the relative values of the indices for the *o* and *e* rays. The index of refraction for the ordinary ray is designated by the Greek letter ω (omega); that for the extraordinary ray, by ε (epsilon). If the value for ω is greater than that for ε, the crystal is said to be optically negative; it is called positive if ε exceeds ω. Calcite is negative, ω = 1.658, ε = 1.486; zircon, positive, ω = 1.92, ε = 1.98. The difference between the values for ε and ω is called the strength of the *double refraction* or *birefringence.* For calcite the double refraction is high, 0.172 (1.658 — 1.486); for quartz it is low, only 0.009 (1.553 — 1.544).

The other group of anisotropic crystals includes those which have two isotropic directions or optic axes. These crystals are called *biaxial.* To this group belong all orthorhombic, monoclinic, and triclinic crystals. They possess three principal optical directions, at right angles one to another. For each such direction there is a principal index of refraction, these three indices being: α (alpha), the smallest; β (beta), the intermediate; γ (gamma), the largest. Examples are: topaz (orthorhombic), α = 1.619, β = 1.620, γ = 1.627; orthoclase (monoclinic), α = 1.518, β = 1.524, γ = 1.526; albite or moonstone (triclinic), α = 1.525, β = 1.529, γ = 1.536. In general, if the value of β is nearer to α than to γ, as in topaz, the mineral is optically *positive;* if β lies nearer to γ (orthoclase), it is optically *negative.* The double refraction or birefringence is equal to γ — α; for orthoclase it is 0.008 (1.526 — 1.518). In the following table, the optical properties are briefly summarized.

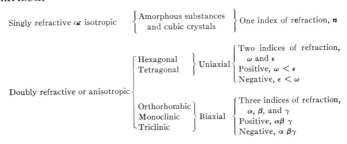

Singly refractive or isotropic	Amorphous substances and cubic crystals	One index of refraction, *n*
Doubly refractive or anisotropic	Hexagonal / Tetragonal } Uniaxial	Two indices of refraction, ω and ε / Positive, ω < ε / Negative, ε < ω
	Orthorhombic / Monoclinic / Triclinic } Biaxial	Three indices of refraction, α, β, and γ / Positive, αβ γ / Negative, α βγ

Polarizing Microscope.—The polarizing or mineralogical microscope (Fig. 95) differs materially from the ordinary biological instrument. The stage rotates in a horizontal plane, adding greatly to the usefulness of the instrument. The essential difference, however, lies in the fact that polarized light may be used, instead

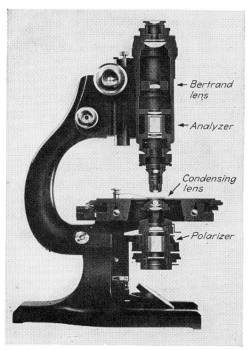

Fig. 95.—Sectional view of polarizing microscope.
(*Courtesy of American Optical Company.*)

of ordinary light. This kind of light is produced by the polarizing prisms (Fig. 95), the *polarizer* and *analyzer,* respectively. Both prisms may usually be rotated, and in addition the analyzer is so mounted that it may be easily moved in and out of the microscope tube.

Polarized Light.—According to the undulatory theory, light is considered to be a form of energy transmitted by waves. Light travels with the great velocity of approximately 186,000 miles or 300,000 kilometers per second. It is propagated by the vibrations which are perpendicular to the direction in which the light travels.

With ordinary light the vibrations are in a plane at right angles to the direction of propagation of the light, but the vibration direction in this plane is continually changing. If in Fig. 96 a ray of light is considered as traveling in a direction perpendicular to the plane of the page, then the vibrations may be in the directions *AA'*, *BB'*, *CC'*, and so forth. In Fig. 97 this is shown in perspective.

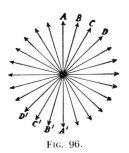

FIG. 96.

In *plane polarized* light, which is ordinarily designated simply as *polarized* light, the vibrations are still in a plane at right angles to the direction in which the light is propagated, but they take place in only one definite direction in that plane. This type of light may be produced: (1) by *reflection* from glass plates or other smooth surfaces; (2) by the partial *absorption* of ordinary light in passing through certain substances, such as polaroid; and (3) by means of *refraction,* as is the case with Nicol prisms. The third method is the most efficient and is usually employed in the polarizing microscope and other optical instruments. Since the development of polaroid, the second method is sometimes used for the production of polarized light in these instruments, which are, however, somewhat less efficient than those with Nicol prisms.

Polarized Light by Reflection.—When ordinary light is reflected from a smooth surface, it is found to be partly plane polarized, the

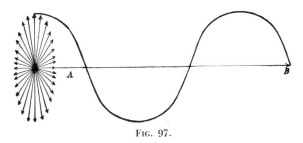

FIG. 97.

vibration directions being at right angles to the direction of propagation. In Fig. 98, the plane *ABCD* contains the incident and reflected rays *ax* and *xy*. The plane, *MPON,* in which the polarized ray *xy* vibrates is called the plane of vibration. These planes are perpendicular to each other. This method of producing polarized light was formerly used much more extensively than at present.

Polaroid Plates.—When ordinary light passes through substances with highly selective absorption, the light which emerges is plane polarized. This is because such substances permit light to pass through readily when the light vibrates in a given direction xy (Fig. 99). Light vibrating in other directions is absorbed. This can be demonstrated by placing a second plate of the sub-

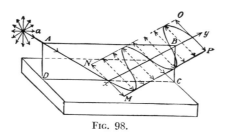

FIG. 98.

stance in the path of the polarized ray, so that the favorable direction for passage $x'y'$ is at right angles to the vibration direction of the ray. When this is done, no light will emerge from the second plate. The commercial product polaroid is a substance which can be used for the production of plane polarized light in this manner, although the light which emerges is not completely polarized. Plates of polaroid have been substituted for the Nicol prisms in many optical instruments, with satisfactory results.

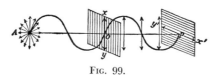

FIG. 99.

Nicol Prism.—A Nicol prism is represented in Fig. 100. It consists of a clear, elongated cleavage piece of calcite or Iceland spar. The dotted outline at A and F represents the original outline of the cleavage piece. The angles at these points, originally 71 degrees, are ground down to 68 degrees, producing the outline represented by $BCED$. The piece of calcite is then cut along the plane CD into two parts. The cut faces are polished, and then the two parts are cemented together in their original position by means of a thin layer of Canada balsam or thickened linseed oil, which have indices of refraction of about 1.54.

A ray of ordinary light *MN* falling upon *DE* is resolved into two rays *NR* and *NS* by the doubly refracting calcite. Each of these rays is plane polarized in this operation. The ordinary ray *o* has a constant index of refraction of 1.658. This ray strikes the film of balsam or oil at *S* with an angle of incidence greater than the critical angle and is therefore totally reflected in the direction *ST*. It is absorbed by the side of the case containing the Nicol and hence does not emerge at the upper end.

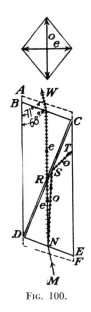

FIG. 100.

The index for the extraordinary ray *e* of calcite varies with its direction through the mineral, namely, from 1.486 to 1.658. In the direction *NR* its index is practically the same as that of the film *DC;* hence the light passes through with little or no deviation along *RW*, and emerges from the Nicol as a plane polarized ray.

Nicol prisms find extensive use in polarizing microscopes and all other optical instruments in which plane polarized light is employed. In the microscope one prism, called the *polarizer,* is placed below the stage, and a second, the *analyzer,* is mounted in the tube above the objective (Fig. 95). Observations may be made with the vibration directions of the two Nicols either *parallel* or *crossed*. The Nicols are crossed when their vibration directions are at right angles to each other. Most observations are made with crossed Nicols. Only the polarizer is used in making general observations, determining the indices of refraction by the Becke method, or observing pleochroism. Other types of prisms made of Iceland spar, especially the one devised by Ahrens, are also used.

Parallel and Convergent Polarized Light.—Polarized light may be either parallel or convergent. In the first case the rays of light pass through the substance under examination in a direction parallel to the axis of the microscope tube. Convergent polarized light is produced by placing a condensing lens above the polarizer (Fig. 95). This causes the rays to converge in the substance. The use of the polarizing microscope in the identification of gemstones will now be discussed.

Behavior of Isotropic Substances.—If the analyzer is removed from the tube of the microscope and an isotropic substance, either cubic or amorphous, be viewed in parallel polarized light, the field will be illuminated, and will remain illuminated in all positions of the stage, when it is rotated. However, when the analyzer is replaced, the field is dark in all positions of the stage, provided that the vibration directions of the upper and lower Nicols are crossed. This latter observation is characteristic of isotropic substances, and serves to distinguish them from those which are anisotropic. Also, in convergent light, with crossed Nicols, an isotropic substance is always dark, exactly the same as with parallel polarized light. When under strain, due to the development of anomalous double refraction, isotropic substances exhibit some optical properties which simulate those of anisotropic crystals.

Behavior of Uniaxial Substances.—With parallel polarized light and the analyzer removed, uniaxial substances are illuminated for all positions of the stage. With crossed Nicols such substances are always dark, only when the optic axis is perpendicular to the stage. However, if the optic axis is inclined or parallel to the stage, uniaxial substances are four times light and four times dark during a complete rotation of the stage. In daylight or artificial white light an *interference color* is observed in the four positions of illumination, whereas with monochromatic light some shade of the color employed is seen in those positions. The positions of greatest darkness are known as those of *extinction*. The crosshairs in the ocular of the microscope should be parallel to the vibration directions of the Nicols, and are used in the determination of the extinction or vibration directions of the substances. These observations may also be made on strained isotropic substances which show anomalous double refraction. The extent of the anomalous double refraction is dependent upon the intensity of the strain.

If extinction takes place when the crosshairs are parallel or perpendicular to the edges or cleavage cracks in the specimen (Fig. 101), the substance is said to have *parallel extinction*. Uniaxial substances may also possess *symmetrical extinction* (Fig. 102).

Uniaxial substances with the optic axis perpendicular to the stage exhibit a characteristic uniaxial *interference figure* (Fig. 103) with crossed Nicols in convergent polarized light. In monochromatic light this figure consists of a dark cross superimposed upon a series of light and dark rings. In white light the rings are of different colors. The figure remains stationary when the stage is rotated. If, however, the optic axis is not perpendicular to

FIG. 101.

FIG. 102.

the stage but is inclined, the interference figure will be eccentric, as in Fig. 104. The greater the inclination, the more eccentric will the figure be. When the stage is rotated, the arms of the dark cross in eccentric figures move across the field parallel to the crosshairs, and in the same direction as the movement of the stage. This observation is of great importance in distinguishing uniaxial from certain biaxial figures. Whether a mineral is optically posi-

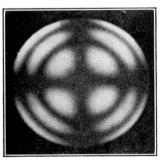

FIG. 103.

FIG. 104.

tive or negative may be determined from the effect of test plates on the interference figure. Depending upon the inclination of the optic axis to the stage, the interference figure may lie outside the field of the microscope and hence will not be visible.

In order to observe interference figures under the polarizing microscope, either the Bertrand lens (Fig. 95) must be inserted into the tube above the analyzer, or the eyepiece must be removed.

Interference figures from small fragments or thin sections are best obtained when a high-power objective is used. In examining cut stones, which are much thicker, a low-power objective is necessary. Such stones should be immersed in a suitable liquid such as mineral oil or glycerine, to reduce the internal reflections from the facets. To observe the interference figure, the stone should be rotated or turned in the liquid until it is in the proper position, for interference figures are observed only when light passes through the stone in certain directions.

FIG. 105.

Behavior of Biaxial Substances.—With crossed Nicols and in parallel polarized light, biaxial substances are in general four times dark and four times light during a complete rotation of the stage. However, when the substance is so placed that one of the optic axes is perpendicular to the stage, the substance remains dimly but uniformly illuminated during the rotation. In orthorhombic substances extinction is either parallel or symmetrical. Monoclinic substances may show parallel, symmetrical, or inclined extinction. When the crosshairs of the microscope are at an angle to the crystal edges of a substance in the position of extinction, the sub-

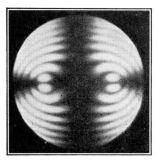

FIG. 106.

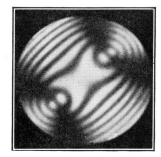

FIG. 107.

stance is said to possess *inclined* extinction (Fig. 105). Triclinic substances always have inclined extinction. These facts enable one to differentiate the crystal systems among biaxial substances.

The interference figures observed in biaxial crystals, in convergent light with crossed Nicols (Figs. 106 and 107) differ from those of uniaxial substances. Biaxial figures vary markedly with the direction in which the substance is viewed. Figure 106 illustrates, in the *normal position,* the biaxial figure observed when the substance is so placed that the line bisecting the acute angle between the two optic axes is perpendicular to the stage. The direction bisecting the optic axes is called the *acute bisectrix.* If the substance is now rotated 45 degrees to the *diagonal position,*

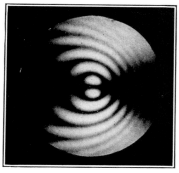

FIG. 108.   FIG. 109.

the interference figure appears as illustrated in Fig. 107. The two "eyes," indicating the emergence of the optic axes, the oval curves, and the hyperbolic brushes, are to be noted in these figures. If one of the optic axes is perpendicular to the stage, the interference

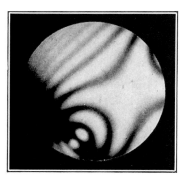

FIG. 110.

figure will resemble those illustrated in Figs. 108 and 109, the normal and diagonal positions, respectively. In these figures one axis and one brush are visible. Figure 110 represents the figure observed, if the orientation of the substance is such that the plane which includes the acute bisectrix and both optic axes is inclined to the stage. As already indicated, these figures do not remain stationary when the stage is rotated, and the brushes move in a direction opposite to that of the stage. With test plates it can be determined whether a biaxial substance possesses positive or negative optical character. Isotropic and uniaxial substances, when strained, may exhibit optical properties which resemble those of biaxial crystals.

Summary.—From the foregoing brief treatment of the optical properties of crystals it is evident that by means of the microscope much important optical data may be obtained.   In most cases the crystal system can be determined as well.   Such an examination is of great value in the identification of cut gemstones and gem minerals, especially if the latter are poorly crystallized or are in fragments or powder.   In the following table are summarized the criteria by which the determinations may be made:

BEHAVIOR OF SUBSTANCES IN PARALLEL POLARIZED LIGHT BETWEEN CROSSED NICOLS

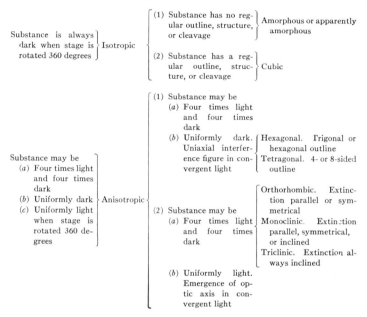

Shipley Polariscope.—This instrument (Fig. 111) may be used to determine whether a substance is singly or doubly refractive. It consists of a cylindrical shell with polaroid plates at the ends, whose favorable directions for transmission of light are at right angles to each other.   These polaroid plates act as the polarizer *P* and analyzer *A* in a manner similar to the Nicol prisms in the polarizing microscope.   The gemstone is mounted on a removable section of an inner cylinder which is free to rotate.   The support on which the gem is mounted may also be rotated about its axis with the knurled knob *B*.   When the removable section is placed in the proper position in the instrument, the gem is in

the beam of polarized light which enters through the lower polaroid plate.

If a singly refractive substance is viewed through *A* while *P*
is illuminated by a strong light, the substance will always remain

dark even though the inner cylinder and the support are rotated. If a doubly refractive
substance is similarly examined,
it will in general appear four
times light and four times dark
during a complete rotation of
the inner cylinder. However, if
an optic axis should happen to
coincide with the axis of the two
cylinders, the substance would
remain dark during the rotation

Fig. 111.—Shipley polariscope. (*Courtesy of Gemological Institute of America.*)

of the inner cylinder because the direction of the optic axis is a
singly refractive (isotropic) direction. If the knob *B* is then rotated, the position of the optic axis is changed and the stone
would appear four times light and four times dark on rotating
the inner cylinder.

A low-power loupe or hand lens which will bring the gemstone in focus while holding the polariscope close to the eye is
often of material assistance.

Fig. 112.

Fig. 113.

Enantiomorphism and Circular Polarization.—Right- and left-
handed crystals of substances are found, which bear the same relationship to each other as do the right and left hands. The crystals
are exactly similar but cannot be superimposed one upon the

other, just as one's hands are exactly alike but cannot be made to fit over each other, palm to back, thumb over thumb. Figures 112 and 113, respectively, show left- and right-handed crystals of quartz. This phenomenon is the result of a peculiar arrangement of the atoms of which the crystals are built up. It is as if, with the same kind, size, and shape of building stones, in one case a spiral stairway were built winding up to the right, in another, winding up to the left. This condition has its effect on the optical properties. *Enantiomorphous crystals,* as these are called, exhibit *circular polarization;* that is, they rotate the plane of polarization of light. Quartz is the best-known example of such minerals. Figure 114 illustrates the type of interference figure to be observed on quartz and quartz

Fig. 114.

gems. This figure differs from the normal uniaxial interference figure, in that the arms of the dark cross do not extend in to the center of the figure. By the use of test plates the right- or left-handed character of the crystals may be determined. This can also be done by superimposing a section of a right-handed over

Fig. 115.

Fig. 116.

one of a left-handed crystal (Fig. 115), or vice versa (Fig. 116). Such interference figures are sometimes observed when enantiomorphous crystals are twinned.

Pleochroism.—The color of a substance is due to the absorption of certain portions of white light in its passage through it. This is known as *selective absorption.* The remainder of the white light, namely, that which is not absorbed in the substance, blends to produce the color seen. In isotropic substances light is equally absorbed irrespective of the direction in which it travels. But in anisotropic substances the absorption of light varies with the direction, as is also the case with the velocity of light. This variation in absorption with direction is termed *pleochroism*.

The ruby well illustrates pleochroism. When looked at in a direction parallel to the vertical, or optic, axis, a ruby has a much deeper red color than when viewed in a direction perpendicular to this axis. For this reason rubies are usually cut with the table

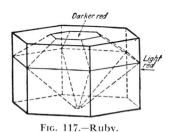

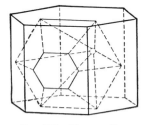

FIG. 117.—Ruby.   FIG. 118.—Tourmaline.

FIGS. 117 and 118.—Diagrams showing proper orientations for cutting natural ruby and tourmaline.

(p. 100) parallel to the basal pinacoid, thus producing the best possible color (Fig. 117). Light traveling parallel to the vertical axis is much more strongly absorbed than that traveling in a direction at right angles to it. The paler color seen in the latter direction is a compound hue made by the blending of two colors. One of these is the same deep red observed parallel to the vertical axis; the other is pink. The former is the color for the ordinary ray; the latter, for the extraordinary ray. As both rays are observed simultaneously, an intermediate color is accordingly seen. In tourmaline the conditions of pleochroism are reversed, and hence the table should be placed parallel to the vertical axis (Fig. 118) if a deep color is desired.

Since uniaxial substances have two principal indices of refraction, they possess two corresponding principal colors, when viewed in transmitted light. These substances are called *dichroic*. Ruby is an example of a substance showing *dichroism*. Similarly, biaxial substances, which possess three indices of refraction, show three principal colors and are said to be *trichroic*. The phenomenon is called *trichroism*. *Pleochroism* is the general term covering both dichroism and trichroism. Many minerals, like the ruby, are pleochroic in two shades of the same color. In others, however, the colors may be entirely unlike when the substance is viewed in different directions. Thus cordierite, sometimes called dichroite, shows three principal colors, yellow, light blue, and dark blue.

In order to separate the combined colors as seen by the eye, a simple instrument called the *dichroscope* (Fig. 119) is used. This

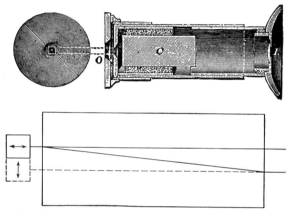

Fig. 119.—*Above:* cross section of dichroscope. *Below:* diagram showing passage of light rays through Iceland spar C (enlarged) and images with vibration directions.

consists of a transparent section of calcite or Iceland spar, *C,* mounted in a cylindrical case. At one end is a small square opening *O,* and at the other end an eyepiece *L.* Another and very convenient form of this instrument is shown in Fig. 120.

When the dichroscope is held to the eye, two images of the opening at the opposite end are seen side by side. This is due to the very strong double refraction of the calcite. The rays producing these images are polarized at right angles to each other (Fig. 119) and correspond to the ordinary and extraordinary rays (pp. 63 and 68).

If a pleochroic substance is placed in front of the opening, the two images are, in general, differently colored. The colors of the images correspond to the colors transmitted by the two rays in the substance. For example, if the ruby be viewed in this way, one image will be dark red, while the other is lighter in color. In one direction, however, namely, parallel to the vertical axis,

which is an isotropic direction, the two images will have the same color. In a direction at right angles to the vertical axis the two images will show the maximum difference in color.

In biaxial substances there are three principal directions at right angles to each other in which the absorption is different (Fig. 121). The dichroscope obviously can reveal only two of the colors at one time. To observe the three principal absorption colors the specimen must therefore be viewed parallel to two of the principal directions. When thus studied four images will be observed which will

FIG. 120.—Dichroscope with stone for testing.

include the three principal colors. One of the colors will be seen twice.

Pleochroism may also be observed with the microscope by using only the polarizer. On rotating a pleochroic substance on the stage of the microscope, first one color and then another will be seen at intervals of 90 degrees. But in this case it is necessary to carry in mind one of the colors for comparison with the other. However, in the dichroscope the colors are to be seen side by side, and very slight variations are thus more easily recognized. Because pleochroism is an absorption phenomenon, the colors observed will vary with the thickness of the specimen (p. 45).

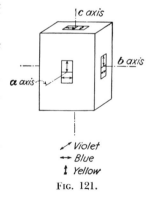

FIG. 121.

The property of pleochroism is another aid in the determination of gems. In many cases the character of the pleochroism is decisive in making an identification.

For example, red garnet and spinel have been used to imitate the ruby, but on account of their total lack of pleochroism these stones are easily distinguished from the ruby.

Absorption Spectra.—The color of a mineral is the result of the blending of all the portions of white light not absorbed. Two minerals may absorb light in entirely different ways and yet show the same color. By means of the spectroscope, an instrument described in all standard texts on physics, exactly what particular portions of white light are absorbed by any substance may be determined. The unabsorbed light is dispersed (p. 54) in its passage through the prism of the spectroscope, forming a band of colors known as an *absorption spectrum.* Dark lines or bands crossing the spectrum indicate the light which has been absorbed. Certain gems have typical and unique absorption spectra, and the

Fig. 122.—Absorption spectrum of a Burma zircon. (*Adapted from Anderson.*)

determination of these spectra is often of value in the differentiation of precious stones. For example, the absorption spectrum of a Burma zircon (Fig. 122), shows prominent dark lines and bands for the following wave-lengths, given in millimicrons, mμ: [1] 691, 683, 663, 660, 654 (in the red); 621, 615 (orange); 589, 563 (yellow); 538, 516 (green); 484, 460 (blue); 433 (violet).

Other gem minerals possess distinctive absorption spectra with strong lines and bands, as follows:

Ruby—strong lines in the red, 694, 693, 639; wide band in orange, yellow, and green, 595 to 520; lines in the blue, 476, 475, 468 mμ.

Emerald—strong lines in the red, 683, 681, 662, 646; broad band in orange and yellow, 630 to 580 mμ.

Alexandrite—strong lines in the red, 680, 678; broad band in orange, yellow, and green, 620 to 540 mμ.

Almandite—strong bands in yellow and green, 576, 505; weaker ones in the orange, 617, and blue, 462 mμ.

Synthetic blue spinel—strong bands in orange, yellow, and green, 633, 580, 544 mμ.

---

[1] These wave-lengths are also designated in terms of angstrom units, Å: 6,910 Å., 6,830 Å., 6,625 Å., and so forth; see footnote, p. 55.

In the case of an allochromatic mineral (p. 41) the character of the absorption spectrum may offer a clue as to the nature of the pigmenting impurity, which might not be detected in any other way. The *pocket spectroscope* and *microspectroscope* may be used for the approximate determination of absorption spectra.

Chapter V

CRYSTAL STRUCTURE AND X-RAY METHODS

Crystal Structure.—The popular conception of a crystal is that of a solid bounded by natural plane surfaces, called faces. Thus, the diamond commonly occurs in forms bounded by well-developed faces (Fig. 123). These forms are the external expression of a definite internal arrangement of the atoms making up the

Fig. 123.—Diamond crystal with well-developed dodecahedral faces (enlarged). (*Courtesy of Lazare Kaplan.*)

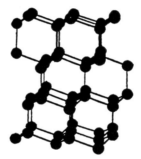

Fig. 124.—Model showing arrangement of carbon atoms in the diamond.

solid. Owing to the advances made in the study of crystal structure during the last half century, a marked change in the conception of a crystal has taken place.

The external forms of crystals will always be the subject of serious investigation, for they are of much value in the identification and classification of crystals. However, the scientist today places great emphasis upon the internal structure of crystals, that is, upon the arrangement of the atoms of which they are composed. Accordingly, *a crystal is defined as a solid whose component atoms are arranged in a definite three-dimensional pattern.* Figure 124 shows the arrangement of the carbon atoms in the diamond.

The atoms making up crystals are arranged according to basic patterns, called *space-lattices.* In these space-lattices there is a regular repetition of atoms, represented by points, at constant

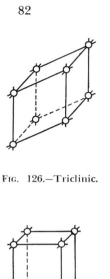

FIG. 126.—Triclinic.

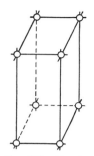

FIG. 127.—Simple monoclinic.

FIG. 128.—Base-centered mono-clinic.

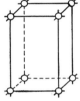

FIG. 129.—Sim-ple orthorhom-bic.

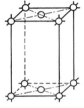

FIG. 130.—Base-centered ortho-rhombic.

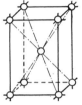

FIG. 131.—Body-centered ortho-rhombic.

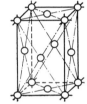

FIG. 132.—Face-centered ortho-rhombic.

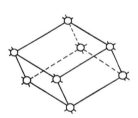

FIG. 133.—Rhombohedral.

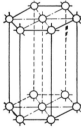

FIG. 134.—Hex-agonal.

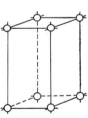

FIG. 135.—Sim-ple tetragonal.

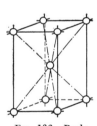

FIG. 136.—Body-centered tetrag-onal.

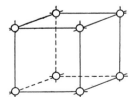

FIG. 137.—Simple cubic.

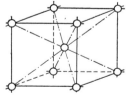

FIG. 138.—Body-centered cubic.

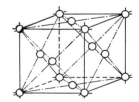

FIG 139.—Face-centered cubic.

FIGS. 126–139.—The fourteen space-lattices.

intervals for a given direction, Fig. 125. Fourteen space-lattices are geometrically possible, and these fourteen lattices are in harmony with the six crystal systems. If planes are passed through the points of the lattices, space is divided into identical parallelepipeds, called *unit cells*. Figures 126 to 139 on page 82 illustrate the unit cells of the fourteen space-lattices. As the drawings indicate, these cells are the basic units of the various structures which continue in all three directions. Many crystal structures

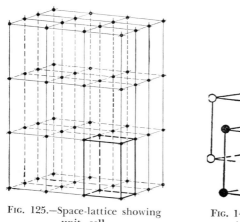

FIG. 125.—Space-lattice showing unit cell.

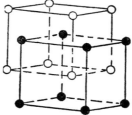

FIG. 140.—Interpenetrating unit cells.

must be interpreted as consisting of space-lattices interpenetrating in various ways (Fig. 140).

Since the internal arrangement of the atoms is fundamental in crystal structure, it is evident that a specimen of quartz, bounded by natural plane surfaces (Fig. 310), and an irregular grain of quartz, as found in sand, are both to be considered as crystals in the broad sense.

X-ray Methods.—The internal structure of crystals may be determined by various X-ray methods. Brief reference will be made to the Laue, Bragg, powder, and rotation or oscillation methods.

Laue Method.—A beam of heterogeneous or polychromatic X-rays is transmitted through an oriented section of a crystal (**Fig.** 141). The emergent rays consist of a strong, undeviated beam and of fainter beams which have been diffracted or reflected by the different layers of atoms. These beams are directed upon a photographic plate, and a spot photograph, known as a *Laue pho-*

tograph or *Laue diagram,* is produced (Fig. 142). From the distribution and intensity of these spots, the internal structure of the crystal under consideration may be determined.

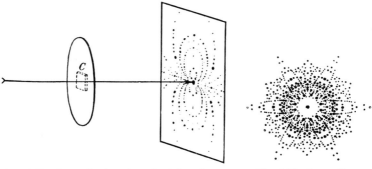

FIG. 141.—General plan for obtaining Laue diagrams. (*Adapted from Rinne.*)

FIG. 142.—Laue diagram of beryl parallel to the *C* axis. (*After Rinne.*)

Bragg Method.—While the Laue method involves the transmission of X-rays through the crystal, the Bragg method depends upon the reflection of a beam of homogeneous or monochromatic X-rays from the successive layers of atoms, corresponding to simple crystal faces, such as the cube, dodecahedron, and octahedron in the cubic system.

An X-ray beam with wave-length λ is directed upon a crystal at a small angle. The crystal is then slowly turned. The angles at which reflections of maximum intensity take place, called the

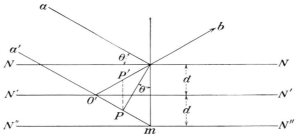

FIG. 143.—Diagram showing reflections from parallel layers of atoms and determination of Bragg angle.

Bragg angles, can be determined (Fig. 143). By means of the formula $n\lambda = 2d \sin \theta$, it is possible to calculate the actual distance between the successive layers of atoms parallel to the crystal face.

By determining the Bragg angles and the relative intensities of reflections from several simple faces, the spatial relations of the atoms within the crystal, that is, the structure of the crystal, may be deduced. This method is especially applicable to the determination of the more simple crystal structures. The apparatus is called the X-ray spectrometer.

W. H. and W. L. Bragg (father and son), who devised the method, were the first to determine the structure of the diamond (Fig. 144). The carbon atoms are located both at the positions of a face-centered cube (Fig. 139) and at the corners of a tetrahedron within the cube.[1] Moreover, the Braggs determined the length of the edge of the unit cell of the diamond containing the equivalent of eight carbon atoms as 3.55×10^{-8} centimeters, or 3.55 angstrom units.

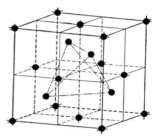

FIG. 144.—Unit cell of diamond.

Powder Method.—In this method finely powdered material is used, in contrast to the Laue and Bragg methods, which require a definitely oriented crystal specimen. Monochromatic X-rays are transmitted through a thin layer of the fine powder (Fig. 145), and the reflected rays are recorded on a semi-circular photographic film, producing a diffraction pattern (Fig. 146), called a *powder photograph*. The lines of the pattern are due to reflections from definite crystal planes. If the reflecting crystal planes can be identified, the structure of the substance may be determined. This method greatly extended the use of X-rays in the study of crystal structure.

Rotation or Oscillation Methods.—In these methods monochromatic X-rays are directed upon a single small crystal, which is rotated or oscillated through a definite angle about some important crystallographic direction. As the crystal is rotated, reflection will take place from all the planes that come into proper position. The number of reflections is large. They are recorded on a photographic film (Fig. 147). By graphical methods the planes responsible for the reflections can be identified. These methods

---

[1] Figure 124 (p. 81) shows the structure model of the diamond so placed that the layers of atoms parallel to an octahedron face are horizontal.

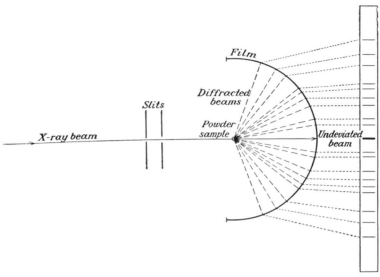

FIG. 145.—Diagram showing method for obtaining powder photographs.

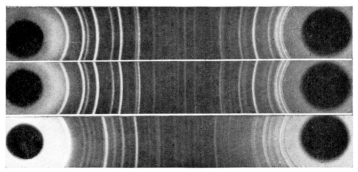

FIG. 146.—Powder photographs of natural (*top*) and synthetic rubies, which are identical, and of rose quartz.

CRYSTAL STRUCTURE AND X-RAY METHODS

Fig. 147.—X-ray diffraction pattern of apatite by the rotation method.

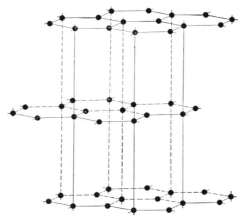

Fig. 148.—Model showing the widely separated parallel layers of carbon atoms in graphite.

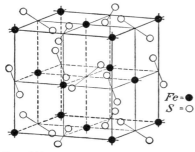

Fig. 149.—Unit cell of pyrite, FeS₂.

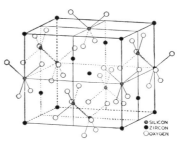

Fig. 150.—Unit cell of zircon, ZrSiO₄.

are serviceable in interpreting complex crystal structures and those of low symmetry.

Crystal Structure of Elements.—Crystals of 21 elements, which include copper, silver, gold, and platinum, have the face-centered cubic arrangement (Fig. 139). The body-centered cubic structure is possessed by crystals of 14 elements (Fig. 138). Iron at ordinary temperatures has this type of structure. Sixteen elements have structures based either upon the rhombohedral or hexagonal arrangements (Figs. 133 and 134). Figure 148 illustrates the structure of graphite, which is the hexagonal modification of the element carbon (p. 90). The structure of some elements, for example, sulfur, is very complex.

Structure of Compounds.—The different types of structures among minerals are very numerous and many are extremely complex. Two comparatively simple structures are illustrated, namely, those of pyrite, FeS_2 (Fig. 149), and zircon, $ZrSiO_4$ (Fig. 150).

Value of X-ray Analysis.—Since 1912, when the Laue method was first described, great progress has been made in developing new methods and techniques. Accordingly, our knowledge of the crystal structure of minerals and chemical compounds has been greatly expanded. Not only have the general theories of crystal structure based upon space groups been confirmed, but important relationships between crystal structure and the chemical and physical properties of crystallized solids have been established.

Since X-ray methods require elaborate equipment as well as highly specialized techniques, their application to the study and identification of gemstones and pearls will of necessity be restricted to a few centers having adequate facilities and trained personnel.

Chapter VI

CHEMICAL PROPERTIES

Every mineral has a characteristic chemical composition and may be either an element or a chemical compound. The elements gold, silver, platinum, and carbon commonly occur uncombined. The diamond is crystallized carbon. When two or more elements are in chemical combination, a chemical compound results. Rock crystal (quartz) consists of the elements silicon and oxygen. Its composition is indicated by the formula SiO_2, silicon dioxide. The formulas of many gem minerals are exceedingly complex, for example, turquois (see below).

With regard to chemical composition, minerals are classified under the following divisions.

1. *Elements*

Diamond.. C

2. *Sulfides*

Pyrite.. FeS_2

3. *Oxides and Hydroxides*

Corundum (ruby and sapphire)............................... Al_2O_3
Quartz... SiO_2
Opal... $SiO_2.xH_2O$

4. *Carbonates*

Smithsonite.. $ZnCO_3$
Malachite.. $CuCO_3.Cu(OH)_2$

5. *Sulfates*

Gypsum (satin spar)....................................... $CaSO_4.2H_2O$

6. *Aluminates*

Spinel... $Mg(AlO_2)_2$ or $MgO.Al_2O_3$
Chrysoberyl.. $Be(AlO_2)_2$ or $BeO.Al_2O_3$

7. *Phosphates*

Turquois... $H_5[Al(OH)_2]_6Cu(OH)(PO_4)_4$
Apatite.. $Ca_5(F, Cl)(PO_4)_3$

8. *Silicates*

Beryl (emerald).................... $Be_3Al_2(SiO_3)_6$ or $3BeO.Al_2O_3.6SiO_2$
Orthoclase......................... $KAlSi_3O_8$ or $K_2O.Al_2O_3.6SiO_2$
Garnet....................... $M''_3M'''_2(SiO_4)_3$ or $3M''O.M'''_2O_3.3SiO_2$
$(M'' = Mg, Ca, Fe, or Mn; M''' = Al, Fe, or Cr)$

89

It should be noted that the formulas of the minerals belonging to the aluminate and silicate groups may be expressed in two ways.

Minerals commonly used as gems are given as examples for each group. The elements, oxides, aluminates, and silicates are the groups which contain most of the important gem minerals. The minerals referred to in the classification are all of inorganic character. Certain substances which are also used as gems, such as jet, amber, pearl, and coral, are of organic nature, having been formed through the agency of live organisms.

Some chemical substances occur in different modifications each having distinct physical and chemical properties, although the chemical composition is the same. Thus, the element carbon occurs as the diamond and graphite, and iron disulfide, FeS_2, as pyrite and marcasite. When a chemical substance occurs in two distinct modifications, it is said to be *dimorphous;* in three modifications, *trimorphous;* in many, *polymorphous.* The element sulfur is an excellent example of a polymorphous substance, as at least six modifications are recognized. Synthetic corundum is also polymorphous. These modifications are often called *allotropic forms.*

Chapter VII

FORMATION AND OCCURRENCE OF GEM MINERALS

Formation of Gem Minerals.—There are four important modes of formation of gem minerals: (1) from solution; (2) from fusion; (3) by metamorphism; and (4) by organic processes.

Formation from Solution.—Minerals may be formed from solutions in several ways: (1) by the evaporation of the solvent, (2) by change of temperature or pressure, or (3) by chemical action involving solutions, gases, or solids. Sometimes several of these methods may be effective simultaneously. Malachite, quartz, opal, and gypsum are examples of gem minerals which have been derived from solutions in one or another of the foregoing ways.

Formation from Fusion.—Igneous rocks (p. 95) are formed by the solidification of molten masses of rather complex composition, called *magmas.* During the solidification of the magma, various minerals crystallize one after another. In general, the slower the cooling of the mass, the larger the crystals which are formed. *Mineralizers,* which include water vapor and other gases, are also important in influencing the size and character of the crystals formed. Mineralizers are very important in the formation of gem minerals, which are usually only minor constituents of igneous rocks and among the last minerals to crystallize as the magma cools. The diamond, emerald, sapphire, topaz, and tourmaline have been formed in this way.

Formation by Metamorphic Processes.—The action of heat, pressure, and moisture upon rocks produces marked changes in their character and mineral composition. Thus, rocks are often profoundly changed by the intrusion of igneous masses, as a result of the action of the heat and the gases emanating from the igneous body. This process is called *contact metamorphism.* Shales and limestones are especially susceptible to alteration by this type of metamorphism. Emerald, garnet, spinel, and diopside are commonly the result of contact metamorphism. Mountain-making processes, largely dependent for their effectiveness upon pressure, cause the metamorphism of very large areas of rocks. This is known as *regional metamorphism*. Among gems formed in this way are staurolite, cyanite, and garnet. Evidences of these two

FIG. 151.—Beryl: variety, emerald. Bogota, Colombia.

FIG. 152.—Titanite. Arendal, Norway.

types of metamorphism, which may have been simultaneous in their action, are often observed in the same mineral locality.

Formation by Organic Processes.—Some gems are strictly organic substances, for example, amber and jet. Pearl and geyserite are formed by the action of organisms on solutions, and opalized or petrified wood by the reaction of solutions with organic material.

Occurrence of Gems.—Gem minerals may either be *disseminated* through other minerals or rocks (Figs. 151 and 152) or found as

FIG. 153.—Attached crystal of diopside. Ala, Italy.

attached crystals (Fig. 153). Disseminated minerals sometimes are well crystallized, though more often they are of irregular shape. Garnet, beryl, and diamond are commonly found disseminated. Attached crystals are usually *singly terminated* (Fig. 153), whereas disseminated crystals may be *doubly terminated,* having well-developed faces at both ends of the crystal (Fig. 152).

A *vein* is a crack or crevice filled with mineral matter (Fig. 154). A rock crevice becomes a vein by the gradual deposition within it of one or more minerals, usually from solutions. If the composition of the solution changes from time to time, different minerals may be deposited in the same vein, giving it a *banded* appearance (Fig. 155). Veins may be either *symmetrically* (Fig. 155) or *unsymmetrically* banded. In the former case the same minerals appear in the same relative positions on both sides of the vein. The valueless portions of veins are spoken of as the *gangue,* as, for example, the quartz in gold-bearing quartz veins. The solutions commonly involved in the filling of veins may be either

Fig.   154.—Vein   of   serpentine.

Fig. 155.—Banded vein of sphalerite *(dark),* fluorite and calcite.

descending solutions, which have obtained their mineral matter by leaching out the more soluble constituents of the overlying rocks; or hot *ascending* solutions, the mineral content of which has come from igneous masses or other deeply buried rocks. Mineralization by solutions which have traveled in a *lateral* direction may also occur.

Geodes are cavities lined with minerals, often well crystallized (Fig. 156). These cavities may be large enough to be called caves. They were once filled with a solution from which the mineral matter slowly crystallized out. Quartz crystals, agate, and opal commonly form geode fillings (Figs. 325, 326, and 327). The term geode is restricted to cavities in rocks, especially sedimentary rocks. Similar cavities in veins or pegmatites (p. 95) are called *vugs* and are often the source of excellent gem material, for example, aquamarine, topaz, and tourmaline.

The occurrences of gems are classified in still another way. If the minerals are found in the place in which they were originally formed, they are said to occur *in situ* or in *primary deposits*. Beryl and tourmaline in pegmatites are examples of the *in situ* type of occurrence. Quite often gems have been weathered out of the mother rock, and carried away by the streams. By being constantly rolled about in the stream bed the stones become worn and rounded. Minerals with low specific gravity are obviously more readily transported than the heavy ones. Hence, the heavier minerals are deposited at those places along the stream where the velocity has been decreased. In this way, by natural processes

Fig. 156.—Geode of calcite crystals.

the heavy and resistive minerals, which include many of the gems, are sorted and segregated in sands and gravels. Such occurrences are known as *placer* or *secondary deposits*. The first South African diamonds were found in placers in the stream beds of the Vaal and Modder rivers. Rubies and sapphires frequently occur in such deposits, as also do native gold and platinum. Minerals occurring in placer deposits are often called *alluvials*.

Because placer or secondary deposits commonly consist of loose sands and gravels, gem minerals occurring in them are usually easily recovered with no danger of fracturing them by blasting, as is frequently the case in other deposits. Moreover, precious stones obtained from placer deposits are generally of high quality; for during their transportation by the stream, minerals with incipient fractures, inclusions, and other flaws tend to break along these lines of weakness. The more resistive fragments thus formed are very apt to be free from imperfections and hence of good quality.

Rocks.—The rocks of the earth's crust may be classified as (1) *igneous,* (2) *sedimentary,* and (3) *metamorphic.*

Igneous Rocks.—As mentioned previously (p. 91), igneous rocks are formed by the solidification of magmas, which are molten masses of mineral matter with a complex composition. The temperature of these masses is usually high. The minerals found in igneous rocks are of two types, *essential* minerals, which make up the larger part of the rock, and *accessory* or minor minerals, including gems and ores.

Magmas may reach the surface through volcanic vents. The rocks formed by the solidification of such magmas are called *volcanic* or *extrusive* rocks. Not many gems are found in these rocks. Because they cooled rapidly on the surface of the earth, their texture is glassy, cellular, or very fine-grained. Igneous bodies, which have solidified at depth, have cooled slowly, and are therefore coarse and fairly well crystallized. They are known as *plutonic* or *intrusive* rocks. The diamond, tourmaline, and quartz occur in plutonic rocks; olivine, turquois, and opal in volcanic rocks. Topaz and pyrope garnet may be found in either type of rock.

Igneous rocks may be subdivided in another way, that is on the basis of mineral and chemical composition. One group is characterized by a high content of silica, and contains orthoclase, acid plagioclase, more or less quartz, and some dark-colored mineral. Rocks of this group are generally light-colored. They are referred to as *acid* or *salic* rocks. Rocks of the other group contain less silica, with basic plagioclase, no quartz, and a large amount of dark minerals. These are usually dark in color, and are called *basic* or *femic* rocks. It must be pointed out here that rocks intergrade gradually and completely. The distinctions between rocks are by no means so hard and fast as those between minerals.

The acid rocks include *granites, syenites, diorites, pegmatites,* and *rhyolites,* and others of less importance. The very coarse and well-crystallized rocks known as pegmatites are important because of the many gem minerals they frequently contain, some of which may be quite rare. Beryl, tourmaline, several forms of quartz (such as rock crystal, smoky and rose quartz, and amethyst), spodumene, topaz, and a great variety of other gems often occur in this kind of rock. Pegmatites are the segregations of the most soluble constituents of granites. Before solidification they contained large amounts of vapors and gases, which aided in the formation of the good crystals so characteristic of this type of rock. Pegmatites and *dikes* are similar. They are fissures filled with igneous intrusions.

The basic igneous rocks include *gabbro, basalt, peridotite,* and *pyroxenite.* Peridotites are extremely important as the original source of the diamond.

Sedimentary Rocks.—These are characterized by a stratified or bedded structure and have been deposited, generally by the aid of water. The materials of which they are composed have been derived from igneous, metamorphic, or older sedimentary rocks by the processes of weathering and transportation. Sedimentary rocks are divided into (1) mechanical, (2) chemical, and (3) organic sediments.

The *mechanical sediments* are those which have been deposited in bodies of water by settling due to gravity. The particles were not dissolved in the water, but were mechanically suspended. Some examples of mechanical sediments are *shales,* composed of consolidated mud or silt; *sandstone,* made up of sand grains; and *conglomerates* composed of rounded and *breccias* of angular fragments in a finer ground mass. These have occasionally been formed by the consolidation of the materials in placer deposits (p. 94). *Chemical sediments* include some limestones, gypsum, and salt, all of which were deposited from solution by chemical means. The *organic sediments* are composed of the remains of animals or plants, and include some limestones and coal. Many sedimentary rocks which are loose or consolidated mechanical deposits are important sources of the diamond, ruby, sapphire, zircon, and amber. Moreover, in the veins which may traverse the various kinds of sedimentary rocks, such minerals as opal, quartz, and gypsum may be found.

Metamorphic Rocks.—These are formed from igneous or sedimentary rocks by the action of heat, pressure, and moisture, commonly at depth. As explained on page 91, there are two types of metamorphism, *regional* and *contact.* The more important metamorphic rocks have been formed by regional metamorphism. They include *gneisses,* banded rocks derived mainly from igneous rocks; *schists,* finely laminated, with a good cleavage, and made up chiefly of one mineral, such as mica, hornblende, talc, or chlorite; *quartzite,* a very firm and compact metamorphosed sandstone; *slate,* derived from shale, and possessing an excellent cleavage into large, flat sheets; *marble,* which is recrystallized limestone or dolomite; and *serpentine,* a soft, green rock, formed by the metamorphism of basic igneous rocks or impure dolomitic limestones. Lapis lazuli, ruby, sapphire, and spinel are found in contact metamorphic marbles. Schists and gneisses frequently contain emerald, garnet, jadeite, nephrite, staurolite, and others.

Geological Occurrence.—The geological sources from which the most important gem minerals are obtained may be summarized as follows:

Igneous rocks:
Basic Rocks.—Diamond, garnet, olivine.
Pegmatites.—Emerald, beryl, tourmaline, topaz, spodumene, quartz.
Secondary deposits:
Sands and Gravels (Alluvials).—Diamond, sapphire, ruby, amber, jadeite, rock crystal, tourmaline, beryl, agate, chrysoberyl, amethyst.
Deposits from water:
By Various Methods.—Opal, quartz, turquois, malachite.
Metamorphic rocks:
Crystalline Limestones.—Ruby, sapphire, spinel, lapis lazuli, emerald.
Schists and Gneisses.—Jade, garnet, chrysoberyl, emerald.

Because of the great value of the diamonds and other gemstones obtained from them, the alluvial deposits, that is, sands and gravels, are at present the most important sources.

Geographical Occurrence.—As the continent of Africa is the principal source of the diamond, it has produced annually 90 to 95 per cent of the world's gems, by value. The countries of Africa that are the most important in this respect are the Belgian Congo, Gold Coast, Union of South Africa, Sierra Leone, Angola, and South-West Africa. Other countries producing gems in appreciable amounts are Brazil, Siam, Burma, Ceylon, Russia, Germany, British Guiana, Colombia, and Australia. Since the more valuable gems do not occur in any abundance in the United States, the annual production of gem minerals in this country has always been relatively small, and especially so in recent years.

Statistics of Production.—For many years the value of the world's production of rough gem minerals varied from $80,000,000 to $100,000,000. During the period of depression, beginning about 1930, production dropped approximately one-half. Accordingly, the value of the gem minerals mined annually was estimated at about $50,000,000, of which rough diamonds accounted for about 95 per cent. During the Second World War there was further curtailment, for the diamond pipe mines of Africa were not operated, and the mining of other gem minerals practically ceased throughout the world. However, owing to the unprecedented demand of the war effort for industrial diamonds, production of diamonds from the alluvial deposits of Africa continued, especially from those of the Belgian Congo.

The following table gives the world's production of diamonds in carats and their value for the years 1938 to 1944, as reported by S. H. Ball.[1]

Year	Carats	Value
1938	11,755,243	$43,000,000
1939	12,485,320	40,360,000
1940	14,140,200	31,000,000
1941	9,345,075	28,000,000
1942	9,254,200	28,000,000
1943	8,140,000	29,000,000
1944	11,400,000	40,000,000

The value of the annual production of gem minerals does not indicate the volume of the retail trade in gemstones, which is much larger. This is due to many factors, such as (1) the cost of fashioning the rough minerals into finished gemstones, (2) the drawing upon the reserves of previous years, and (3) the fact that annually many cut stones are placed upon the market and are resold. In recent years the resale of gems has been very large.

[1] "The Diamond Industry," Annual Review, *Jewelers' Circular-Keystone*, N. Y.

Chapter VIII

CUTTING AND POLISHING OF GEMS

Beautiful as some gems are in their natural form, they may all be much improved by judicious cutting and polishing. It frequently happens that only a small portion of the gem crystal is transparent, flawless, and of good color. Even if the entire crystal is of gem quality, its value may be greatly enhanced by the proper cutting of facets, so disposed as to bring out most effectively its color, fire, and brilliancy. At the same time an endeavor is made to produce a symmetrical stone with an outline pleasing to the

FIG. 157.   FIG. 158.

eye. Moreover, amorphous and cryptocrystalline gem materials must obviously be cut and polished so as to enhance their attractiveness.

Cabochon Cuts.—Before the art of gem cutting was well developed, the naturally occurring gem minerals were smoothed or rounded off and polished, by crude methods. At an early date gems were drilled or pierced and used as drops. The old, rounded forms of cutting still survive in the various types of *cabochon* cuts. These include the double or convex cabochon, the lentil cut, high cabochon, simple, plain, or single cabochon, and hollow or concavo-convex cabochon. The outline of gems cut in any of the above cabochon styles may be circular, elliptical, or oval, as one looks down upon the stone.

In the *double-cabochon* cut (Fig. 157), both the upper and lower parts of the stone are convex, though the curvature of the upper portion is the greater. If both parts have the same convexity, the cut is known as the *lentil* (Fig. 158). The *high-cabo-*

99

chon (Fig. 159) is cut with the upper portion very high.   The *simple-cabochon* style has a flat lower surface, which is mounted as the underside of the stone (Fig. 160).   In the *hollow-cabochon* cut the lower surface is hollowed out, being concave, and the upper portion is convex (Fig. 161).

The cabochon cuts are especially desirable for use with gems which have a chatoyant sheen, as shown by tiger's-eye; a play of colors, as in opal; opalescence, as in moonstone; or asterism, as seen in star rubies and star sapphires.   Stones whose charm depends upon their color or upon peculiar mottlings or markings are also cut in this way, garnet, turquois, tourmaline, chlorastrolite, and thomsonite being examples.   Some stones, as, for example, the

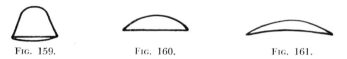

FIG. 159.   FIG. 160.   FIG. 161.

dark garnets, are so deeply colored that they appear almost black when cut in the ordinary way.   For such gems the hollow cabochon cut may be used to considerable advantage, for the thickness of the stone is thereby so reduced that a more pleasing color may be seen.

Faceted Cuts.—The art of cutting smooth plane surfaces of pleasing geometrical outline symmetrically placed on gems, has generally been credited to Louis de Berquen, of Bruges, Belgium.   Berquen's name is variously given in different languages as Ludwig von Berquen or van Berquem.   The discovery of this method is supposed to have been made during the latter part of the fifteenth century, 1456 to 1476.   But, it is now well established that faceted cuts were known and used at an earlier date, especially in Italy and France.   According to Henri Polak, the Venetian craftsman Vincenzo Peruzzi was probably the first to cut the diamond in the shape now known as the *brilliant*.

The original *table cut* was much used for the diamond.   The upper and lower points of a natural octahedral crystal were smoothed off and polished, the upper facet, known as the *table,* being much wider than the lower facet, called the *culet* (Fig. 162).

The *rose cut* was then developed and was much employed in the cutting of the diamond.   It is not used to any great extent at present except for small stones. The rose cut has a flat base, with triangular facets to the number of twelve to twenty-four, or even thirty-two, terminating in a point, grouped about the upper part of the stone (Figs. 163 and 164). Stones cut with few facets (twelve or less) are called *roses d'Anvers* and were a specialty at Antwerp; those with more facets are known as *roses couronnées*. The outline of these stones may be circular, elliptical, or oval. Sometimes a *double-rose cut* is used. It consists of an upper and lower portion, each of which has the rose cut.

About the end of the seventeenth century the *brilliant cut* was introduced. It has been extensively used for the diamond, since

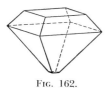

FIG. 162.   FIG. 163.   FIG. 164.   FIG. 165.

it brings out to marked advantage the remarkable fire and brilliancy of that gem. The finished gem retained a fairly high percentage of the weight of the original stone, and showed a marked improvement in brilliancy and fire over the older cuts. The octahedron, either natural or the result of cleavage, was made the basis of this cut. This type of cutting is now referred to as the *old mine cut* (Fig. 165) and is commonly observed on stones which were marketed up to the close of the nineteenth century. Later, more emphasis was placed on brilliancy and fire rather than on retaining the highest possible percentage of the original weight of the uncut stone and the modern brilliant cut was developed.

The general relationships between an octahedron and the finished gem are shown in Figs. 166 to 169. Approximately six-sixteenths of the height of the stone is removed from the upper point, and three-sixteenths from the lower. If the stone is of considerable size, this is done by sawing. The removed portions may be used for smaller stones. Cut in this manner the portion above the *girdle G* (Fig. 169) should be about 40 per cent as thick as that below the girdle. The upper portion of the stone is called the *crown, top,* or *bezel* (Fig. 167); the lower part, the *pavilion, back,* or *base* (Fig. 168). The uppermost facet *T* is the table, and *C* is the culet. Exclusive of the table and culet there are usually fifty-six facets, though in some cases the number is increased by groups of eight to sixty-four, seventy-two, or even eighty facets. All the facets of a brilliant have definite names. The fifty-eight facets of the usual brilliant include one table *T*, eight star facets *S*, four bezel or top main facets *B*, four top corner facets *TC*, sixteen top half (break or girdle) facets *TH*, sixteen bottom half (break or girdle) facets *BH*, four bottom corner facets *BC*, four pavilion or bottom main facets *P*, and one culet *C*.

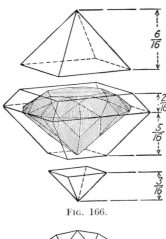

Since the four top corner facets *TC* may be of the same shape and size as the four bezel facets *B*, as is the case on the round brilliant, they also may be called bezel facets. Such stones are then said to have eight bezel facets. Similar conditions may apply to the bottom corner *BC* and the pavilion *P* facets. In such cases, stones are said to have eight pavilion facets.

Fig. 166.

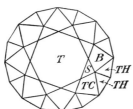

Fig. 167.

The girdle of the stone is formed where the top half and the bottom half facets (*TH* and *BH*, Figs. 167 and 168) meet in a sharp edge. In order to retain as much as possible of the original weight of the uncut stone the experienced diamond cutter may leave a very small portion of the rough original surface of the diamond crystal at one or two points around the girdle. These are known as *naturals* and generally do not de-

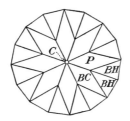

Fig. 168.

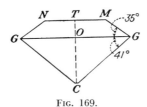

Fig. 169.

tract from the value of the stone if they are minute, because they are evidence of careful workmanship. However, if they are easily recognized the stone is said to have a *thick girdle*. At times the girdle is polished, or a series of small facets may even be placed around the entire circumference of the stone. For a given weight, stones with a polished or faceted girdle obviously have a smaller spread than those with knife-edge girdles.

The cutting of the diamond so as to exhibit its optical properties most advantageously is based upon long practical experience. Accordingly, it is common practice to cut stones so that the thickness TC (Fig. 169) from the table to the culet is about 60 per cent of the width or *spread* GG at the girdle. The distance TO of the table above the diameter through the girdle may vary from about one-third to slightly less than one-half of the distance OC that the culet is below it. The width of the table NM may be from 40 to 60 per cent of the spread.[1]

Under the foregoing conditions the angle that the main upper facets make with the plane through the girdle will be from 35 to 37 degrees, whereas the lower main facets will be inclined at about 41 degrees. Depending upon the character of the stones to be cut, a variation of 5 to 7 degrees may be observed in the inclination of the upper main facets, that is, from 30 to 37 degrees. The permissible variation in the inclination of the lower main facets is much less; for when stones are cut with these facets at angles less than 40 degrees, they have a *fish-eye* appearance, that is, they look dead. This is especially true if, at the same time, the upper main facets are cut at too low an angle, namely, at less than 30 degrees. On the other hand, when the angle of the lower main facets is greater than 42 degrees, the cut stone is too thick and is said to be *lumpy*. This applies also to stones with the table cut "too high," that is, with too great a depth from the table to the girdle. Stones cut in this way have a blackish, glassy appearance. Sometimes stones are sawed so that the removed portion, called the *sawed top*, is too large, and hence the depth from the table to the girdle is materially reduced and the spread of the table increased. Stones cut in this manner have less brilliancy and give the impression that they are larger than they actually are.

[1] For a detailed discussion, consult "Diamond Design," by Marcel Tolkowsky, London, 1919.

Such stones are said to be *swindled*. This term is now also applied to all cut stones with too large a spread of the table, and consequently with a shallow upper portion.

Krumbhaar, Johnsen, and Rösch endeavored to determine the theoretical form of the ideal brilliant cut in order that the cut diamond may show the maximum brilliancy. In making their determinations it was found that maximum brilliancy can be obtained when the incident and emergent rays are perpendicular to the table. Under these conditions the proportions of the stone and the angles of inclination of the main facets vary considerably

Gem	Index of refraction	Critical angle	Diameter of table, per cent	Height of crown, per cent	Height of pavilion, per cent	Total height, per cent *	Inclination of main facets	
							Upper	Lower
Diamond...........	2.42	24.5°	56.0 †	19.0 †	40.0 †	59.0 †	41.1°	38.5°
Zircon..............	1.95	30.9°	59.0	22.0	40.7	63.0	47.0°	38.8°
Corundum.........	1.77	34.5°	60.0	24.0	40.9	64.9	50.2°	38.9°
Spinel								
$p = 5$ ‡..........	1.73	35.3°	60.5	24.6	41.0	65.6	51.0°	39.0°
$p = 1$............	1.72	35.6°	60.5	24.7	41.0	65.7	51.2°	39.0°
Topaz §............	1.63	37.8°	61.0	26.0	41.1	67.0	53.0°	39.1°
Tourmaline.........	1.62	38.1°	59.0	27.3	40.7	68.0	53.1°	39.1°
Emerald...........	1.58	39.3°	56.6	28.1	41.1	69.2	52.3°	39.4°
Rock crystal........	1.54	40.5°	44.2	27.5	42.9	70.4	44.5°	40.6°

* These values do not take into account the thickness of the girdle. According to Eppler this amounts to about 2 per cent. The values given should be increased by 2 if it is taken into consideration.

† Percentage of the long diameter through the girdle *GG* (Fig. 169).

‡ Indicates parts of Al_2O_3 with respect to MgO. Thus, $p = 5$ means 1 MgO to $5Al_2O_3$ (p. 164).

§ These values also hold good for flint glass.

from those given above. The ideal cuts for other gemstones have been studied and calculated by Rinne and Eppler.

The table above, which is based largely upon the results obtained by the foregoing investigators, gives the various angles and relationships that should be observed in order to secure what they consider the ideal brilliant cut for the different gems.

Although these theoretical values are of general and scientific interest, it must be remembered that a mounted cut stone is viewed from many directions and under varying conditions and not merely in the manner indicated above, upon which the calculations are based. Furthermore, there are certain economic factors of importance which must be considered along with the production of brilliancy, such as the ratio of the weight of the cut to that of the original stone. Accordingly, it will undoubtedly continue to be the general practice in cutting gems to use data that experience has shown to be very effective.

Figure 170 illustrates the course of rays of light in passing through a brilliant-cut diamond. The light, which enters through the crown, will then strike the lower facets at an angle greater than the critical angle, which is about 24 degrees for the diamond

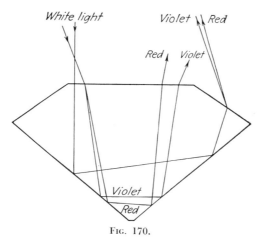

FIG. 170.

(p. 56), and will undergo repeated total reflection. When this reflected light emerges from the stone, the ever-changing flashes of color known as *fire* are to be observed, due to the strong dispersion of the mineral (p. 54).

The modern brilliant cut slowly evolved until it reached its present form in the early years of the twentieth century. By far the greatest majority of diamonds have been cut in this form, but from time to time it has been modified to produce novelty cuts, which have often enjoyed considerable vogue. In these cuts the number of facets is commonly increased by replacing one or more of the facets of the standard brilliant by pairs of smaller facets, thus adding new facets in multiples of eight.

The *double-brilliant* or *Lisbon cut* has seventy-four facets. The *twentieth-century cut* has eighty or eighty-eight facets. In addition to doubling some of the normal facets, eight very low facets replace the flat table of the regular brilliant cut. The *multi-*

facet cut may have as many as one hundred and four facets.   The
Portuguese cut has two rows of rhomboidal and three of triangular facets on both the crown and base.

Another departure from the standard brilliant cut is the use
of five-fold or six-fold symmetry to replace the eight-fold symmetry shown in Figs. 167 and 168.   In the *star cut* the hexagonal
table is bordered by six facets in the shape of equilateral triangles,
forming with the table a six-rayed star.

The *trap-brilliant* or *split-brilliant cut* has forty-two facets.   The
half-brilliant, Old English, single, or *eight cut* is a simple form
used on smaller stones.   These commonly have eighteen facets

Fig. 171.   Fig. 172.   Fig. 173.

including the table and the culet, eight facets above and eight
below the girdle (Fig. 171).   The culet is often omitted.

In order that as much of the stone as possible may be retained
in the finished gem, the outline varies considerably.   But symmetry and beauty of design are always kept in mind and rarely
sacrificed for size.   Rectangular, circular, oval, elliptical, pear-
shaped or pendeloque, triangular, and drop-shaped outlines are,
therefore, frequent.

The brilliant cut is also used for stones other than the diamond,
such as the ruby, sapphire, emerald, and zircon.   Many of these
minerals are also cut with a square outline and relatively few
facets (Fig. 178).   This is commonly true of the emerald.   Diamonds with the *emerald cut* (Figs. 172 and 173) have been popular in recent years.   This cut has fifty facets including the table
and culet.   Less of the original weight of the stone is sacrificed in
this cutting.

At present, fancy shapes are not uncommon, of which the following are the more important: *baguette, cut-corner triangle,
epaulet, half-moon, hexagon, keystone, kite, lozenge, marquise*
or *navette, pentagon* or *bullet, square, trapeze,* and *triangle* (Figs.
174 to 187).   These new shapes have given designers greater lati-
tude in the creation of modernistic jewelry.

FIG. 174.—Trapeze.   FIG. 175.—Half-moon.   FIG. 176.—Epaulet.

FIG. 177.—Triangle.   FIG. 178.—Square.   FIG. 179.—Cut-corner triangle.

FIG. 180.—Cut-corner triangle.   FIG. 181.—Lozenge.   FIG. 182.—Kite.   FIG. 183.—Pentagon or bullet.

FIG. 184.—Hexagon.   FIG. 185.—Keystone.   FIG. 186.—Baguette.   FIG. 187.—Marquise.

FIGS. 174–187.—Modern diamond cuts. (*Adapted from "The Glorification of the Diamond" by Ansen and Company, Inc., New York City.*)

The term *melee* is applied to stones cut from small diamonds, or from fragments, the result of either cleavage or sawing. Many of these small stones, of which 8 to 16 are required to make a carat, are cut with the usual fifty-eight facets and are called *full cut.* Smaller stones are called *small melee.* These stones may be so small that 400 are required to make a carat. These very small stones, both cut and uncut, are sold by the carat and not as

FIG. 188.   FIG. 189.

individuals. Small uncut diamonds weighing 60 or more to the carat are called *sand.*

The *step, trap,* or *cushion cut* (Figs. 188 and 189) is commonly used with colored stones such as emerald and tourmaline. The stone is cut rather flat, with one or more rows of facets arranged parallel to the girdle. A similar style, the *table cut,* differing somewhat from the older table cut (p. 100), has a very large table which joins the girdle in beveled edges. Occasionally the style of cutting used for the top differs markedly from that of the back.

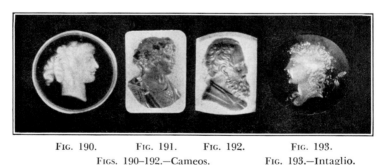

FIG. 190.   FIG. 191.   FIG. 192.   FIG. 193.
FIGS. 190–192.—Cameos.   FIG. 193.—Intaglio.

In order to increase the brilliancy of colored stones the ideal angles for some of them have recently been calculated (see table, p. 104).

Cameo.—The term *cameo* is used to designate those stones generally composed of two differently colored layers, in one of which a raised figure or design has been cut, the layer of the second color forming a background (Figs. 190 to 192). Cameos are cut principally from onyx, a variety of quartz having parallel layers of different colors, and are often called *stone cameos*. Shells with a similar structure are also employed. These are termed *shell cameos*. An *intaglio* is a gem with an incised design (Fig. 193).

A stone with a raised design and a depressed or somewhat hollowed background (Fig. 194) is called a *cuvette, curvette,* or *chevee*.

Cutting of Gems.—Because of its superior hardness, the cutting of the diamond presents a difficult problem, and *diamond cutters* form an aristocracy of talent among those who cut precious stones. Men who fashion stones other than the diamond are called *gem cutters, lapidaries,* or *lapidists.* For many years the principal diamond-cutting centers were located in Belgium, Germany, and the Netherlands. Prior to the Second World War, Antwerp and the Flemish provinces of Belgium had the largest number of diamond cutters (20,-000 to 21,000). Germany ranked second with Idar-Oberstein, Hanau, Odenwald, and the Palatinate as the important

FIG. 194.—Cuvette.

districts (6,500). Amsterdam, the Netherlands, which had long been an important center, ranked third with about 4,000 cutters. Paris and Saint-Claude, France; Geneva and Biel, Switzerland; and Genoa and Rome, Italy, are other centers in Europe. The war greatly disrupted the industry in Europe, but much progress has been made in rehabilitating it.

In Great Britain and the United States the number of diamond cutters increased during the war; some of these were engaged in the shaping of diamonds for industrial purposes. Birmingham and London are the principal centers in Great Britain. At present New York, Cincinnati, Detroit, Chicago, and Hazleton, Pennsylvania, have many diamond-cutting shops. It is reported that diamond cutting in the United States was started as an industry in New York in the early 1870's.

Diamonds are also cut in Johannesburg, Kimberley, Cape Town, and Pretoria, South Africa; and in Borneo, Palestine, Puerto Rico, Cuba, and Brazil.

Gem cutting has flourished for several centuries at Idar-Ober-stein, Germany, where there is abundant water and electric power. At first, agates were the principal stones that were cut and pol-ished, but later all gems, including the diamond and synthetic stones, were handled (p. 127). In the order of the number em-ployed, gem workers are classified as (1) diamond cutters, (2) gem cutters, and (3) lapidaries (p. 130). Before the war this district had about 1,600 establishments of varying sizes, many of them in

FIG. 195.—Cutting gems with hand-driven apparatus.

private homes. Other important gem-cutting centers are Saint-Claude in the Jura Alps and Royat in Puy-de-Dôme, France; Waldkirch, near Freiburg, Ger-many; Turnov, Czecho-Slovakia; also various places in China, Ceylon, India, and Japan.

Much fine lapidary work is done in Russia, largely in the fashioning of or-namental objects. In China and Japan crystal balls of quartz are laboriously cut and polished by hand. Canton, China, is an important center for the cutting and carving of jade; Bangkok, Thailand (Siam), for zircon; Biel and Locarno, Switzerland, for jewels and bearings for watches and scientific instruments. In many localities gems are cut by very primitive methods. Figure 195 shows a lapidary using a simple apparatus driven by hand.

Professional lapidary shops are scattered throughout the United States, especially in those states with well-known gem localities, such as Maine, Rhode Island, California, Oregon, and Montana. There are also many lovers of gems in this country who, as so-called *amateur lapidaries,* have become very skillful in the cutting and polishing of gem minerals (p. 131).

Diamond Cutting.—The process of diamond cutting may be di-vided into five stages, as follows: (1) *inspection,* (2) *cleaving,* (3) *sawing,* (4) *cutting,* (5) *polishing.*

1. *Inspection.*—The rough stones are first carefully examined with respect to crystal form and shape, for many of them are dis-torted, rounded, or twinned (p. 21). Inclusions, cleavage cracks,

or other flaws, if present, must be accurately located. The style of cutting that will permit the stone to be worked to the best advantage, and as far as possible eliminate imperfections, must also be decided upon. If the inspection shows that the stone must be cleaved or sawed, the directions in which this is to be done are marked upon it with India ink (Figs. 196 and 197).

2. *Cleaving.*—Rough stones with shapes unsuited for advantageous cutting, as well as those with inclusions, cleavage cracks,

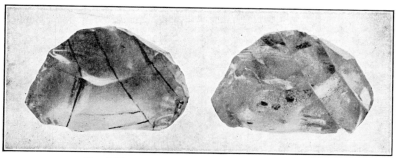

Fig. 196.   Fig. 197.

Fig. 196.—Jonker diamond marked for cleaving and sawing. About two-thirds natural size.

Fig. 197.—The diamond after being cleaved twice and fitted together. (*Photographs by F. H. Pough.*)

or other flaws, are commonly cleaved. This can be readily done by means of the highly perfect octahedral cleavage possessed by the diamond. Moreover, large stones may be readily subdivided into smaller ones suitable for commercial purposes. This is especially true of large stones which are slightly off-color, for, by cleaving, the thickness of the resulting portions is greatly reduced, and accordingly the color is much improved.

Figure 198 shows a model illustrating the arrangement of the atoms of carbon in a diamond crystal (see also Fig. 144). It is easily seen that successive horizontal layers are alternately closely and widely spaced. The closer the spacing, the greater the attractive forces between the atoms; the wider the spacing, the weaker the forces. Accordingly, cleavage readily takes place in the direction indicated by the arrow *A*. This direction is parallel to one of the faces of the octahedron. Although there are four different directions of such cleavage in the diamond, only two, *A* and *B*, are readily seen in the figure.

To cleave a diamond it is first necessary to mount the stone on the end of a specially designed stick, by means of a suitable hard cement. Next, an incision or groove is made in the direction of the cleavage as determined by the inspection. If the stone has

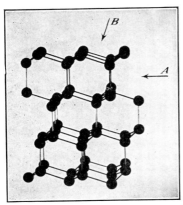

FIG. 198.—Model of the crystal structure of the diamond.

well-developed octahedron faces, the octahedral cleavage directions can naturally be easily recognized; otherwise, it is necessary for the cleaver to study the stone carefully for lines of growth, commonly called the *grain.* These growth lines are shown in Figs. 199 and 207.

The groove is cut by using the edge of a small cleavage or sawed fragment of a diamond, called a *sharp,* also mounted on a stick so that it may be easily handled like a pencil (Fig. 200). The stick with the diamond to be cleaved is then placed in a support with the tapered edge of a steel plate, the *cleaving iron,* held with one hand in the groove or notch. With the other hand the steel plate is struck a sharp blow with a small hammer or cleaving implement (Fig. 201). The stone is thus caused to cleave or separate into two parts, parallel to a face of the octahedron.

Although this process is apparently a simple one, cleaving in reality exacts the most careful workmanship, since a good diamond may be easily ruined by improper cleaving or careless handling. The cleavage surfaces should be as smooth as possible. Great care must also be exercised so that even the minutest particles are not lost. Small cleavage fragments are called *chips.* They should not be confused with melee (p. 108).

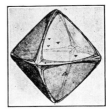

FIG. 199.—Diamond from South Africa. (*After Goldschmidt and Fersmann.*)

3. *Sawing.*—In order to convert as much as possible of the original rough diamond into a finished gem, the stone is generally subdivided into smaller ones. This is usually done by sawing it through the middle so as to obtain two stones of about equal size.

When sawed above the middle, stones of unequal size result (Fig. 166). As indicated under Inspection (p. 110), the shape of the stone and the position of flaws or imperfections determine the manner in which the stone is sawed. Sometimes both sawing and cleaving may be used, especially with large or imperfect stones.

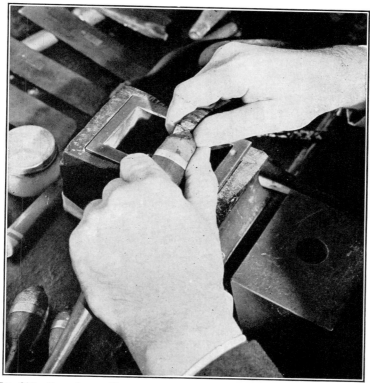

FIG. 200.—Grooving a diamond for cleaving. (*Photograph by courtesy of Harry Winston, Inc.*)

The smaller portions of the stone thus formed may be cut and polished as melee.

The sawing is done by means of a thin phosphor-bronze disk, called the *diamond saw*, two or three inches in diameter, which revolves at a speed of 2,500 to 4,000 revolutions per minute. The diamond to be sawed is embedded in a metal cup-like holder with a mixture of plaster of Paris and glue. Only the portion to be removed is exposed. The stone is then held mechanically against the edge of the diamond saw, which has been impregnated with diamond dust and oil (Fig. 202). To make the first incision or groove, a thicker or *starting saw* is generally used. To saw a one-carat stone usually takes about eight hours. Larger stones may require several days. Generally one attendant can supervise the operation of twenty sawing machines.

FIG. 201.—Cleaving a diamond. (*Photograph by courtesy of Harry Winston, Inc.*)

Diamond dust can be used to saw or polish the diamond in some directions because in the random distribution of the dust in the saw or on the skeif (p. 118) some of the particles will have hard surfaces and directions exposed (p. 119). These particles are able to abrade the stone in directions of inferior hardness. Sawing is therefore best accomplished in directions parallel to the faces of the cube, commonly called the *sawing grain*. Experience shows that it is almost impossible to saw the diamond if the plane of the cut varies more than a few degrees from that of a cube face. There

are also sawing grains parallel to faces of the rhombic dodecahedron which are sometimes used. Since in each sawing grain
there is a favorable direction for sawing, the direction of revolution of the saw must be controlled. By using a high-voltage electric current the diamond may be sawed in directions other than
in the sawing grains.[1]

FIG. 202.—Sawing the Jonker diamond. (*Photograph by courtesy of Harry
Winston, Inc.*)

4. *Cutting.*—In general, the expression the *cutting of a gem*
includes the shaping and polishing of a rough stone into a finished
gem, that is, the whole fashioning process. In a more restricted
sense, cutting refers only to the process of roughly shaping and
outlining the stone, and is sometimes called *girdling* or *rounding*.
This was formerly done by rubbing together the appropriate portions of two stones over a small box so as to catch the powder and
minute fragments produced during the process. The stones were
mounted on the ends of conveniently handled sticks. This process is called *bruting*.

[1] PETERS, C. G., K. F. NEFFLEN, and F. K. HARRIS, "Diamond Cutting Accelerated
by an Electric Arc," *Research Paper* RP1657, *Journal of Research, National Bureau
of Standards,* vol. 34, June 1945

Cutting is now more rapidly accomplished by mechanical means. The stone to be cut or shaped is mounted with a hard cement in a brass holder, called the *dop*. The dop is then screwed to the chuck of a motor-driven lathe. A second stone cemented in another dop and fastened to the end of a stick of special design is then held against the stone revolving rapidly in the lathe. The

FIG. 203.   FIG. 204.

FIG. 203.—Diamond cutter at work. (*Photograph by courtesy of Asscher and Company, Amsterdam.*)

FIG. 204.—Close view of the cutting process. (*Photograph by courtesy of Harry Winston, Inc.*)

stone mounted on the stick acts as the cutting tool (Figs. 203 and 204).

In mounting diamonds for cutting, a special non-metallic cement is used. It softens and melts easily in the flame of a Bunsen burner but hardens almost immediately when removed from the flame. The hardening of the cement is often hastened by dipping it into a pan of water.

The diamond cutter has two principal tasks. First, he must skillfully remove imperfections, and second, he must give the stone the desired shape or outline without sacrificing more of the gem than is absolutely necessary. In this work the cutter is greatly aided by the use of a special chuck, which permits the stone to revolve either centrally or eccentrically. If the chuck with the stone is centered, a sharp tap will cause the chuck to revolve eccentrically. Thus, round, oval, and other shapes may be cut.

The process of diamond cutting is, as a whole, somewhat similar to lathe turning. The cutter must shape the stone so that, when finished, its outline and form will be attractive and pleasing to the eye. Great care must also be exercised to collect all powder and small fragments, as these are valuable as abrasive and polishing material.

5. *Polishing.*—The fashioning of the various facets, one by one, and the imparting to them of a high polish is called *polishing*. In order that the finished stone may not only be pleasing to the eye but also possess the maximum amount of brilliancy and fire, the facets must be symmetrically arranged and accurately inclined. The tasks of the diamond polisher require much experience and skill and a keen artistic sense. There are two

Fig. 205.—Diamond cutter's gauges. *(Courtesy of Fera and Kadison.)*

groups of diamond polishers, namely, (1) *lappers* (Dutch *loppers*) and (2) *brillianteerers*.

The task of the *lapper* is the fashioning of the eighteen fundamental facets. These are the four top corner *TC* and the four bezel *B* facets and the table *T* above the girdle, and the four bottom corner *BC* and four pavilion *P* facets and the culet *C* below the girdle (Figs. 167 and 168). They must all be precisely placed at given angles in order to obtain the best effects (p. 103). Moreover, since similar facets must be of the same size and have the same angular positions, the lapper is required to have a fine sense of and feeling for proportion and symmetry.

Gauges are used by the lapper as an aid in establishing the proper angles between the facets (Fig. 205) and in maintaining exact parallelism between the table, girdle, and culet.

After the fundamental facets have been completed by the

lapper, the stone is finished by the *brillianteerer,* who adds forty facets.   Of these additional facets, the eight star *S* and sixteen top half *TH* facets are above the girdle, and the sixteen bottom half *BH* are below (Figs. 167 and 168).   This produces a stone with the usual fifty-eight facets.   In fashioning these additional facets it is not necessary to use gauges, since the fundamental pattern of facets has been established by the lapper.

FIG. 206.—Polishing one of the Jonker diamonds.   (*Photograph by courtesy of Harry Winston, Inc.*)

Lapping and brillianteering are accomplished by holding the stone, properly mounted, against a rapidly revolving horizontal circular plate of cast iron, known as the *skeif, scaife,* or *lap.*   Diamond dust mixed with oil is smeared upon the wheel, which makes 2,000 to 3,000 revolutions per minute.   The dust is carefully prepared from the diamond powder and fragments obtained from the other operations or from fragments of poorer diamonds, known as *bort.*   The dust should be sized and graded to ensure uniformity.   Usually four stones can be polished on one skeif at a time (Fig. 206).

The skeif is made from high-carbon cast iron.   The surface used for polishing has many minute pits, and it is frequently scoured, whereby fine radial grooves are produced. The diamond dust lodges in the pits and grooves.

The experience of diamond cutters clearly indicates that there are significant variations in hardness in different directions. The optimum directions for polishing are those parallel to a crystallographic axis. Since the faces of the cube *h* (Fig. 207) are parallel to two crystallographic axes, on each of these faces there are two optimum polishing directions. Facets parallel to these faces are easy to polish. Faces of the rhombic dodecahedron *d* are parallel

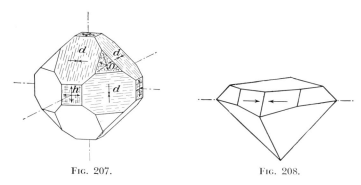

FIG. 207.   FIG. 208.

to one crystallographic axis, and consequently each face has one optimum direction, namely, parallel to the short diagonal. Octahedron faces *o* are equally inclined to three crystallographic axes and hence show the greatest divergence from parallelism with an axis. These faces are therefore the most difficult to polish. In the determination of these directions the diamond polisher is greatly aided by the recognition and accurate determination of the growth lines or grain. To obtain the most rapid rate of polishing, the rotation of the skeif must be perpendicular to the grain (p. 112).

Since facets are not as a rule parallel to a crystallographic axis, the most favorable direction across the facet will always be the one that most nearly approximates parallelism to an axis. In such instances the *sense of direction* is important. That is, in one direction across the facet, for example, from right to left, the rate of polishing may be more rapid than from left to right, or vice versa. In practice, the sense of direction is determined by trial; in theory, it should always be toward a possible face of the rhombic dodecahedron (Fig. 208). The expertness of the polisher depends to a very great extent upon his ability to recognize, quickly and accurately, these important features. By applying a high-voltage electric current to the lap and the dop, the fashioning of the facets can be expedited since lapping and polishing may be done in directions which are otherwise unfavorable.[1]

These observations on the variation of hardness with direction, which have long been known in the diamond-cutting industry, are

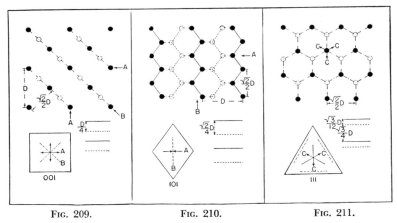

FIG. 209.   FIG. 210.   FIG. 211.

FIG. 209.—Diagrams showing (1) distribution of atoms in cube planes, (2) spacing of successive parallel planes, (3) optimum directions for polishing and sawing *A*, and (4) directions of greatest resistance *B*.

FIG. 210.—Same for rhombic dodecahedron planes.

FIG. 211.—Same for octahedron planes. The three optimum polishing directions are indicated by *C*.

in full accord with the modern views of the crystal structure of the diamond as developed from X-ray studies. The ease of polishing a crystal is largely determined by the arrangement of the atoms. The more closely spaced the atoms in a given plane, that is, the greater the reticular density, the greater will be the attractive forces between the atoms, and hence the greater the resistance to cutting and polishing a facet parallel to that plane. Then, too, the spacing of successive similar layers of atoms exerts great influence upon these processes (Figs. 209 to 211).

Diamonds are cut so that the table is approximately parallel to a face of the cube, octahedron, or rhombic dodecahedron. In the diamond-cutting industry these planes are referred to as the

[1] See footnote on p. 115.

four-, three-, and two-point faces or directions, and, accordingly,
diamonds that are cut with the table parallel to them are desig

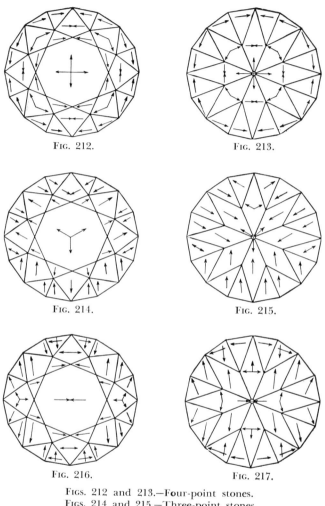

FIG. 212.   FIG. 213.

FIG. 214.   FIG. 215.

FIG. 216.   FIG. 217.

FIGS. 212 and 213.—Four-point stones.
FIGS. 214 and 215.—Three-point stones.
FIGS. 216 and 217.—Two-point stones.

nated as *four-point, three-point,* and *two-point* stones, respectively
(Figs. 212 to 217). The theoretical optimum polishing directions
for the crown and pavilion facets are indicated in the figures. In
practice, however, the orientation of the stone with respect to
faces of the cube, octahedron, and rhombic dodecahedron usually

shows considerable deviation. This is because diamond crystals are not ideally developed and because of the desire to obtain as large a finished stone as possible. Hence, the optimum polishing directions for some facets may differ from those shown in the diagrams.

For the mounting of the stones to be polished, holders, called *dops*, are used. These are of two kinds, namely, (1) *solder dops* and (2) *mechanical dops*.

FIG. 218.   FIG. 219.

FIGS. 218 and 219.—Mechanical dops. (*Courtesy of Asscher and Company, Amsterdam, Holland.*)

The *solder dop* consists of a basin-like holder which is filled with an easily fusible alloy of tin and lead. While still hot and pliable the solder is shaped into a hemispherical mound, and the diamond to be polished is placed in the summit of the mound (Fig. 206). When the solder is cooled, it becomes rigid and the diamond is held securely in position. Only a small portion of the stone is exposed at a time, so that in the grinding and polishing of the numerous facets frequent remountings are necessary.

While formerly all diamonds were mounted in solder dops, at present *mechanical dops* are used extensively, especially in lapping. They are also employed in the brillianteering of larger stones. In the mechanical dop the stone is rigidly held with prongs and clamps, and even though the stone becomes heated during the long grinding and polishing process it cannot change its position. This is an advantage over the solder dop. Then, too, remounting can be more easily made with mechanical dops. Furthermore, the lapper always has a full view of the stone. Figures 218 and 219 show mechanical dops with stones in position for grinding and polishing of facets and the girdle, respectively. There are several other types of mechanical dops.

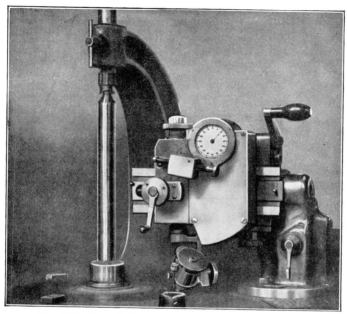

FIG. 220.—Stern-Coleman diamond-polishing machine.

Semi-automatic machines for the polishing of diamonds have been devised. The Stern-Coleman machine (Fig. 220), which was used during the 1920's in the establishment of Messrs. Stern Brothers and Company, New York, had ingenious mechanical devices consisting of a micrometer gauge and a degree finder in combination with a tripping device. The angles and planes to be polished on the diamond were predetermined, and the machine was set by the operator. When the desired depth and angle of the stone were attained, the tripping device automatically removed the stone from the polishing lap. One attendant could operate several machines at a time, and it was claimed that the highest technical skill was no longer required.

Formerly somewhat more than one-half of the rough stone, 55 to 58 per cent, was lost in the cutting of the diamond. With the introduction of the sawing process this loss has been reduced and may now be slightly less than one-half, namely, 45 to 48 per cent. An unwise attempt to save a large part of the stone may result in an ill-proportioned cut and consequently a great decrease in the value of the gem.

Evaluation of Cut Diamonds.—Aside from the size or weight, the *color, make,* and *perfection* of the stone are the important factors for determining its value.

1. *Color.*—In the trade, diamonds are classified according to color in various ways. The following is an accepted classification, the groups being arranged in order of descending values: (1) *blue* (fancy blue), (2) *river* (Jaeger), (3) *Wesselton* (fine white), (4) *top crystal* (blue white), (5) *crystal* (off white), (6) *Premier* (oily body), (7) *very light brown,* (8) *top Cape* (silver Cape), (9) *Cape* (light yellow), (10) *yellow* (very dark), (11) *brown.*

In determining the grade of color, the stone should be viewed through the girdle over neutral white paper; that is, it is placed on edge ("edge up"). In this position the color is commonly of a lower grade than when it is viewed through the table, that is, "face up."

A *top crystal* has been referred to in the trade as a *blue white,* but it shows no tinge of blue. A *Premier* viewed in sunlight will have a bluish cast because of the slight blue fluorescence which is produced by the ultraviolet rays of sunlight.

The color which one observes is dependent not only upon the object but also upon the light in which it is viewed (p. 44). Hence, it is desirable to determine the grade of color of a diamond in daylight or under a special light which simulates daylight. Even under these conditions the light is not constant because daylight varies with the weather. Moreover, the color of the walls and of the ceiling are reflected within the stone when viewed indoors. Lighting conditions are best controlled with special units such as the diamolite (Fig. 221).

The variation in the shades of color of the diamond is slight from one grade to another. Accurate color grading cannot be made except by matching with a stone or a series of stones which have been standardized as to color. The use of a standardized set often allows accurate color determinations to be made even though the lighting is not controlled. In the matching of diamonds more precise determinations can be made if the stones are of the same or approximately the same size and are unmounted.

2. *Make.*—The term *make of the stone* includes an evaluation of the details of the cutting. These are *adherence to proper pro-*

FIG. 221.—Diamolite. (*Courtesy of Gemological Institute of America.*)

portions, symmetry, and *finish.* Diamonds are sometimes classified according to seven grades, which may be designated as follows: (1) *correct,* (2) *very slightly thinner crown,* (3) *very slightly thinner pavilion,* (4) *very slightly thinner crown and pavilion,* (5) *heavier pavilion,* (6) *heavier crown,* (7) *heavier crown and pavilion.*

3. *Perfection.*—Under this heading, cognizance is taken of the presence or absence of inherent blemishes, flaws, or other imperfections. As many as eight grades of perfection or imperfection are recognized by some dealers: (1) *flawless,* no internal flaws; (2) *flawless,* with small external nicks and chips; (3) *very, very slightly imperfect* (V.V.S.I.); (4) *very slightly imperfect* (V.S.I.); (5) *slightly*

imperfect; (6) *first piqué* (1st **P.K.**), with larger flaws; (7) *second piqué* (2nd **P.K.**), with many flaws and cloudy; (8) *badly imperfect,* with large flaws. While all these factors should be carefully considered in evaluating a cut stone, the grade of color is always stressed.

In order properly to evaluate a diamond a long period of training and much practice are necessary. There are, however, some observations that the layman can make which will assist him in judging the quality of a stone. Since in all diamond-cutting establishments the best stones are entrusted to the most skillful cutters, the visible evidences of good workmanship should be sought. The expert workman will endeavor to produce a cut stone, (1) with a thin, uniform horizontal girdle; (2) with the crown facets intersecting in well-defined points; and (3) with a small, even minute, symmetrical culet. The presence of one or more naturals (p. 102) on the girdle is not to be considered as being detrimental if the rest of the girdle is well made, since naturals indicate that the stone was cut by a workman well grounded in the art. If the crown facets are not accurately placed, a short, thin edge instead of a sharply defined point will be observed where the facets should intersect. Similarly, if the pavilion facets are not all cut uniformly, this departure from good practice will be revealed in an unsymmetrical culet. When the culet is very small, any lack of symmetry is emphasized, which may, however, be made less evident by enlarging the culet. If the layman has the opportunity to examine the cut stone under the diamondscope (Fig. 222), he should be able to see these evidences of the character of workmanship, which otherwise are not readily observed.

Fig. 222.—Diamondscope. *(Courtesy of American Gem Society.)*

The diamondscope is a binocular microscope with a specially designed substage in which the stone is held in an easily movable and rotatable tongs. As the stone is uniformly illuminated from all sides, it can be viewed as a whole, including the interior. Accordingly, inclusions, cracks, and other flaws, as well as the character of the cutting, can be readily observed. The diamond-scope is very helpful in examining unmounted stones and also those mounted in rings.

FIG. 223.—Gem-cutting mill, Idar-Oberstein, Germany.

Cutting of Other Gems.—The methods of cutting the diamond, described above, are not used in cutting other gemstones. This is because their physical properties differ materially from those of the diamond, and as they are all softer they can be more readily worked.

Although the cutting of gem minerals is carried on in many places in a small way, the most important center has been Idar-Oberstein, Germany, where the industry has long flourished. Before the war, most of the inhabitants of Idar-Oberstein were engaged in this work, some phases of which were conducted as a home industry (p. 110). Usually those artisans who cut gems other than the diamond are called *lapidaries,* but in this district two groups are distinguished, namely, (1) *gem cutters* and (2) *lapidaries.* The first group, the gem cutters, work on sandstone wheels driven by water or electric power and cut agate and other varieties of quartz, as well as opal and other gem minerals with a hardness of 7 or less. The second group, the lapidaries, generally use carborundum wheels and electric power and cut all types of gems other than the diamond.

1. *Gem Cutters.*—In the Idar-Oberstein district the gem cutters work in small gem-cutting mills located on the banks of the Idar

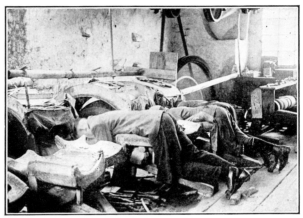

FIG. 224.—Interior of gem-cutting mill, Idar-Oberstein, Germany.

FIG. 225.—Interior of gem-cutting mill, Waldkirch, near Freiburg, Germany.

brook or other streams, which furnish abundant water power (Fig. 223). These mills contain four or five large sandstone wheels mounted parallel. Only a part of each wheel is above the level of the floor. They are about 5 feet in diameter and 14 to 18 inches in thickness. They are driven by water wheels and make about 150 revolutions a minute.

In the fashioning of gems in these mills the larger, rough material is first carefully examined. After being roughly shaped by hewing with a hammer or cutting with a diamond saw or carborundum wheel the specimen is held in the hand against one of the revolving sandstone wheels. Upon the surfaces of these wheels small streams of water are constantly playing. The operator, in working at one of these wheels, lies face down upon a specially constructed support. Both hands are free to handle the specimen. In order to hold the stone against the wheel with sufficient pres-

FIG. 226.—Sandstone wheel with grooves.

FIG. 227.—Interior of gem-cutting mill, Royat, France.

sure, he braces his toes against cleats on the floor behind him. In this way great pressure can be exerted, which is often necessary to cut the larger and harder materials (Figs. 224 and 225).

For the sake of economy each wheel may be used by two cutters. When the grindstone is new, these cutters start to work at opposite edges, which in time, as the result of abrasion, are replaced by broad sloping surfaces. In order to produce the different cabochon cuts uniformly and rapidly some of the wheels have grooves of suitable curvatures and sizes ground into them (Fig. 226).

This method of gem cutting has been used in the Idar-Oberstein district for several centuries with but few changes. Although at first it was introduced to cut agates, it has subsequently been used for other soft minerals. In some of the more modern gem-cutting mills the operators sit upright instead of lying face down (Fig. 227). Owing to cheap electric power, motor-driven sandstone wheels are now more common than those dependent upon water power.

In these methods the shape of the gem and its facets are determined wholly by the eye, while the material is held and manipulated in the fingers. The stones are given a high polish by holding them against rather large revolving cylinders of wood or against canvas-covered laps. Tripoli or rouge is used in the polishing process (Fig. 231).

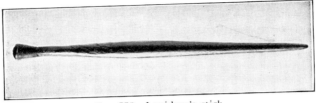

FIG. 228.—Lapidary's stick.

FIG. 229.—
Top view of
lapidary's
stick.

Although some of these gem cutters use methods which seem very primitive, they have acquired unusual skill and gems of great beauty and pleasing symmetry are readily cut at small cost. These methods are also used in a limited way in other localities, among which Waldkirch, near Freiburg, Germany (Fig. 225), and Royat, Puy-de-Dôme, France, may be mentioned (Fig. 227).

FIG. 230.—Lapidary at work.

2. *Lapidaries.*—In general, the artisan who cuts gems other than the diamond is called a *lapidary* or *lapidist.* In the Idar-Oberstein district, however, where the industry is very highly specialized, the term is restricted to those who use carborundum wheels and electric power.

For the slitting or sawing of the rough material the lapidary commonly uses a rapidly revolving disk impregnated with diamond dust or a thin carborundum wheel. By these means the specimen is sized and roughly shaped. The stone is then mounted with hard cement upon a wooden stick in size and shape much like a penholder (Figs. 226, 228, and 229). Thus mounted, the stone is further shaped by holding it in the hand against a revolving horizontal wheel of cast iron, called a *lap,* fed with diamond dust or other abrasives (Fig. 230). The facets are now ground upon the stone. This is done by placing the pointed end of the lapidary stick in a hole in an upright support at one side of the lap (Fig. 230). The stone at the other end of the stick is now held by the hand against the lap. As the upright support is provided with a series of holes at various heights, the facets may be cut at the proper angles by adjusting the inclination of the

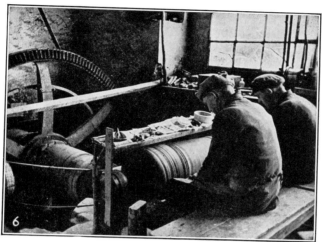

FIG. 231.—Wooden cylinder for polishing gems, Idar-Oberstein, Germany.

stick to the lap. Carborundum wheels of suitable grain size are now often substituted for the laps, for they tend to simplify the process and in general cut more rapidly. Gem cutters who use the large sandstone wheels often mount stones to be cut cabochon on lapidary sticks, as they are more readily handled (Fig. 226).

After the facets have been cut, the stone is then polished with tripoli or rouge on wooden cylinders or on canvas-covered wheels (Fig. 231).

In recent years much interest has been taken in the United States in amateur and professional lapidary work. Some improved mechanical devices (Fig. 232) as well as compact and efficient lapidary shops have been developed (Fig. 233). Those desiring information concerning some of the technical details of this fascinating hobby should consult "The Art of Gem Cutting" by Dake and

FIG. 232.—Facet-cutting device. (*Photograph by the Mineralogist Gem-cutting Laboratories, Portland, Oregon.*)

FIG. 233.—Gem-cutting shop, Portland, Oregon. (*Photograph by courtesy of H. C. Dake.*)

Pearl,[1] (third edition, 1945); "Quartz Family Minerals" by Dake, Fleener, and Wilson [2] (first edition, 1938, pp. 276 to 294); "Jewelry, Gem Cutting and Metalcraft," by William T. Baxter [2] (first edition, 1938, pp. 133 to 178); "Revised Lapidary Handbook," by J. H. Howard [3] (first edition, 1946).

Engraving.—A specialized branch of gem cutting is engraving, for the cutting of cameos, intaglios, or cuvettes (p. 108) requires great skill. The engraving is done by means of a small lathe into which suitable cutting tools may be fitted. The stone, freely manipulated in the fingers, is held against the rapidly revolving cutting tool. The shape, size, and symmetry of the figure are all determined by the eye (Fig. 234). Gem engravers are noted for their patience and remarkable workmanship and skill. In fact, some are able to cut cameos with great accuracy directly from photographs (Figs. 235 and 236).

FIG. 234.—Engraving a cameo.

Boring of Beads.—In the making of beads the boring process is most essential. A very simple and primitive hand process has generally been used, for the piercing of beads requires careful handling. The gem borer sits at a table with the beads before him cemented in orderly rows upon a rectangular metal plate and arranged in the proper position for boring (Fig. 237). Under his left arm is placed a lever. Into a hole near the middle of this lever a drill with a diamond point at the lower end is fitted in an upright position. A movement of the arm or shoulder controls the pressure and position of the drill. A thin cord wound around the drill is fastened to the ends of a bow held in the right hand. By drawing the bow backward and forward the drill is rotated. A slight pressure is exerted by the shoulder upon the drill when the bow is drawn so as to cut into the bead, and with the opposite movement it is released. In

[1] Mineralogist Publishing Company, Portland, Ore.
[2] Whittlesey House, McGraw-Hill Book Company, Inc., New York.
[3] J. H. Howard, Greenville, S. C.

recent years this hand-boring method has been replaced to some extent by mechanical drilling using electric motors. Engraving and boring have been long conducted as home industries in the Idar-Oberstein district, Germany.

Fig. 235.   Fig. 236.

Figs. 235 and 236.—Original photograph and finished cameo.

Ornamental Objects.—Gem minerals are frequently cut and engraved so as to serve as ornamental objects. The cutting of balls and spheres requires much skill. Special grinding wheels are necessary for the shaping of hollow objects, such as dishes (Fig.

Fig. 237.—Gem borer.   Fig. 238.—Cutting an agate dish.

238). Quartz and jade are often cut in a great variety of forms (Figs. 316 and 334).

Size and Weight of Gems.—In the sale of gem minerals four units of weight are used, namely, (1) *carat,* (2) *gram,* (3) *penny-*

weight, and (4) *grain.*   In addition, some gemstones are sold in terms of size, as expressed in *millimeters* or *inches.*   Of these units, only the carat needs to be defined, and accordingly it will be discussed in some detail.

1. *Carat.*—The carat now in use in the principal countries of the world is 200 milligrams or two-tenths of a gram, 0.200 gram. It is often called the *metric carat.*   It was adopted as the standard in the United States in 1913.   Generally the value of a gemstone, per carat, increases rapidly with weight.

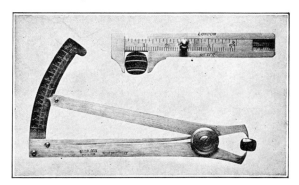

FIG. 239.—Slide (*above*) and caliper gauges.

Originally grains or leguminous seeds were used as units of weight for gems, and naturally they were not of uniform size. Consequently, down to comparatively recent times the weight of the carat varied greatly in different centers.   Thus, for many years it was taken as 0.2053 gram in London, whereas in Florence it was 0.1972 gram, in Madras 0.2073, Amsterdam 0.2057, and so on. In 1871 an attempt was made to establish as the standard the *international carat* of 0.205 gram.   Later the metric carat was proposed, and it is now the accepted unit.

Before the introduction of the metric carat, the weight of a gem was expressed by a series of fractions, such as 2, ½, ¼, 1/16, and 1/64 carats.   In the metric system this weight, so clumsily expressed by the older method, is simplified to 2.83 carats, the sum of the fractional parts of a carat being indicated by the more convenient decimals.

The weight of a diamond is often expressed in points.   Thus, a stone weighing 65 points actually weighs 0.65 carat.   That is, a *point* is 0.01 carat.

The application of the term carat as a unit of weight must not be confused with its use in indicating fineness or purity of the gold in which gems are mounted. In this latter connection a carat means one twenty-fourth part. Thus, pure gold is said to be 24-carat fine. The amount of baser metal alloyed with gold is indicated by a proportional decrease in the number of carats fineness. That is, 18-carat gold is eighteen twenty-fourths gold

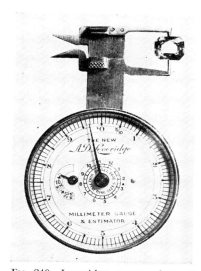

Fig. 240.—Leveridge gem and pearl gauge.

Fig. 241.—Gauge for round brilliant-cut diamonds.

and six twenty-fourths base metal, whereas 12-carat gold is twelve twenty-fourths or half gold. When used in this sense, the term is commonly spelled *karat* and abbreviated as K. Thus, an 18-carat ring may be stamped 18K.

The carat is the unit of weight for the diamond, natural and synthetic rubies and sapphires, emerald, aquamarine, tourmaline, zircon, spinel, precious opal, superior opal doublets, topaz, and garnets. Pearls are sometimes sold by the carat.

2. *Gram.*—The following gem minerals are commonly sold by the gram: lapis lazuli, citrine, moonstone, amethyst, and superior grades of malachite.

3. *Pennyweight.*—In some countries the minerals listed under Gram are sold by the pennyweight (troy), which equals 24 grains or 1.56 grams.

4. *Grain.*—Pearls are commonly sold by the grain. A *pearl grain* is a twentieth of a gram; hence, four pearl grains equals one carat. The pearl grain (0.05 gram) is not the same as the troy grain (0.0648 gram).

5. *Millimeter or Inch.*—Minerals such as amazonite, most of the varieties of quartz, malachite, Swiss lapis, and the cheaper grades of garnet, opal, and opal doublets are sold according to size, as expressed in millimeters or inches. Convenient forms of gauges for measuring the size of gems in either inches or millimeters are shown in Fig. 239. Other gauges are shown in Figs. 240 and 241. Accompanying some of these gauges are tables which permit fairly accurate estimates to be made of the weight of stones from their dimensions.

Chapter IX

THE NAMING OF GEMS

Many of the popular names of gems are a heritage, having been in use long before mineralogy was developed as a science. They do not conform to the modern technical usage. But they are firmly established, and it would be quite impossible to replace them in a short time with the more accurate scientific names. Among these older names may be cited, for illustration, agate, from the Greek; amber, Arabic; amethyst, Greek, the name meaning "without drunkenness," since the stone was regarded as a remedy for intoxication; beryl, Greek, probably from the Sanskrit originally; diamond and emerald, Greek; garnet, Latin; jade, Spanish; opal, Sanskrit; quartz, German; ruby, Latin; sapphire, Sanskrit; and turquois, French. It is interesting to note that the names of the majority of gem minerals are of the old form, especially those which are the most precious. This indicates that they were known at an early date. The names now given to minerals usually end in *-ite,* for example, azurite, chrysolite, fluorite, malachite, smithsonite, and vesuvianite.

Considerable ambiguity has been occasioned by the use of popular gem names by jewelers, simultaneously with the employment of the scientific nomenclature by the mineralogist. Although the popular names are in some respects desirable and ought to be retained, and indeed for some minerals there are no other names, they lack the precision and accuracy of those employed by scientists. Some gem minerals, however, possess many varieties, to which distinctive names have been given. Thus, over twenty varieties of the common mineral quartz have long been used for gem purposes (p. 220). The popular garnet is recognized by the mineralogist as occurring in six distinct varieties (p. 210). Ruby and sapphire are differently colored varieties of the mineral corundum (p. 200), whereas emerald and aquamarine are varieties of beryl (p. 203).

Popular names lend themselves more readily to unscrupulous practices in the selling of gems. To increase its sale value, a cheap stone is often sold under a name closely resembling that of a valuable gem. For instance, some red stones are not infrequently given names which suggest to the uninformed purchaser that they are a variety of ruby. Thus, red pyrope garnets are sold under such trade names as *American ruby, Arizona ruby, California ruby, Cape ruby, Colorado ruby, Montana ruby,* and *Rocky Mountain ruby.* Likewise, red and orange spinels are called *balas ruby* or *rubicelle.* A mineral as different from the true ruby as rose quartz is frequently offered under the name *Bohemian ruby.* Rose and pink topaz may be sold as *Brazilian ruby,* and red or pink tourmalines are called *rubellite* or *Siberian ruby.* Bluish or greenish corundum is often called *Oriental aquamarine.* Although these stones are perfectly good in their own right and are very attractive as gems, the purchaser should know exactly what he is buying. This knowledge is hardly likely to be his when such deceptive names are used.

Furthermore, there is the deceptive and misleading use of *topaz* for yellow quartz with either a natural color or one the result of heat treatment. Although yellow quartz has long been called *false* or *Spanish topaz,* in recent years the qualifying terms are commonly dropped by the trade, and these stones designated simply as *topaz.* Naturally, the deception is much more flagrant when the term *topaz, genuine stone,* is used (pp. 206 and 222).

Likewise, the introduction of special or trade names for stones with some unusual property, especially color, should be discontinued. As an example, the calling of blue zircon, the result of heat treatment, *starlite* may be given. Such names serve no useful purpose, for they do not convey to the purchaser the information concerning the true nature of the stone to which he is entitled. It is obvious that all ambiguity would be avoided by the use of the scientific names as accepted by the mineralogist.

In recent years much progress has been made in this country and Europe toward the standardization of gem names. The Federal Trade Commission has promulgated Trade Practice Rules, which should contribute very materially toward clarifying a most confusing use of terms.[1] In Europe, also, material advances have been made, notably through the activities of the international association called the B.I.B.O.A., with headquarters at The Hague.

[1] For a discussion and interpretation of these rules, see *The Jewelers' Circular-Keystone,* April, 1938, p. 46.

Chapter X

MANUFACTURED GEMS

As previously indicated, gems have been used from earliest antiquity for personal adornment and ornamentation. Because many of the more precious gems are very expensive, their use has obviously been limited to those able to purchase them. Hence, to satisfy the equally strong desire on the part of those financially less fortunate, various types of rather inexpensive manufactured stones are annually placed upon the market in comparatively large quantities. In this chapter some of the more important kinds of material used in this way will be described.

Manufactured gems may be classified as follows:

1. Treated gems.
2. Synthetic gems.
3. Imitation gems.
4. Doublets and triplets.

Accordingly, the term *manufactured gems* includes those natural stones whose gem qualities have been improved by artificial means and whose value has thus been increased. The term also includes those gem materials which are entirely the products of the laboratory, for example, synthetic rubies, sapphires, and spinels. Moreover, materials which are clearly imitations or have been "doctored" for the purpose of deception are also discussed.

Treated Gems.—Treated gems consist of genuine material which has been subjected to some process to increase its beauty and selling qualities. The processes include (1) *artificial coloring or staining,* (2) *heat treatment,* (3) *heat and pressure,* (4) *radiation with radium,* and (5) *special mountings.* Examples of each of these processes will be given.

1. *Artificial Coloring or Staining.*—Agates frequently occur in pale and unattractive colors, which may be greatly improved by artificial coloring. This can be accomplished by soaking natural agate in the proper solutions. Because of the fact that the different layers possess varying degrees of imperviousness, they may

140

PLATE II

First row: 1, rose quartz, Brazil; 2 to 4, artificially colored agates, Brazil.
Second row: 1, moss agate, India; 2, tree agate, Brazil; 3, petrified wood, Arizona;
4, moss agate.
Third row: 1, aventurine, India; 2, tiger's-eye, Africa; 3, heliotrope, India; 4, brecci-
ated jasper, Africa.
Fourth row: 1, banded jasper, Madagascar; 2, jasper-agate, Africa; 3, rhodonite,
Russia; 4, malachite, Ural Mountains.

be colored in various shades which stand out in pleasing contrast. This imperviousness may be due to the porosity of the layers and to the amount of colloidal silica in them. For example, the agate may first be soaked in a solution of sugar or honey, followed by a treatment with concentrated sulfuric acid. The acid chars the sugar taken up by the agate, coloring the more porous layers in different shades of brown and black, the denser layers remaining grayish or white.

The artificial improving of the colors of agate has been developed on a relatively large scale at Idar-Oberstein, Germany. The use of honey or sugar solutions and sulfuric acid dates back to 1819. In order to secure good colors, the agate must be soaked for two to three weeks in the sugar solution.[1] It is then placed, with or without rinsing, in concentrated sulfuric acid, which is slowly heated for about an hour and then boiled for fifteen to twenty minutes. The container is allowed to cool slowly, when the agate may be removed and washed. It is then heated gently for several days in an open crucible in order to remove all traces of sulfuric acid. Because of the marked differences in the structure of agates, considerable variation in the colors produced may result. Accordingly, it is advisable to determine the periods of soaking and heating by experimenting with small chips. Moreover, a preliminary treatment with nitric or hydrochloric acids or with a solution of sodium carbonate to remove deleterious substances is usually necessary before the coloring procedure is begun. Generally the best results are obtained with smaller-sized specimens, either roughly shaped or completely finished.

Some agates may be colored lemon yellow by soaking in hydrochloric acid and heating. Reddish colors may be produced by simple heat treatment or soaking in a solution of ferrous nitrate and subsequently heating. Shades of green may be obtained by using solutions of chromium and nickel salts. A great variety of blue colors may be developed by soaking the agate first in a solution of potassium ferrocyanide and then treating it with a solution of ferric sulfate. Organic dyes and solutions of other colored inorganic salts may also be used. It is nearly always safe to assume

---

[1] Three hundred seventy-five grams of sugar dissolved in a liter of water.

that agates with vivid colors have been treated in one of the foregoing ways (Fig. 242).

Artificial coloring sometimes makes possible the substitution
of one stone for another. Thus, lapis lazuli (p. 243), an attractive
blue stone which is rather popular for decorative purposes, may
be imitated by staining cracked quartz. This blue imitation is
known as *Swiss lapis*. When jasper is colored blue by means of

| 1
Aniline | 2
Chromium
and
nickel
solutions | 3
Hydro-
chloric
acid | 4
Ferric
ferro-
cyanide
solution | 5
Ferrous
sulphate
solution | 6
Honey
and sul-
phuric
acid | 7
Natural
colors |

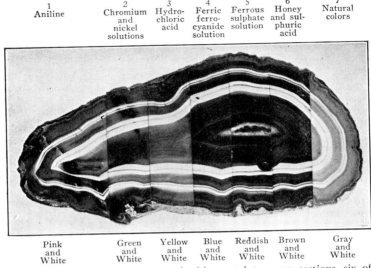

| Pink
and
White | Green
and
White | Yellow
and
White | Blue
and
White | Reddish
and
White | Brown
and
White | Gray
and
White |

FIG. 242.—Agate, naturally gray and white, cut into seven sections, six of
which have been variously colored artificially, at Idar-Oberstein, Germany.

ferric ferrocyanide or Prussian blue, it is called *German lapis* or
blue onyx. The color of turquois and opal is sometimes artificially intensified in order to enhance the value. Alabaster, a
variety of gypsum (p. 256), is often artificially colored so as to
improve its attractiveness.

Although Idar-Oberstein has long been the chief center for the
coloring and staining of gem materials, the methods described
above have recently been successfully introduced in the United
States, notably at Providence, Rhode Island.

2. *Heat Treatment.*—The improving of the color of gem minerals by heat treatment, that is, by being fired or baked, has long
been practiced. For centuries the imparting of an attractive red
color to slightly colored chalcedony by heat treatment, and thus

producing carnelian, has been done in India. Heat treatment has also been applied to many gem minerals in the Idar-Oberstein district in Germany since 1813. In some cases moderate temperatures of about 150°C. are necessary, while in others the temperature must be as high as 800°C. to bring about the desired change in color.[1]

By carefully heating some nearly colorless chalcedony at about 150°C. the reddish color of carnelian is induced. In the process known as *pinking,* yellow topaz is gently heated. This causes the color to change from yellow to an attractive pink. The stone to be pinked is packed in asbestos or magnesia and carefully brought to a low red heat. It is then slowly cooled. The temperatures at which these changes take place are between 300° and 450°C. With too low a temperature the stone becomes salmon-colored, while if the heat is too great the color is lost entirely.

When transparent crystals of quartz, which vary in color from amethyst to smoky quartz, are heat-treated, beautifully light or dark yellow stones may be obtained. As these artificially colored stones strikingly resemble precious topaz, they are erroneously called *Spanish topaz, false topaz, gold topaz,* or *Madeira topaz* (p. 206). The qualifying terms are often omitted, and these heat-treated yellow quartz gems are then unfortunately sold as *topaz.* Such material should properly be designated as *citrine.* Some crystals of quartz become milky when heated and then resemble moonstone in appearance.

When some brownish or reddish zircons are heated, marked changes in color result. Some may become colorless; others assume a beautiful blue color. Heat-treated colorless zircons have long been known and used as gems. Because of the very high indices of refraction and the strong dispersion, colorless zircon simulates the diamond to a marked extent. Colorless zircons, the result of heat treatment, have unfortunately been sold as *artificial matara diamonds* or *matura diamonds* (p. 214).

In 1921 blue zircons began to be marketed in appreciable quantities. This very attractive gem at once became very popular. For several years the source of these stones was unknown, and it was thought that the color was natural. It is now known that the

[1] MACKOWSKY, MARIE-THERESE, *Deutsche Goldschmiede Zeitung,* No. 23, pp. 217-220, 1939.

color has been induced by heat treatment. According to Eppler [1] these zircons are found in the Mongka district of Indo-China and are treated and cut at Bangkok, Thailand. The simplified diagram (Fig. 243), based upon the one devised by Eppler, clearly indicates the conditions under which the naturally colored brownish or reddish stones should be heated to obtain blue and colorless gem material.

From the diagram it is evident that the heating is carried on in either an oxidizing or a reducing atmosphere, that is, with or

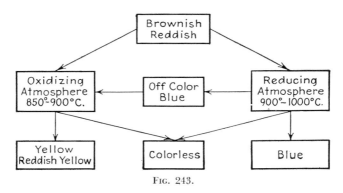

FIG. 243.

without the access of air. Treatment in an oxidizing atmosphere yields colorless, yellow, and reddish-yellow stones. Upon heating in a reducing atmosphere colorless and blue stones are obtained, together with some that have off colors. When the off-colored material is treated in an oxidizing atmosphere some of the stones become colorless; others, yellow or reddish yellow. The stones are generally subjected to two treatments. They may also be heated after cutting. If the deep-blue color fades, it may be restored by careful heating in the flame of a Bunsen burner.

In the treatment of zircon in Thailand, crude charcoal furnaces are used, and the changes in color take place without the addition or use of chemicals. The use of the term *starlite* for the blue zircons obtained by heat treatment has been practically discontinued, as it does not indicate the nature of the stone.

Heat treatment may also be used to improve the color of streaky rubies and of certain amethysts. Yellow sapphires tend to become colorless when heated. Heated in an electric furnace to

[1] *Deutsche Goldschmiede Zeitung*, No. 51, pp. 531-534, 1936.

450°C. greenish beryl from Brazil and Madagascar assumes the bluish color so highly prized in aquamarine. Some dark-blue tourmalines from South-West Africa can be changed to the pleasing green which is so characteristic of emerald. Dark-green stones may be given a lighter, more attractive color.

3. *Heat and Pressure.*—The manufacture of *pressed amber* or *ambroid* furnishes a splendid illustration of the application of heat and pressure in the treatment of gem materials. By this process large quantities of the small pieces and fragments which accumulate when amber is prepared for the market are utilized.

Before being heated and pressed, the small pieces and fragments of amber are carefully selected according to color. They are also cleaned by scraping the surfaces and removing all impurities. After being graded according to size the material is heated with the exclusion of air in specially designed receptacles to about 200° to 250°C. At these temperatures it becomes soft and can be forced under great pressure, about 50,000 pounds per square inch, through perforated plates into molds of the desired shape and size. On cooling it hardens. Special colors and tinting may be given to the product. Many important details of the process are trade secrets. Pressed amber is easily worked and finished for the market. It was first made in Vienna. Königsberg, East Prussia, has long been the most important center for natural and pressed amber.

In general appearance pressed amber is very much like natural amber and is often mistaken for it. There are, however, some characterizing features which permit the accurate identification of pressed amber (p. 283).

4. *Radiation.*—When exposed to radium emanations, cyclotron bombardment, X-rays, cathode rays, or similar radiations, many gemstones show some changes in color. Thus, with long-continued, direct radiation of the diamond by means of radium, colorless stones become green, and artificial "carbon spots" may be produced. Colorless and rose quartz become smoky brown after such treatment, and the original color of heat-decolorized smoky quartz and amethyst may be restored by the action of radium. The colors produced by radium are not always permanent, especially if heated to redness. Gems which have been exposed to radium emanations generally become radioactive. De-

pending upon the length of exposure the radioactivity may be very strong and may be retained for a long period, even several years (Fig. 244). It is not dispelled by heating.

Color changes are also induced in some gems by exposure to deuteron radiation as generated by the cyclotron. This color change may be either superficial, that is, "skin-deep," or it may be a change in the body color. When thus exposed, the diamond assumes a green color, which may be very attractive, depending upon the original color of the stone. Colorless diamonds show

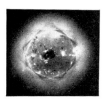

less tendency to change than do those with some original color. The induced color, which is only skin-deep, may be dispelled by heating to 900° C.

Bombardment by deuteron radiation induces a change in body color in rose quartz to purplish brown. The change in rock crystal is only a surface darkening. Radioactivity induced by deuteron bombardment is short-lived.

FIG. 244.—Self-photograph of diamond with induced and long-retained radioactivity.

Changes in color are also produced in many gems by exposure to cathode or X-rays. These changes are not as significant as those induced by radium or cyclotron radiations. Moreover, many of the colors tend to fade.

In all probability many profound changes in the color of gems may be induced when it becomes possible to expose them to the intense radioactivity which is generated by the fission or splitting of the uranium atom.

5. *Special Mountings.*—Cases are on record in which yellowish diamonds were given a thin coat of a blue dye in order to neutralize their natural yellow tint. Being soluble in alcohol, the dye may easily be removed. Color may also be improved by mounting stones over stained foils or colored enamels. Asterism (p. 47) may be produced artificially by ruling fine parallel lines on the back of a cabochon stone and covering them with enamel. Three sets of lines intersecting at 60 degrees will produce a very distinct six-pointed star. Such stars differ in appearance from those of the true star sapphires and rubies and are not apt to be confused with them.

Synthetic Gems.—Aside from the fact that artificial or synthetic gems are made in the laboratory, they are in other respects essentially the same as the natural stones. The elements composing these artificial stones are combined by chemical processes. A synthetic ruby, for example, consists of Al_2O_3 just as does the natural ruby. Besides having the same chemical composition, synthetics have the same physical properties as natural stones. The hardness, specific gravity, cleavage, index of refraction, and so on, are identical in synthetic and natural gems. But the process by which they are made usually causes the development within the stones of certain incidental and characterizing features which may be used for purposes of identification.

In the development of the manufacture of synthetic gems, one of the earliest attempts consisted of fusing together fragments of the natural material. The larger stones produced in this way were called *reconstructed gems*. This process was applied to the ruby, especially. At first the product was not clear. Moreover, it was poor in color, and often brittle. Later, in 1895, Michaud succeeded better, and his reconstructed rubies found a market in France, Germany, America, and India. It is suspected that in India some of the reconstructed rubies were mixed with the natural gems and sold as such. In Michaud's process a fairly large fragment of natural ruby was placed in a revolving platinum crucible and heated to about 1800°C. Smaller chips were added from time to time, and were fused to the original fragment. In this way stones of fairly large sizes were obtained, even though the product would sometimes burst asunder. Reconstructed rubies are no longer manufactured. They have been displaced by the more successful synthetic stones described on pages 150 to 167.

The term *scientific gem* is sometimes heard. It is often applied to an artificial product which is substituted for the natural gem and may be very different from it in composition. "Scientific emeralds," for instance, are nothing more than green lead-glass imitations (p. 168).

Synthetic Diamonds.—Because of its great value, many attempts have been made to produce the diamond in the laboratory. The process generally followed is to dissolve some form of carbon in a suitable solvent and then to allow it to crystallize out. Of the many attempts, perhaps those of Moissan (1893) and of Noble and Crookes (1906) are most worthy of a brief description.

Moissan thought that he had succeeded in producing artificial diamonds of microscopic size by dissolving carbon, prepared by the ignition of sugar, in molten iron and suddenly cooling the mass. The iron was melted in an electric furnace, and a temperature of about 4000°C. was attained. At this temperature the iron quickly melted and became saturated with carbon. The crucible was then suddenly cooled in a water bath. A rigid crust of iron was formed, while the interior of the mass remained molten. As a result of this condition within the mass it was assumed that an enormous pressure was developed and that part of the carbon had crystallized out as the diamond, the rest as graphite. The iron ingot which was formed was dissolved by successive treatments with nitrohydrochloric acid. There was a bulky residue which consisted of graphite, some black flakes, and a few microscopic, transparent, colorless crystals. The graphite and other impurities were chemically removed, leaving behind the unattacked crystals. The crystals were rarely if ever whole, but appeared to be broken, as if liberation from the intense pressure prevailing when they were formed had allowed them to burst. It is interesting to note that diamonds from South Africa have also been known to burst asunder when removed from the blue ground.

From the evidence available, Moissan seemed to be convinced that he had actually produced minute crystals of the diamond. This experiment has since been repeated many times by other scientists who apparently succeeded in obtaining similar products. However, by the use of modern methods of examination it has always been conclusively demonstrated that the crystals obtained were not diamonds.

Sir William Crookes in 1906 reported another method for the production of the diamond artificially. Sir Andrew Noble had previously shown that, when the powerful explosive cordite is exploded in a closed steel cylinder, a pressure of 50 tons per square inch and a temperature of 5100°C. are momentarily attained. These conditions should be favorable for the liquefaction of carbon. It was thought that, if the explosion were to extend over a sufficient period to permit the carbon to be liquefied, it might then solidify in the crystalline form of the diamond. In the experiment Noble used cordite containing a slight excess of carbon, and collected the residue after the explosion. This residue was examined by Crookes, who identified minute crystals of the diamond, the largest being only 0.5 millimeter in length. The success of this experiment has also been questioned.

Numerous experiments were also conducted by Hannay, Parsons, Friedlander, Van Hassinger, and Ruff.[1] In all cases no proof was furnished that the products were actually diamonds. In order that the evidence be convincing, the experiments should be well controlled throughout and the product subjected to the accurate determination of its properties by modern optical, chemical, and X-ray methods.

According to Rossini and Jessup, the relation between the diamond and graphite, the two modifications of carbon, is such that a pressure of approximately 200,000 pounds per square inch is necessary to convert graphite into diamond at ordinary temperatures. The formation of the diamond at higher temperatures is possible only under greatly increased pressures.[2]

In 1943 Guenther, Geselle, and Rebentisch [3] repeated Moissan's experiment with improved apparatus and methods using extremely high pressures and with temperatures up to 3200°C. The product was examined by X-ray methods. There was no evidence that the diamond had been produced. These experimenters confirm the opinion previously expressed by various writers that it is doubtful that synthetic diamonds have ever been produced.

By some scientists it is suggested that the presence of a suitable agent might sufficiently alter the conditions of the process and permit the formation of the diamond at lower pressures.

On various occasions the diamond has been reported as occurring in microscopic crystals in steels, especially in those which had been cooled under pressure. The hardness of certain steels has accordingly been attributed to the presence of this crystalline form

[1] "The Quest for Synthetic Diamonds," *Jewelers' Circular*, vol. 102, pp. 39, 48, 1932.
"Supposed Synthetic Diamonds Tested," *Gems and Gemology* (Los Angeles), vol. II, pp. 195-198, 1938.
"Did J. B. Hannay Produce 'Laboratory Diamonds' in 1880?" *Jewelers' Circular-Keystone*, vol. 114, No. 7, pp. 120, 122, 124, 1944.
[2] *Journal of Research of the United States Bureau of Standards*, vol. 21, No. 1, p. 509, 1938.
[3] "Untersuchungen zum Diamantproblem," *Zeitschrift für anorganische und allgemeine Chemie* (Leipzig), vol. 250, pp. 357-372, 1943; English translation, *Industrial Diamond Review* (London), vol. 6, pp. 42-46, 1946.

of carbon. However, the presence of minute diamonds in iron meteorites has been definitely demonstrated.[1]

The Verneuil Process.—Attempts to produce artificial rubies chemically have been many. Gaudin was one of the first in this field. In 1837 he made microscopic rubies by fusing alum at a high temperature, with the addition of a little chromium as a pigment. Ebelmen in 1847 produced the white sapphire by fusing alumina in boric acid. Frémy and Feil were able, in 1877, to produce crystallized corundum from which small stones could be cut. A lead aluminate was first formed by fusing together Al_2O_3 and PbO. This was kept molten for some time in a fire-clay crucible, whereby silica from the crucible combined with the lead of the aluminate to form lead silicate. During this process alumina was liberated, which crystallized as white sapphire. By adding 2 to 3 per cent of a chromium compound the ruby was obtained. Frémy and Verneuil manufactured the artificial ruby by a reaction at red heat between BaF_2 and Al_2O_3 containing a little chromium. Other workers who attacked this problem were Elsner, De Senarmont, Sainte Claire-Deville, Caron, and Debray. In their processes the general plan was to form a molten mixture of salts in which alumina was soluble. These mixtures were then saturated with alumina, and on long heating, sometimes for weeks, the solvent volatilized, allowing alumina to crystallize out.

In 1902 Verneuil announced in Paris an entirely new process by which the ruby could be manufactured artificially on a commercial scale. At present it is also used to produce many of the other varieties of corundum, as well as those of spinel. It is common practice to call these manufactured stones *synthetic* gems, thus, for example, *synthetic rubies, sapphires,* and *spinels.* Synthetic gems are chemically and physically identical with the natural stones, except for certain features incidental to the process (p. 157). The essential details of the Verneuil process will be given below under the description of the manufacture of synthetic white sapphire.

Synthetic White Sapphire.—Figures 245 and 246 show the Verneuil apparatus, which is essentially an inverted oxyhydrogen

---

[1] KSANDA, C. J., and E. P. HENDERSON, "Identification of Diamond in the Canyon Diablo Iron," *American Mineralogist*, Vol. 24, pp. 677-680, 1939.

blowpipe. Purified and finely divided alumina is placed in a receptacle *A*, the bottom of which is a fine sieve *S*. The receptacle is tapped by a mechanism as shown in the cut. This causes a small amount of the powder to pass through the sieve and into a flame

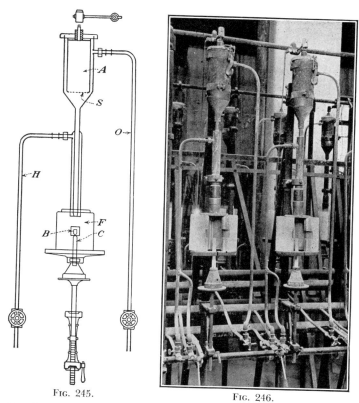

FIG. 245.　　　　　FIG. 246.

FIGS. 245 and 246.—Cross section and general view of apparatus for the manufacture of artificial rubies and sapphires. (*Swiss Jewel Company, Locarno, Switzerland.*)

produced by a mixture of hydrogen and oxygen. The hydrogen enters through the tube *H;* the oxygen, through *O*. The alumina is fused in the intense flame at *F* and collects on a fire-clay support *C*. A pear- or carrot-shaped mass of alumina *B*, called *boule* or *birne* (Figs. 245 and 247), slowly forms, the broader part being uppermost. Sometimes the boule is rotated during formation. When the desired size is attained, which may vary from 150 to 400 carats, the furnace is shut down. The furnace is allowed to cool for a short period; the boule is then removed with suitable tongs. Further cooling takes place rather rapidly. Boules weighing as much as 750 carats have been made. When no pigmenting material is added to the alumina, a colorless, transparent product called *white sapphire*, is obtained.

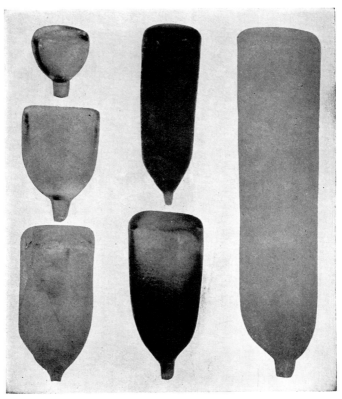

Fig. 247.—Pear- and carrot-shaped *boules* or *birnes* of different colors varying in weight from 37 to 560 carats. Natural size.

In the manufacture of synthetic corundum very pure ammonium alum, $NH_4Al(SO_4)_2.12H_2O$, is used as the raw material. By the direct ignition of the alum in fused quartz dishes in a suitable furnace, finely powdered alumina, Al_2O_3, is produced. As great care must be exercised at all stages to ensure the absence of deleterious impurities, some of the manufacturers prepare the alum from pure metallic aluminum, sulfuric acid, and ammonia.

Although these boules have the same crystal structure as natural corundum (α-alumina), which belongs to the hexagonal system, there is generally no definite external evidence of crystallization. Occasionally a hexagonal outline or cross section may be observed (Fig. 248). This may occur when the crystallographic c axis is parallel to the axis of the boule. Because of the general lack of external evidence of crystallization the orientation of the boule cannot be readily determined except in polarized light. By this

FIG. 248.—
Boule of synthetic
ruby with hexag-
onal outline, top
and side views.

FIG. 249.—Rods of
synthetic ruby and
sapphire.

means the direction of the optic axis can be located, which in hexagonal crystals coincides with the crystallographic c axis.

In most boules one of the sides is somewhat flattened. In such cases the optic axis lies in the plane which passes through the axis of the boule and is normal to the flattened side. The position of this plane which includes the optic axis may be determined by examining the sets of fine lines which are often observed on the blunt end of the boule. The set of longer lines indicates the direction of the plane. In boules of European manufacture the position of the optic axis in this plane varies considerably. In 1941, the Linde Air Products Company succeeded in controlling the crystallographic orientation of the boule. Another achievement of the company is the production of slender rods of considerable length, up to 30 inches (Fig. 249).

The rate at which boules can be produced varies considerably with the materials used as pigmenting agents. Boules weighing 250 to 400 carats can be made in about four hours. Generally about twenty-five furnaces, although in some instances as many as sixty, are operated by one person. In the successful operation of the furnaces much technical skill is necessary (Figs. 250 and 251).

Fig. 250.—Interior of plant showing furnaces for manufacture of synthetic gems. (*Swiss Jewel Company, Locarno, Switzerland.*)

Synthetic Ruby.—By adding to the alumina varying amounts of chromium oxide, up to 7 per cent, boules with different shades of red are produced. The darker varieties are called *synthetic ruby*. Light varieties are designated by various names (p. 156). As revealed by chemical analysis, these synthetic rubies contain only about one-half of the chromium oxide that was mixed with the alumina. The color is uniformly distributed throughout the product. Natural ruby contains only 0.10 to 1.25 per cent of chromium oxide, according to Papish.

Synthetic Sapphire Proper.—When about 2 per cent of iron oxide and 1 per cent of titanium oxide are added as the coloring matter, boules of a blue color are obtained. This product is known as the *synthetic sapphire proper,* or simply as *synthetic* *sapphire.* The presence of iron in the boule is easily detected by analysis, whereas titanium may be entirely absent or present only in slight traces. The color is quite uniformly distributed in the boules that are now made. Formerly the blue color was often confined to a comparatively thin superficial layer, about 2 millimeters thick, while the interior of the boule was much paler or even quite colorless. When the color is unevenly distributed,

Fig. 251.—Interior of plant of Linde Air Products Company, near Chicago.

the material should be cut so that the blue portions are either the table or culet of the finished gem (p. 42).

Synthetic Green Sapphire.—When a mixture of the oxides of vanadium and cobalt is used, the boules are colored green. During the process of manufacture the oxide of cobalt volatizes, and hence only vanadium can be detected in the product. The color is uniformly distributed throughout the boule. This material is properly designated as *synthetic green corundum* or *green sapphire.* The term *scientific emerald* is misleading and should not be used.

Synthetic Alexandrite-like Corundum.—A product simulating to a marked degree the mineral alexandrite, $Be(AlO_2)_2$ (p. 231), is obtained when about 3 per cent of vanadic oxide is used as the coloring agent. This interesting synthetic corundum behaves much like natural alexandrite in that its color is not the same in natural and artificial light. Thus, this material is gray-green in daylight, while in artificial light the color is distinctly a wine red. It is often erroneously called *synthetic alexandrite*.

Other Varieties.—There are a number of other colored varieties of synthetic gem corundum. These are produced by varying the amounts of the pigmenting agents or by mixing them. Thus, smaller amounts of chromium oxide than are necessary to give the dark-red colors essential for the ruby yield material which is light or pale red. These are called *pink* or *rose sapphire*. The misleading terms *synthetic rose topaz, danburite,* and *kunzite* are sometimes given to these lighter red synthetic corundums. Furthermore, when a mixture of the substances causing the red and blue colors is used, a *violet sapphire* is obtained. Similarly *orange sapphire* results when a mixture of the materials that ordinarily produce red and yellow boules is used. This orange-colored material is frequently called *padparadschah sapphire*.

Properties of Synthetic Rubies and Sapphires.—As previously pointed out, natural and synthetic rubies and sapphires possess essentially the same chemical and physical properties. Owing, however, to the great differences in the processes by which the two types of stones have been formed, there are certain definite criteria which in general permit their true character to be recognized.

Composition of Sapphires.—The following table, by A. J. Moses, of analyses of natural and synthetic sapphires, shows that they are the same chemically. Indeed, the artificial product is the purer.

	Synthetic			Natural		
	Verneuil			India	Ceylon	
Al_2O_3	99.84	99.85	99.83	97.51	99.33	99.26
Fe_2O_3	trace	trace	trace	1.95	0.92	0.97
TiO_2	0.11	0.12	0.13			
SiO_2	none	none	none	0.80		
	99.95	99.97	99.96	100.26	100.25	100.23

Indices of Refraction.—Similarly, the following table shows the striking agreement of the indices of refraction and birefringence of the natural and the synthetic stones:

	ω_{Na}	ϵ_{Na}	$\omega - \epsilon$
Synthetic sapphire, Verneuil (Moses)	1.7680	1.7594	0.0086
Natural sapphire, Ceylon (Brauns)	1.7693	1.7610	0.0083
Natural sapphire, Burma (Melczer)	1.7692	1.7609	0.0083
Synthetic ruby, German (Brauns)	1.7709	1.7629	0.0080
Natural ruby, Burma (Melczer)	1.7715	1.7632	0.0083
Synthetic white sapphire, German (Brauns)	1.7681	1.7599	0.0082
Natural white sapphire, Burma (Melczer)	1.7686	1.7605	0.0081

Specific Gravity.—The following table is of interest in that it shows that the specific gravities of synthetic and natural stones are to all intents and purposes identical:

Synthetic sapphire, Verneuil, boule (Kraus)	4.03
Synthetic sapphire, Verneuil, cut stone (Moses)	4.01
Synthetic sapphire, German, boule (Brauns)	3.96
Natural sapphire (Bauer)	4.08
Synthetic ruby, German (Brauns)	3.99
Synthetic ruby, Verneuil, boule (Kraus)	3.96
Natural ruby (Bauer)	4.08
Synthetic white sapphire, Verneuil, boule (Kraus)	4.00
Synthetic pink sapphire, Verneuil, boule (Kraus)	3.99
Synthetic yellow sapphire, Verneuil, boule (Kraus)	3.97

Also with respect to the other physical properties, such as hardness, crystallization, and the property of parting, the same close agreement between the synthetic and natural stones is to be observed.

Characteristics of Synthetic Rubies and Sapphires.—Although in all essentials synthetic rubies and sapphires manufactured by the Verneuil process are identical with the natural stones, they differ in some features, which, though minor, are nevertheless of great importance in revealing the artificial character of the stones. Among these features are *structure lines, gas bubbles, strain and internal cracks,* and *orientation of cut stones.*

Structure Lines.—The synthetic stones often show fine *structure lines* (Fig. 252). That is, the material appears to be built up of thin layers parallel to the surface of the boule. This may be due to fluctuations in temperature during the formation of the boule or to an *uneven distribution of the pigment.* This structure cannot commonly be observed in faceted stones without recourse to the microscope, although it may be apparent when the gem is cut *en cabochon,* that is, with a comparatively large curved surface. These structure lines are characteristically curved, conforming to the shape of the boule. They can usually be readily distinguished

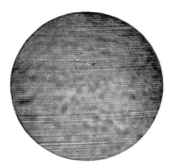

FIG. 252.—Synthetic ruby with structure lines and gas bubbles (black). (*Photograph by Swiss Jewel Company.*)

FIG. 253.—Montana sapphire with hexagonal pattern. (*Photograph by Swiss Jewel Company.*)

from the more nearly straight, parallel bands due to the zonal distribution of color in natural stones (Fig. 253). This distinction can obviously be best made under the microscope with the stone immersed in a suitable liquid. Surface striations produced dur-

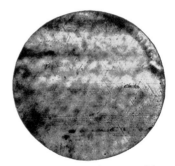

FIG. 254.—Ceylon sapphire with liquid inclusions. (*Photograph by Swiss Jewel Company.*)

FIG. 255.—Ceylon sapphire with needle-like crystals of rutile and liquid-filled cavities. (*Photograph by Swiss Jewel Company.*)

ing the cutting and polishing processes, as well as lines due to repeated twinning, may also be observed on natural stones, but these differ materially from the structure lines of synthetic material.

Gas Bubbles.—Rounded and not infrequently elongated gas bubbles are sometimes to be found in the boules (Fig. 252).

Sometimes portions of a synthetic gem show pronounced *cloudiness*. It was formerly thought this cloudiness was caused by minute quantities of the unfused powder becoming disseminated in the boule. It is now believed that it is caused by gas bubbles being massed together in limited areas. Cloudiness is commonly regarded as indicative of faulty handling of the furnace. With the development of greater skill in the manipulation of the furnaces, products are now made that contain few gas bubbles which are of much smaller size than formerly. This is especially true of white sapphire.

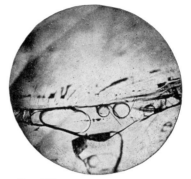

FIG. 256.—Natural sapphire with liquid inclusions and movable bubbles.

Although gas bubbles are characteristic of synthetic corundum, they are not observed in natural corundum, which may contain inclusions of liquids (Figs. 254 and 256), rutile (Fig. 255), or hematite. The liquid inclusions commonly contain bubbles of gas, which may be movable in the liquid. The inclusions of rutile are usually in the form of microscopic needle-like crystals with a characteristic hexagonal grouping. Hematite may be observed as small hexagonal plates. If any of these inclusions are present, the stone is without doubt natural.

Strain and Internal Cracks.—As these synthetic gems are formed at high temperatures and allowed to cool rather quickly, the boules are generally under great strain. They must therefore be handled with care and not be permitted to rub against one another; otherwise, they will fracture badly. When this happens, usually all the boule is lost.

When cold, the boules can generally be made to split lengthwise. This is accomplished by exerting pressure with a pliers in the appropriate direction upon the stem of the boule or by striking the boule with a hammer as shown in Fig. 257 or with some other implement. The plane of splitting includes the optic axis and the long axis of the boule. The halves are then sawed (Figs. 258

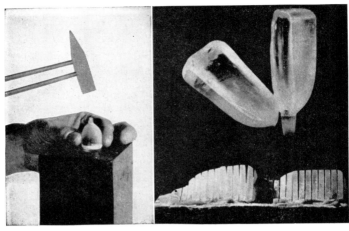

FIG. 257.—Splitting a boule.　　FIG. 258.—Split boule before and after sawing. (*Photographs by Swiss Jewel Company.*)

FIG. 259.—Sawed sections of boules, "half moons," mounted for fabrication into jewel bearings. (*Courtesy of Linde Air Products Company.*)

and 259) so as to yield the largest possible return in cut gems, watch jewels, or instrument bearings. No attention has generally been paid to the crystallographic orientation or to the dichroic properties of the stone.

Once the strain is relieved by splitting, these synthetic stones will not commonly fracture further while being sawed, cut, or polished. On account of their extreme brittleness and due to some residual strain, however, *internal cracks* may develop during these processes or even later (Fig. 260). These are sometimes notice-able at the junction of the facets, especially near the culet. These flaws may at first sight give the impression that the stone has been chipped, but a closer examination will reveal that the facets are perfect and that the flaw is within the stone.

Fig. 260.—Cut synthetic sapphire with many internal cracks.

Boules which have been grown with a definite orientation (p. 153) are less likely to develop excessive strains, and consequently the man-ufacturing losses can be reduced. A preferred orientation is one in which the axis of the boule is normal to one of the rhom-bohedral parting planes. When the position of the optic axis approximates or coincides with the axis of the boule, splitting does not readily take place. If such boules are sawed, the result-ing sections tend to rupture or fracture easily. It is thought that this is due to polysynthetic twinning which develops during the cooling process. When boules are under strain, they show an abnormal biaxial character. The degree of strain is revealed by the size of the angle of the optic axes, which may be as large as twenty degrees.

Some stones possess what may be designated as *feathers,* which are fairly large internal cracks so situated as to be easily visible.

Orientation of Cut Stones.—As has been pointed out (p. 156), synthetic rubies and sapphires are identical in composition and physical properties with the natural stones. Colored varieties must therefore show pleochroism. Consequently, as indicated on page 76, in order to cut them to the best advantage, that is, so that the deepest color will be obtained, the table of the stone should be cut parallel to the basal pinacoid. In the case of natural rubies and sapphires this can easily be done, since they are usually well crystallized, and the direction of the vertical axis is readily recognized.

Although cut natural rubies and sapphires are generally properly oriented, most synthetic stones are not. This is because the positions of the principal crystallographic and optic directions in the boules are not constant. They are generally inclined to the long axis of the boule, at angles which vary considerably. Another reason is the peculiar way the boules split lengthwise, parallel to the long axis (Fig. 258) and in the direction of deeper color. The optic axis (vertical crystallographic axis) lies, however, in the plane of splitting. For these reasons it is obvious that synthetic rubies and sapphires cannot be economically oriented so as to give the best color.

In fact, to orient these stones properly for cutting would entail time, for each boule would need to be carefully studied before being sawed preparatory to cutting. Moreover, lapidaries are generally not well enough versed in crystal optics to do this. Then, too, the proper orientation of each piece for cutting would cause a very large percentage of the boule to be wasted, and would necessitate the production of smaller stones. The colored varieties with a random orientation therefore show dichroism when examined through the table. On the other hand, the natural stones are almost always properly oriented and hence are not dichroic when examined in the same way. This difference in behavior is an important factor in recognizing synthetic cut stones.

General Statement.—Although the differences, described above, between natural and synthetic rubies and sapphires are obviously not readily recognized by the untrained observer, the expert is in general able to pass judgment on the character of the material. In the case of rather small stones, however, which have been selected, oriented, and fashioned with great care, the distinguishing criteria may be entirely absent. Also, it is of interest to point out that the production of synthetic rubies and sapphires on a commercial scale was not begun until after the opening of the present century. Consequently, rubies and sapphires with a history considerably antedating the year 1900 are in all likelihood natural.

Prior to September, 1947, synthetic star rubies and sapphires had not been produced. The Linde Air Products Company now manufactures stones of excellent quality (p. 200).

Synthetic Spinel.—The Verneuil process also lends itself to the manufacture of a product with the chemical composition and

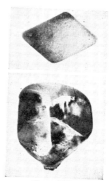

FIG. 261.   FIG. 262.   FIG. 263.

FIG. 261.—Well-developed spinel boule in furnace. (*Courtesy of Linde Air Products Company.*)

FIGS. 262 and 263.—Top and side views of boules of synthetic spinel (blue), showing distorted cubical (Fig. 262) and octahedral (Fig. 263) development, and pronounced cubical cleavage cracks.

physical properties of gem spinel (Fig. 261). Very beautiful synthetic spinels in a variety of colors are now on the market. They were first introduced about 1926.

Process of Manufacture.—Chemically, gem spinel may be considered as magnesium aluminate, $Mg(AlO_2)_2$, or as a multiple oxide of magnesium and aluminum, $MgO.Al_2O_3$. For the synthetic stone a mixture of magnesium oxide and alumina, in the ratio 1 to 1, serves as the raw material. This mixture is placed in the receptacle A (Fig. 245), and the process is then carried out essentially as in the manufacture of the ruby and sapphire.

Although true gem spinel has the composition given above, a series of synthetic products is manufactured in which the ratio between the magnesium oxide and alumina varies from 1 to 1, as in normal spinel, to 1 to 5.

Character of Boules.—Spinel crystallizes in the cubic system. The boules generally show marked external evidences of crystallization, since they are often square in cross section and also possess large well-formed surfaces (Figs. 261 and 262). These surfaces are faces of the cube and sometimes those of the octahedron (Fig. 263). Smaller faces have been identified as those of other forms of the cubic system. Cracks indicating a cubical cleavage may also be recognized.

Synthetic spinel may also be produced as slender rods, similar to those of synthetic sapphire.

Colored Varieties.—When no pigmenting agent is added to the mixture of the oxides of magnesium and aluminum, the product is colorless. The addition of cobalt oxide produces a blue color, whereas green spinel is obtained when chromium oxide is used. By varying the amounts of these coloring materials many aquamarine- and alexandrite-like shades of color result. Reddish varieties are also marketed.

Specific Gravity.—Since the composition of synthetic spinel may vary greatly, there is also considerable variation in the specific gravity, namely, from 3.48 to 3.71. These values agree well with those of the natural gem (p. 239).

Hardness.—The hardness is 8, the same as for the natural gem. It becomes slightly greater, however, as the percentage of alumina increases.

Indices of Refraction.—According to Rinne, who has investigated synthetic spinel in great detail, the indices of refraction and the dispersion of the two extreme types are as follows:

	Type 1 $MgO:1$ Al_2O_3	Type 1 $MgO:5$ Al_2O_3
n_C line	1.7143	1.7243
n_D line	1.7182	1.7280
n_F line	1.7261	1.7361
Dispersion	0.0118	0.0118

These values are also very similar to those of the natural stones.

Names.—All varieties of this synthetic material should be sold as synthetic spinels. The use of such terms as *synthetic sapphire, synthetic aquamarine, synthetic zircon, rozircon, alexandrite, Brazilian emerald,* and *danburite* for the variously colored varieties of synthetic spinel should be avoided, as they are deceptive and misleading.

General Statement.—Spinel is isotropic, hence singly refractive, and does not show dichroism. These properties distinguish it from synthetic or natural corundums as well as from natural zircon and chrysoberyl (alexandrite), all of which are anisotropic. Anomalous double refraction, due to strain, is generally observed. Synthetic spinel is not so hard as the ruby, sapphire, or chrysoberyl, but it is slightly harder than zircon. By means of its superior hardness synthetic spinel is easily distinguished from glass, which is also isotropic. The various characteristics incidental to the products made by the Verneuil process (p. 157) are also observed on these synthetic gems.

Cut synthetic spinels are rather popular. As the hardness of spinel is inferior to that of the ruby and sapphire, it is not used extensively as jewels in watches or other delicate instruments.

Synthetic Emerald.—Although many attempts had been made to produce the emerald, $Be_3Al_2(SiO_3)_6$, synthetically, it was not until 1930 that Jaeger and Espig of the research staff of the I. G. Farbenindustrie, Bitterfeld, Germany, succeeded in obtaining well-developed crystals measuring up to two centimeters in length. Carroll F. Chatham of San Francisco, California, made synthetic beryl in 1930, and later, in 1935, succeeded in producing emerald crystals weighing one carat in the rough.

Synthetic emerald crystals are of good color and show the characteristic hexagonal forms of the natural emerald (p. 203). The synthetic product simulates very closely the natural in all essential physical and chemical properties. The method of manufacture differs markedly from that used to produce synthetic rubies, sapphires, and spinels. Moreover, no details of the method have been revealed other than that it is a process of slow crystallization.

Synthetic emerald possesses flaws, such as cracks, and characteristic wisp-like spherical inclusions, which are important aids in identification. The specific gravity and the refractive indices of the synthetic product are in general lower than for the natural emerald, but the differences are slight. As the quality of the synthetic product is being improved, it is becoming increasingly difficult to distinguish between synthetic and natural emeralds. However, according to Switzer, synthetic emeralds of both American and European manufacture fluoresce with a deep red color when subjected to ultraviolet rays, while natural emeralds do not. Thus far, stones, not over one carat in weight, have been cut.

The German manufacturers suggested the term *igmerald* for this product, but the term has not been widely used. The product should properly be called *synthetic emerald*. Although synthetic emeralds have not yet become important commercially, their production is a significant scientific achievement.

Some stones sold as synthetic or scientific emerald or aquamarine are synthetic sapphire or spinel or colored glass.

Synthetic Chrysoberyl.—Although this green mineral with the chemical composition $Be(AlO_2)_2$ has been made synthetically with the color of alexandrite, it has not been marketed. This is because the product is inferior to synthetic sapphire or spinel with an alexandrite color, and due to the higher cost of manufacture.

Synthetic Rutile.—Transparent, colorless, and colored boules of synthetic rutile, TiO_2, are made by the Verneuil process. Due to its high indices of refraction and strong adamantine luster (p. 261), synthetic rutile may find use as a gem.

Value and Uses of Synthetic Gem Materials.—Since natural and synthetic rubies and sapphires are alike in all important essentials, naturally the artificial stones are in great demand. Furthermore, this popularity has been stimulated by the fact that cut synthetic stones may be bought at various prices up to $2 or $3 per carat, depending upon the quality, whereas natural stones of corresponding size and quality are obviously much more expensive (p. 202).

It is also worthy of note that comparatively large quantities of cut synthetic rubies and sapphires are now used in place of the natural stones as the jewels in watches and in physical and scientific apparatus where hard bearing surfaces are required, for example, in balances, chronometers, meters of all kinds, precision gauges, and injector nozzles. Automobiles and modern aircraft are equipped with many delicate instruments containing large numbers of these bearing jewels. During the war, the industrial demand for synthetic rubies and sapphires increased enormously. The use of rods of uniform diameter (p. 153) reduces the cost of fabricating bearing jewels, since jewel blanks of the appropriate size are readily obtained by merely sawing the rods transversely. Pointed rods are used for phonograph needles. At temperatures of about 1700°C. crystals of aluminum oxide are plastic; hence, rods can be easily bent. Because of their superior hardness, appropriately bent rods are used for thread guides in the textile industry (Fig. 264). These rods are also used in designing special types of jewelry. Moreover, by flame treatment polished high cabochon stones and tear-drop shapes for jewelry purposes can be fabricated from these rods.

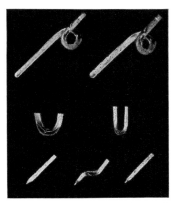

Special care and accurate information concerning the crystallographic orientation are necessary for the successful bending of the rods. The bending takes place in the plane which includes the axis of the rod and c crystallographic (optic) axis. This is the plane in which boules split.[1]

Before the Second World War the most important centers for the manufacture of the various varieties of synthetic rubies, sapphires, and spinels were Locarno and Monthey, Switz

FIG. 264.—Thread guides and phonograph needles of synthetic sapphire. (*Courtesy of Linde Air Products Company.*)

erland; Annecy and Jarrie, France; and Bitterfeld and Freyung, Germany. These plants had a total daily capacity of 750,000 to 1,000,000 carats. With the outbreak of the war in 1939, the supply of rough and fabricated synthetic rubies and sapphires to the United States and Great Britain was greatly reduced. It was consequently necessary to begin their manufacture in these countries. Plants are now located near Chicago and at Salford, England.

Imitation Gems.—Materials classified as imitation gems have compositions differing markedly from the gems that they simulate. They are manufactured principally from glass, although bakelite and other plastics are also used. These materials are well adapted for use in costume jewelry.

[1] See also "Some Properties of Materials Used for Jewel Instrument Bearings" by Insley, H., McMurdie, H. F., Parsons, W. P., and Steierman, B. L., *American Mineralogist*, vol. 32, pp. 1-15, 1947.

Glass.—These imitations are manufactured from special types of glass, often referred to as *paste* or *strass*. These are heavy and very transparent varieties of flint glass with relatively high indices of refraction and strong dispersion. By properly heating the following mixture a glass is obtained which is commonly used to imitate the diamond: 300 parts of quartz, 470 of red lead, 163 of potassium carbonate, 22 of borax, and 1 of white arsenic. If a colored stone is to be simulated, pigments must be added to the mixture. The pigments used are compounds of certain metals. The compounds of manganese give a purple color; of cobalt, blue; of selenium, red; of iron, yellow to green; of chromium, green and red; and of gold, ruby red.

In some cases these stones are very carefully cut, but often the molten glass is simply pressed into properly shaped molds, and allowed to become solid. The facets of such molded stones are apt to be dull, and the edges rounded, unless the stones are subsequently ground and polished to enhance their sale value.

These glass imitations have the following general properties:

1. *Inferior Hardness.*—They are softer (hardness 5 to 6) than the gems which they simulate. They will not scratch ordinary glass. Exposed surfaces soon become scratched, nicked, and dull.

2. *Isotropic Character.*—Being amorphous, these imitations are singly refractive and do not show dichroism.

3. *Index of Refraction.*—Depending upon the composition of the glass, the index of refraction varies from 1.50 to 1.80. To increase the brilliancy and prevent light from passing through the lower facets, the back of the stone, that is, the pavilion and culet, are silvered or foiled, and lacquered. All such imitations are called *chatons* or *chaton foils*. The terms *brilliant* and *rhinestone* are applied to the colorless ones. The use of the term *strass* is often restricted to unsilvered stones.

4. *Specific Gravity.*—This property varies markedly with the composition, especially with the amount of lead oxide used in the manufacture, and may range from 2.5 to 4.0.

5. *Air Bubbles.*—Although great care is taken in manufacturing the glass, air bubbles are usually present. They are sometimes so prominent that they are readily seen by the unaided eye or with the hand lens. Air bubbles are not observed in natural stones.

6. *Heat Conductivity.*—Glass imitations are poor conductors of heat and hence are warm to the touch. This property may be of value in differentiating between these imitations and the diamond and quartz.

7. *Conchoidal Fracture.*—As is characteristic of all amorphous substances, glass has an easy conchoidal fracture, yielding quite brilliant surfaces. The fracture is best seen on exposed surfaces and near the prongs of the setting.

Although all these properties are important, the first four are usually sufficient to determine accurately glass imitations.

A glass imitation of yellow or red aventurine quartz is called *goldstone* or *aventurine glass.* It contains small crystals of metallic copper which reflect light and give the material a very attractive appearance. During its manufacture, air is entrapped, causing the formation of air bubbles, which help to reveal the true character of the goldstone. Frequently the polished surface is pitted where it has been cut through such air bubbles. Glass made to simulate opal is often sold as *Lake Superior fire agate* or by other misleading terms.

Most glass imitations of gems have been made in Germany and Czecho-Slovakia. In Jablonec, Czecho-Slovakia, and the neighboring villages there were many firms engaged, before the Second World War, in manufacturing and fashioning them for personal ornamentation. Turnov, Czecho-Slovakia, has been important for the cutting and polishing of glass imitations and marcasite. The cutting was done by semi-automatic machinery.

Plastics.—These products of synthetic chemistry are finding an increasing use in costume jewelry. They are called plastics because they can be easily molded, shaped, and formed when in a liquid or semi-liquid condition.

For many years *bakelite,* discovered in 1909, was the most important plastic. Bakelite is made by mixing together phenol (carbolic acid) and formaldehyde. Upon heating, a chemical reaction takes place, forming a substance which is viscous when hot, but which hardens upon cooling. This material can be ground and introduced into molds, where under high temperature and pressure it assumes its final form, which is permanent and will not soften when reheated. More recently, other plastics with a formaldehyde base have been developed by combining the formal-

dehyde with substances like urea.   These products are similar to
bakelite in that they harden permanently after being heated and
molded.

There are two classes of plastics, namely, (1) *thermosetting plastics,* and (2) *thermoplastics.*   To the first class belong those plastics
which harden permanently after being molded.   They will not
soften when reheated and hence cannot be remolded.   Bakelite
and other plastics with a formaldehyde base are thermosetting.
The plastics which will soften when reheated, and hence can be
remolded, are called thermoplastics.

The thermoplastics are also complex substances, such as the
"styrene," "vinyl," and "acrylic" resins.   They are prepared in
fine powders or granules which are hard at ordinary temperatures.
These can be introduced into molds, and when heated under pressure the particles soften and fuse together to produce molded
shapes, which are rigid when cooled and have a high polish.   If
necessary, the products can be readily machined.   Unlike the
thermosetting plastics, these finished and hardened materials can
be resoftened by heating and again molded.   In the last two
decades, many thermoplastic products have been developed which
have found use in jewelry.   The acrylic resins have very desirable
optical properties which make them especially suitable and are
sold under such trade names as *lucite* and *plexiglass.*   Many of
the newer plastics are, however, now included in the general
term *bakelite.*

Cellulose nitrate, discovered in 1864, was the first thermoplastic
product to be made.   Because of its many undesirable properties,
especially its high inflammability, it has not been used extensively
in jewelry.   Cellulose nitrate is marketed as *celluloid* and *pyralin.*
Another cellulose plastic is the acetate, which has properties very
similar to those of cellulose nitrate, but has the advantage that
it is not inflammable.   Cellulose acetate is sold under various trade
names, such as *lumarith* and *tenite.*

The specific gravities and the indices of refraction of the various
plastics referred to above are given in the table on following
page.

In view of the rapid development of plastics and the great increase in their use, newer types will undoubtedly be developed.

	Specific gravity	Index of refraction
Phenol formaldehyde:		
Bakelite........................	1.20-1.32	1.5 -1.7
Urea formaldehyde:		
Beetle.........................	1.45-1.50	1.54-1.60
Styrene resin:		
Styron........................	1.05-1.07	1.59
Vinyl resins:		
Vinylite—a....................	1.19	1.47
Vinylite—b....................	1.35-1.37	1.53
Acrylic resins:		
Lucite, plexiglass...............	1.19	1.49
Cellulose nitrate:		
Celluloid......................	1.35-1.60	1.46-1.59
Cellulose acetate:		
Lumarith......................	1.27-1.60	1.47-1.51

Doublets and Triplets.—There are two types of doublets, *true doublets* and *false doublets*. The *true doublet* (Fig. 265) consists of two sections, each of genuine material, joined with an invisible cement to produce a larger stone, the value of which would naturally be greater than the sum of the values of the two smaller pieces. The layer of cement in these doublets may be detected by immersing the stone in a liquid with an index of refraction approximately equal to that of the gem fragments. The cement is frequently soluble in alcohol or chloroform so that when a doublet is soaked in one of these liquids the two portions may fall apart. Diamond fragments are sometimes used in making true doublets, the crown being one piece, the pavilion another. The two sections are so cut that they are cemented together at the girdle, which obviously makes it more difficult to recognize the true character of the stone.

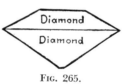

FIG. 265.

The *false doublet* (Fig. 266) has a genuine crown, while the pavilion ordinarily consists of an inferior stone or of glass. For instance, a slice of ruby may be backed with garnet, some other inexpensive red stone, or red glass. When mounted, the exposed portion, being genuine, will stand successfully the usual tests that

might be made upon it.   Further, a thin slice of a comparatively
hard stone, such as garnet, may be used for the upper portion of
the doublet, to withstand abrasion, while the lower portion may
be of glass of any desired color (Fig. 267).   Diamond doublets may
have the lower portions of colorless sapphire, topaz, zircon, or
glass.   Many gems have been imitated in this way.

The character of false doublets may be detected by the methods
applied in the case of true doublets or one may breathe upon
the stone, causing a film of moisture to be formed.   This permits

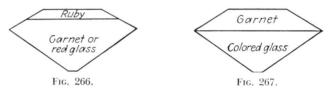

FIG. 266.   FIG. 267.

the boundary between the two portions to be more easily seen.
If the two portions of the doublet are differently colored, the character of the stone may be ascertained by examining it through the
back over a white background.   In case the two parts of a doublet
are fused together, they naturally cannot be separated by soaking,
but here the difference between the sections may be observed by

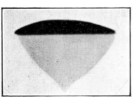

FIG. 268.   FIG. 269.

immersion in a liquid whose index of refraction is approximately
equal to that of one portion of the stone (Figs. 268 and 269).

The *opal doublet* consists (1) of two thin slices of opal, the
upper slice being of superior quality, held together by a colored
cement which tends to improve the attractiveness of the exposed
layer; or (2) of a superior upper layer of opal cemented upon an
inexpensive material, often dark in color.   In the *hollow doublet*
(Fig. 270) the lower side of the crown is hollowed out, and a
colored liquid is placed within this cavity in order to impart the

desired color to the stone. This type is now of little importance, since it is used infrequently.

The term *imitation doublet* is sometimes applied to stones that are nothing but glass, in one piece. The purpose of this term is to enhance the sale value, since doublets consisting in part of genuine stones are naturally considered more valuable than those composed entirely of glass.

Closely related to doublets are *triplets*. These consist of an upper portion of quartz or of another mineral, to withstand wear, and a lower portion of some mineral or glass. These parts are

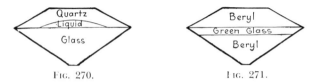

FIG. 270.   FIG. 271.

separated by a piece of foil, a colored layer, or a thin plate of colored mineral, to give the stone a desirable tint. The triplet has been used to imitate the emerald. A layer of green glass, usually of the type known as *paste* (p. 168), is cemented between two thicker layers of pale beryl or quartz (Fig. 271). The beryl gives the stone the proper hardness and index of refraction, while the glass contributes the green color. The upper section of beryl is of sufficient thickness to extend to the girdle, whereby the effectiveness of the deception is greatly increased. By immersion in liquids with the proper indices of refraction, this deception may be readily detected. In this way the three sections of the stone are distinctly seen. According to Liddicoat, the fluorescence induced by ultraviolet light is also helpful in detecting both doublets and triplets.

The term "soldered emerald" has been applied to emerald doublets and triplets, especially to those with fused parts. In recent years, with the increase in the use of synthetic rubies and sapphires in many colors, the demand for doublets and triplets has fallen off to a great extent. The synthetic stones are, of course, much more satisfactory, and are comparatively inexpensive.

Chapter XI

METALS USED FOR GEM MOUNTINGS

The metals used most extensively for gem mountings are gold, platinum, and silver. The more expensive gems are mounted in gold or platinum. These metals do not tarnish as does silver.

Gold.—Pure gold is much too soft (hardness 2½ to 3) and malleable to be durable as a mounting. It must therefore be alloyed with other metals to increase its hardness. The gold content of these alloys, that is, their *fineness* or *purity,* is indicated by the use of the term *carat* or *karat* (p. 135), which means one twenty-fourth part. Thus 18-karat gold, usually stamped 18K, consists of 18 parts of gold and 6 parts of alloyed metals. The use of 6 parts of alloyed metals with 18 parts of gold increases the hardness sufficiently so that the alloyed gold has satisfactory wearing qualities. In order to reduce the cost, alloys of lesser gold content are also used. Although custom and practice permit 10K alloys, when so stamped, to be sold as gold, an alloy with less than 50 per cent gold (12K) is not properly designated as gold.

The term *fine gold* is frequently used to indicate pure gold (24K). Fineness may also be expressed in terms of parts per thousand; thus, 750 fine means that the alloy consists of 750 parts of gold and 250 parts of alloys, in other words, 18K.

When gold is alloyed with different metals, very noticeable changes in color result. These alloys are known as *yellow, white,* and *green* gold.

Yellow Gold.—When equal parts of silver and copper are alloyed with the requisite amounts of the precious metal, yellow gold is obtained. Thus, 18K yellow gold consists of 18 parts of gold, 3 parts of silver, and 3 parts of copper by weight. Lighter shades of yellow may be obtained by increasing the amount of silver and decreasing the copper proportionately without changing the amount of gold used. Darker shades result when the copper content is increased and the silver decreased. In yellow gold of lower karat rating, zinc is sometimes added to improve its working qualities.

White Gold.—This alloy contains nickel, copper, and zinc. Thus, 18-karat white gold commonly consists of 75 per cent pure gold, 17 per cent nickel, 2.5 per cent copper, and 5.5 per cent zinc. This gold alloy is somewhat harder and therefore more durable than those of platinum and iridium and is used as a substitute for them. White gold may also be made by alloying 15 per cent or more of palladium with gold.

Green Gold.—The alloy consisting of 75 per cent gold, 22.5 per cent silver, 1.5 per cent nickel, and 1.0 per cent copper is called green gold. Formerly, it was used quite extensively for mounting purposes.

Gold metal designated as *rolled gold, gold filled, gold plate,* and *gilt* is frequently used for the mounting of gems.

Rolled Gold.—This consists of an outer layer of gold alloy (for example, 18K) and an inner layer of base metal. The layer of gold alloy is "sweated" under proper conditions to a bar of base metal. This composite bar is then rolled into thinner bars or sheets or drawn into wire. In these processes the proportion of gold alloy to base metal is preserved unchanged. Articles made from rolled gold should be properly designated with respect to the proportion of gold alloy to base metal, by weight, as well as to the fineness of the gold alloy. Thus, 1/10 18K, means that the ratio of gold alloy to base metal is 1 to 9 and that the fineness of the gold surface is 18 karat. The term *gold filled* is often used for this type of composite metal. This term does not, however, adequately describe its character. Such metal is well described as *rolled gold plate* and is thus distinguished from metals that are gold-plated electrolytically and are designated as *gold plate.* Metals with very thin coatings of gold, produced either electrolytically or by merely dipping or "washing" the metal in a solution of gold, are commonly called *gilt* or *washed gold.*

Platinum.—Like gold, pure platinum is soft and flexible. For use in jewelry it must be alloyed with a metal which will impart the necessary hardness and rigidity. Alloyed with 10 per cent iridium, the hardness of platinum, which is about 4 to 4½, is materially increased. This iridium-platinum alloy is admirably adapted for the mounting of gems. Because iridium is more expensive than platinum, an alloy with but 5 per cent iridium is often used, but this cheaper alloy is considerably inferior in hardness. The other members of the platinum group of metals, osmium, ruthenium, rhodium, and palladium, can also be alloyed with platinum. Because of their superior hardness, iridium ($6\frac{1}{2}$) and osmium (7) are used for the points of fountain pens. Rhodium alloys find application in the chemical industry.

Silver.—This metal is not used extensively for the mounting of gems for personal adornment. Large quantities, however, are used for articles sold by jewelers and for coinage purposes. Silver, like gold and platinum, is soft ($2\frac{1}{2}$) and must be alloyed with a hardening metal, usually copper. The important alloys are *sterling silver* and *coin silver*.

Sterling Silver.—This alloy consists of 92.5 per cent pure silver and 7.5 per cent copper. It is commonly stamped "sterling."

Coin Silver.—The silver coins of the United States contain 90 per cent silver and 10 per cent copper. The content of silver coins is not uniform for all countries; for example, Great Britain uses sterling silver.

Other Metals.—During the war, restrictions were placed on the use of gold and platinum for jewelry purposes. Consequently, there was a greatly increased use of palladium for gem mountings. Palladium is much like platinum in appearance and hardness, and it is many times rarer than gold. Palladium alloys can be readily distinguished from those of platinum and gold, for palladium is much lighter in weight. The specific gravities of the three metals are platinum 21.4, gold 19.3, and palladium 12. After the close of the war, platinum mountings were again in popular demand.

PART II

GEM MATERIALS

DESCRIPTION OF INDIVIDUAL GEMS

In the preceding chapters the important properties and facts about gem materials in general have been thoroughly discussed. It is now possible to describe in considerable detail and in a systematic manner those minerals that are used in various ways as gems or for ornamental and decorative purposes.

A very satisfactory order of treatment is first to describe the most precious stones, next the semi-precious and ornamental stones, and then the metallic gem minerals. It may be emphasized here that there is no sharp distinction between the precious and the semi-precious gems. It is usual, however, to rank the diamond, ruby, sapphire, and emerald as the precious stones, since they are the most valuable and attractive of all gems. Ornamental stones are those from which decorative objects, such as vases, jewel caskets, table tops, and paper weights are frequently fashioned, or which are used in the beautifying of interiors of buildings, as, for example, in mosaics. All other stones are called semi-precious. There is a tendency to discontinue the classification of gems as *precious, semi-precious,* and *ornamental* and to refer to all of them simply as *gem stones.* In addition, there are described certain natural organic materials which have long been used for personal adornment. These are the pearl, coral, amber, and jet. Manufactured materials have been fully discussed in Chapter IX. The following classification will be used in this chapter: (1) *important gem stones,* (2) *other gem and ornamental stones,* (3) *metallic gem minerals,* and (4) *organic gem materials.*

In the descriptions of the various gem minerals emphasis has been placed upon their important properties and upon the principal localities where they occur. These descriptions are in sufficient detail to give the student and lover of gems the information that is necessary not only to recognize the various gems, especially with practice, but also to stimulate interest in and appreciation of them.

In the following tabulation, the minerals which may be used for gem and ornamental purposes are grouped according to the classification given above:

IMPORTANT GEM STONES

Diamond	Jade
Corundum (ruby and sapphire)	Chrysoberyl
Beryl (emerald)	Tourmaline
Topaz	Olivine
Garnet	Spinel
Zircon	Turquois
Opal	Feldspar
Quartz	Lazurite

OTHER GEM AND ORNAMENTAL STONES
(Arranged alphabetically)

Anatase	Iolite
Andalusite	Lazulite
Apatite	Moldavite
Axinite	Obsidian
Azurite and malachite	Phenacite
Benitoite	Prehnite
Beryllonite	Rhodonite
Brazilianite	Rutile
Calcite	Sepiolite
Cassiterite	Serpentine
Chlorastrolite	Smithsonite
Chrysocolla	Sodalite
Cyanite	Sphalerite
Danburite	Spodumene
Datolite	Staurolite
Diopside	Steatite
Dioptase	Thomsonite
Enstatite, bronzite, and hyper-sthene	Titanite
	Variscite
Epidote	Vesuvianite
Euclase	Willemite
Fluorite	Zoisite
Gypsum	

METALLIC GEM MINERALS	ORGANIC GEM MATERIALS
Chromite	Pearl
Cobaltite	Coral
Gold	Amber
Hematite	Jet
Pyrite	

These gem materials will be described in the order given above.

DIAMOND

The diamond, generally acknowledged to be the most precious of all stones, crystallizes in the cubic system, the more common crystal forms being the octahedron (Fig. 272) and rhombic dodecahedron (Figs. 1 and 273). However, the cube and some of the

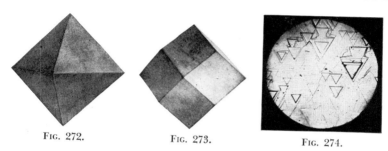

FIG. 272.   FIG. 273.   FIG. 274.

more complex forms of the cubic system are also observed. Any one of these forms may occur alone on the crystal or in combination with other forms. These crystals are often rounded or distorted, and may be twinned. Contact twins according to the spinel law are frequent (Fig. 50). Depressed growth figures, called *trigons,* are commonly observed on faces of the octahedron (Fig. 274). The edges of these characteristic triangular figures are in a reversed position to those of the octahedron. Figure 275 is a photograph of an octahedral diamond crystal in the blue ground from Kimberley, South Africa. Diamond crystals vary in size from microscopic dimensions to over 3,000 carats in weight. Sometimes the mineral is massive, either as crystal aggregates or devoid of external crystal faces.

As has been noted on page 31, the diamond has a very perfect octahedral cleavage, which is of assistance in cutting it. This

cleavage requires that caution be exercised in setting cut diamonds, as well as in wearing them, especially in rings, to guard
against cracking them by accidentally hitting some hard object.
There is also a less perfect cleavage parallel to faces of the rhombic
dodecahedron, which is only rarely used as it is difficult to produce. Because of the dominant octahedral cleavage the apparent
conchoidal fracture, which is sometimes observed, consists of step-
like cleavages, as revealed by the microscope.

FIG. 275.—Diamond in blue ground. Kimberley, South Africa.

The diamond is the hardest substance
known, and hence the value 10 is assigned
to it in the Mohs scale of hardness (p. 26).
The hardness varies on the faces of the different crystal forms. Thus, the hardness is
greater on faces of the octahedron than on
those of the cube. These variations are observed when the diamond is cut and polished
(p. 119).

The reports that the hardness of diamonds
varies with the locality from which the stones
are obtained have originated with diamond cutters and may be
attributed to the following factors: (1) the variation in external
crystallization from that with which the cutter has been familiar,
and the consequent difficulty he experiences in properly orient-
ing the stones; (2) the more frequent occurrence of twinned areas
in diamonds from different localities, and the difficulty in recognizing and properly interpreting the twinned areas; (3) the common tendency to decry the quality of stones from new localities
and thus depress their value, especially if they occur in considerable quantities.

The specific gravity ranges from 3.15 to 3.53, according to the
variety. When the mineral is pure and well crystallized, the value
is nearly constant at 3.52.

Most of the diamonds used as gems are colorless, or nearly so.
The different shades of yellow and brown are the most common.
Green stones are much less common, while those with a red or
blue color are very rare. The colors are usually pale. Gray,
black, milky, and opalescent stones are also found. Diamonds
with distinctive colors and a high degree of transparency are designated as *fancy* stones. In the trade, diamonds are sharply dif-

ferentiated according to color into many different classes (p. 124). If the stone has a tinge of an undesirable color, such as yellow or brown, it is said to be *off color*. The cause of color in diamonds is not definitely known, but is usually ascribed to traces of some of the metallic oxides.

The diamond may be transparent, translucent, or opaque. Only those which are transparent are valued as gems. The luster of the uncut diamond is often dull or greasy, but it is a brilliant adamantine in the cut stone. Carbonado (p. 198) has a dull luster.

The index of refraction and the dispersion of the diamond are high, n for red light being 2.402, for yellow 2.417, for green 2.427, and for violet 2.465. The dispersion is $2.465 - 2.402 = 0.063$ (Fig. 81). The characteristic fire is due to this unusually strong dispersion. Anomalous double refraction, caused by internal strains, is often noted. Because it is an excellent conductor of heat, the

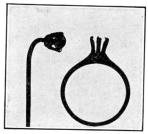

FIG. 276.—X-ray photograph of lead glass imitation (pin) and of diamond (ring).

diamond is cold to the touch. On the other hand, it is a poor conductor of electricity, and becomes positively electrified when rubbed. Many diamonds fluoresce or phosphoresce (p. 49) on exposure to ultraviolet, cathode, and X-rays or to radioactive emanations. Thus, ultraviolet rays may cause some colorless stones to show a light-blue luminescence, while others may glow with a greenish or yellow color. Similar effects are sometimes observed on exposure to sunlight. The mineral is transparent to X-rays, but glass or paste imitations of the stone are not. An X-ray photograph will serve to distinguish the genuine diamond from these imitations (Fig. 276).

The diamond is composed of pure carbon, for when it is burned in an atmosphere of oxygen only carbon dioxide, CO_2, is formed. The colored stones, when burned in this way, leave very small residues which show them to be slightly impure. The stone is unattacked by acids.

Depending upon the uses to which they are put, diamonds are classified as (1) *gem diamonds,* commonly called *cuttables* in the trade; and (2) *industrial diamonds.* These varieties are discussed in detail on pages 191 to 199.

Occurrence and Recovery.—The diamond was known to the ancients and was called *adamas.* From that name the word *adamantine,* used especially in connection with the luster, is derived. The older diamonds came from India and Borneo. In India the diamond was found in three principal localities, (1) in the Madras Presidency of southern India; (2) farther north, in a large area between the Mahanadi and Godavari rivers; and (3) in Bundelkhand in central India. The diamonds were found in alluvial deposits and in a conglomerate, neither of which, of course, represented the original source. In Borneo the most important locality is near the town of Pontianak. At present the annual production of diamonds in India and Borneo is very small.

Tradition has it that diamonds were first discovered in Brazil in 1670, in the gold washings, but they were not positively identified until 1721. The provinces of Minas Geraes and Bahia are the most important producers. The deposits in Brazil are secondary, and the diamond is associated with such minerals as gold, cyanite, tourmaline, pyrope garnet, zircon, and some heavy ore minerals. The Brazilian deposits were very productive between 1721 and 1870, but the present yield is small. It is said that 1,666,569 carats were exported between 1732 and 1871.

The recovery of the diamond in Brazil has been carried on in a primitive way. Material from the diamond-bearing stream beds is usually washed in a hemispherical pan called a *batea,* the larger pieces having been first broken up by sledges. Water is added and, by means of an oscillating, rolling motion, is allowed to spill over the side, carrying with it the lighter constituents of the sand and gravel. The diamond, being comparatively heavy, remains in the bottom along with a number of other heavy minerals, from which it is easily separated by hand.

↑ The most important diamond-producing countries at present are those of Africa, where over 95 per cent of the world's diamonds are being mined. It was in 1867 that diamonds were discovered in Africa. There are several stories of the manner in which the discovery was made. According to one of these, an ostrich hunter and peddler named John O'Reilly, while traveling along the south shore of the Orange River near Hope Town, called at the home of the Boer peasant, Schalk van Niekerk. O'Reilly's attention was called to several stones with which some peasant children had been playing and which they had picked up along the river. When O'Reilly went away, one of the stones was entrusted to him to be identified. He submitted it to various persons but received no decisive information. Some thought that the stone was quartz or topaz. Finally O'Reilly sent it to Dr. W. Guybon Atherstone of Grahamstown, who pronounced it to be a diamond. The stone weighed over 21 carats and sold for $2,500. News of the discovery brought many prospectors to the region about Hope Town.

The first diamonds were found in secondary deposits, that is, in the sands and gravels of stream beds, principally along the Orange, Vaal, and Modder rivers. They were, therefore, called *river diggings.* The separation of the diamonds from the associated sands was by washing, in much the same way that gold is panned.

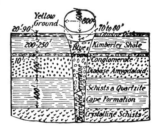

FIG. 277.—Section through the Kimberley Mine.

In 1870, diamonds were discovered in primary deposits, or *dry diggings,* upon a plateau between the Vaal and Modder rivers, at the place now known as Kimberley. The occurrences were limited to circular or elliptical areas, varying in diameter from 20 to 700 meters. Near the surface the diamonds were found in a soft, decomposed material known as *yellow ground.* At a depth of 20 to 25 meters (Fig. 277) the yellow ground passed into a hard, unaltered, basic igneous rock, at first called *blue ground* or earth, but now commonly known as *kimberlite,* a variety of peridotite. The long, narrow funnels of diamond-bearing rock are known as *pipes* or *diamond pipes.* The pipes are of igneous origin. The material of which they are composed was once liquid and welled upward, filling these pipe-like openings. According to Alpheus F. Williams, about forty minerals are found in the diamond-bearing kimberlite. Among these minerals are pyrope garnet, which is placed on the market as *Cape ruby,* and cyanite, olivine, and zircon.

These diamond-bearing areas were staked off into claims about thirty feet square. Separated by two rows of claims, there were roadways across the diggings, which permitted access to the workings. The diamonds were easily recovered from the soft, yellow ground by washing. As the claims were mined deeper and deeper, the roadways became steep-sided ridges between the workings. Landslides often occurred, and the removal of the earth from the claims was obviously expensive, especially when it consisted of barren material.   As time went on, the financial difficulties of the small claim owners became greater and greater, causing them to dispose of their holdings.   In 1888 a consolidation of the diamond-mining properties of the Kimberley district was effected, largely through the efforts of Cecil J. Rhodes.   The powerful organization thus formed is known as the De Beers Consolidated Mines, Ltd.

For a time open-pit mining (Fig. 278) was continued, the blue ground being hoisted to the surface from deep pits.   It finally became evident that such a method was no longer feasible, and underground mining by means of shafts and drifts was inaugurated.   The Kimberley mine has been worked to a depth of about 3,600 feet.

Most of the work is done by natives, who live during the term of

FIG. 278.—Kimberley diamond mine.

their employment in enclosures known as *compounds* (Fig. 279).   This precaution is necessary in order to prevent the theft of stones, as the natives formerly concealed them in various ways and sold them to unscrupulous traders outside the camp.   Hence, at present these native workers are allowed to leave the compound only after a most searching examination.

For many years it was the practice to remove the blue ground from the mines and expose it to the processes of weathering upon open fields called *depositing floors*.   In due time the hard and consolidated blue ground would become soft and friable.   By the use of sledge hammers or tractors the larger pieces could be easily broken up.   The material was then loaded into cars and taken to the crushing and washing plants for concentration.

At present, the blue ground is not exposed on depositing floors but is crushed and washed immediately after being mined.   Although this method involves the risk of crushing diamonds of considerable size, the tying up of large amounts of capital on the depositing floors is avoided. This is known as the *direct-treatment method*.

The various steps in the recovery of the diamonds from the blue ground are (1) *crushing* and *washing*, (2) *jigging*, (3) *greasing* or

FIG. 279.—Bultfontein mine. Compound at the right. (*Photograph by the Aircraft Operating Company of Africa, Ltd. Courtesy of De Beers Consolidated Mines, Ltd.*)

automatic sorting, and (4) *cleaning* and *evaluating*. Each step will be described briefly.

1. *Crushing and Washing.*—The blue ground is first crushed. It then passes to the washing machines. These are large pans or shallow tanks about fourteen feet in diameter into which the finely crushed material is fed. A stream of water flows into these pans, and the mixture is constantly agitated by suitable stirring devices. This causes a mechanical separation, for the heavier constituents of the blue ground settle to the bottom of the pan, the lighter materials flowing away as tailings. By the washing process the material is reduced to about one one-hundredth part of the original volume.

2. *Jigging.*—The concentrates from the washing machines are first sized by passing through screens. They are then conveyed

to the jigs or pulsators.   Here further concentration takes place according to specific gravity.

The jig is a tight box with a screen of suitable mesh fitted across the bottom.   On the screen a layer of metallic balls or rings is placed.   The sized concentrates are fed into the jig, which is stationary, and the various substances in the concentrates are kept in an up-and-down motion by a pulsating stream of water entering the jig below the screen.   The water passes up through the

FIG. 280.—Automatic diamond sorters, Premier mine.

screen and carries away the lighter materials through an opening near the top.   At the same time the heavier minerals pass downward through the pulsating layer of balls and the screen to the bottom of the jig, and are removed from time to time.   At first the concentrates from the jigs were sorted by hand, but now the diamonds are separated mechanically by the greaser.

3. *Greasing or Automatic Sorting.*—In 1896 the *automatic diamond sorter* or *greaser* was devised.   Its use is based upon the fact that, of all the minerals in the concentrates, grease sticks most tenaciously to the diamond.

The greaser (Fig. 280) is a laterally oscillating and sloping corrugated iron table covered with a coat of thick grease, petrolatum. The concentrates from the jigs are fed upon the greaser at the upper end, and everything passes over the grease and off, as tailings, at the other end with the exception of the diamond, pieces of metal, and some metallic minerals.   Practically all the diamonds are removed with one treatment, most of them within six inches of the top of the table. The remainder can be recovered by passing the tailings over the greaser. This mechanical method is practically 100 per cent efficient. These automatic sorters are enclosed in order to safeguard against theft.

Fig. 281.—Premier diamond mine, near Pretoria, Transvaal.

In general, the diamond content of a load of blue ground (1,600 pounds) is less than ¼ carat. That is, the ratio of the occurrence of the diamond in the blue ground is 1 part or unit of the diamond in 15,000,000 or more parts or units of blue ground.

4. *Cleaning and Evaluating.*—At intervals the grease is removed from the automatic sorters, and the diamonds are recovered.

After suitable treatment the grease is used again.   In order to clean the diamonds they are boiled with alkalies and acids.   They are then weighed, sorted, and evaluated.   Finally, they are made up into packets, called *parcels,* ready for marketing.

In the Kimberley district, which is the great diamond center of the world, there are five important mines, the Kimberley (Fig. 278), Dutoitspan, De Beers, Wesselton, and Bultfontein (Fig. 279).   Other important South African mines are the Jagersfontein, in the Orange Free State, and the Premier, near Pretoria

Fig.   282.—Cullinan   diamond   (uncut). Premier mine, South Africa.   Weight 3,106 carats.

in the Transvaal.   Until recently, the Premier was the largest known diamond mine, having a productive surface area of about eighty acres.   It was at this mine that the direct method of recovering the diamond from the blue ground was first introduced. The Premier (Fig. 281) is also famous as the source of the world's largest diamond, the Cullinan (Fig. 282).   In 1941, Dr. J. T. Williamson discovered a mine at Mwadui, in Tanganyika, which is reported to be eight times larger than the Premier mine.

Formerly the diamond pipe mines, of the type just described, furnished most of the world's annual production.   At present, however, the annual production of the alluvial deposits of Africa is much greater than that of the pipe mines, most of which were not operated during the war.   In 1944 the alluvial deposits produced about ten million carats and the pipe mines approximately one-half million carats.   Industrial stones made up 80 per cent (about two tons) and gemstones 20 per cent (about one-half ton) of this production in carats.   As alluvial stones occur in sands and gravel, they are readily concentrated by washing.   Subsequent handling is similar to that of the diamonds obtained from the pipe mines.

The Belgian Congo, Gold Coast, Sierra Leone, Angola, Union of South Africa, and South-West Africa are the most important producers of alluvial diamonds in Africa. The production of the Belgian Congo is by far the largest. About 90 per cent of this production is obtained from the deposits known as the *Beceka* (Société Minière de Beceka). Other localities are Brazil, British Guiana, Borneo, India, New South Wales, Liberia, and Venezuela.

In the United States a few isolated diamonds have been found, either in secondary deposits or in glacial drift, in California, North Carolina, Georgia, Virginia, West Virginia, Michigan, Wisconsin, Ohio, Indiana, Colorado, Idaho, and Nevada. In fact, the occurrence of diamonds has been reported from practically every state. On August 1, 1906, the most remarkable discovery of diamonds in the United States was made in Arkansas, near Murfreesboro in Pike County, about one hundred miles southwest of Little Rock. The rock in which these diamonds are found is strikingly similar to the kimberlite of South Africa. More than 10,000 diamonds have been recovered from this area. The largest of these stones weighed 40.22 carats. It is a flattened, irregular octahedron, and is the largest diamond found to date in North America. About 10 per cent of the diamonds from this district were of gem quality. Kimberlite also occurs in and near Syracuse, New York, where a single diamond has been reported; and in Elliott County, Kentucky. No stones have been found in the latter locality.

In 1943, it was reported that the *"Punch" Jones* diamond, weighing 34.46 carats, had been found in 1928 at Petersburg, West Virginia. This is the largest diamond found in alluvial deposits in the United States.[1]

1. **Gem Diamonds.**—In general the stones of good color and perfection are used for gem purposes. The methods for cutting and polishing and of evaluating gem diamonds are described in detail in Chapter VII. No sharp distinction can be made between the lower quality of gem and the higher quality of industrial diamonds. Many gemstones of poor color could be used equally

[1] For further information concerning occurrence and production consult the annual reports "The Diamond Industry" by Dr. S. H. Ball, *Jewelers' Circular-Keystone*, New York.

well for industrial purposes, whereas some stones of good color, which are used in industry, could be cut as gems of poorer quality.

As is well known, cut gem diamonds retain their beauty indefinitely, as use and wear have little or no effect upon them. Consequently, they may be sold and resold and thus appear many times on the market. However, they are generally held for long periods as highly prized personal or family possessions. The annual production of newly mined gem diamonds is a very small part of the world's total stock.

Fig. 283.—Glass models of the nine largest stones cut from the Cullinan diamond. (One-half natural size.)

Famous Diamonds (Figs. 283, 284, 286, and 287).—Brief mention may be made of some of the historically famous large diamonds. Owing to the fact that in the past the unit of weight used in expressing the size of precious stones, namely, the carat, fluctuated considerably (p. 135), the weights assigned to them have not always been the same.

Cullinan, 3,106 metric carats in the rough (Fig. 282). This, the world's largest diamond, was found at the Premier mine, South Africa, on January 25, 1905 (Fig. 281). In the rough this stone measured 10 by 6.5 by 5 centimeters, and was a cleavage fragment of a still larger stone. It was purchased for £150,000 by the Transvaal government and presented to King Edward VII on his birthday, November 9, 1907. The stone was entrusted to the well-known firm of Asscher and Company, Amsterdam, for cutting. It was cleaved to remove a flaw (Fig. 62). From the cleavage pieces two large stones were cut. The largest, known as *Cullinan I,* and now called the *Star of Africa,* is a drop-shaped stone of 530.2 carats. The *Cullinan II* is a square brilliant of 317.4 carats. In addition,

103 other stones were cut from this large diamond. The total weight of the cut stones was 1,063.65 carats or 34.25 per cent of the original stone. Glass models of the largest 9 stones cut from the Cullinan are shown in Fig. 283.

Fig. 284.—Stones cut from the Jonker diamond. Full size. (*Courtesy of Harry Winston, Inc.*)

Jonker, 726 carats uncut (Fig. 196). This diamond was found on January 16, 1934, by Jacobus Jonker, Sr., at Elandsfontein, Pretoria, in alluvial diggings, about three miles from the Premier mine, where the Cullinan was discovered in 1905. The quality of the stone is superior to that of any of the large famous diamonds. It was purchased by the Diamond Corporation, Ltd., at a reported price of £63,000. The stone was subsequently bought by Harry Winston, Inc., of New York City and was cut by Lazare Kaplan, an experienced diamond cutter, also of New York. Twelve beautiful stones ranging in weight from 142.9 to 5.3 carats (Fig. 284) were obtained. The total weight of the cut stones was 370.87 carats or 51 per cent of the original diamond, which is an unusually high yield (p. 124). The largest stone was subsequently recut and weighs 125.35 carats.

Vargas, 726.6 carats uncut (Fig. 285). It was found in Patrocinio, Minas Geraes, Brazil, July, 1938. The stone was purchased by Harry Winston, Inc., and cut in New York City. Twenty-nine stones were obtained, of which sixteen ranged in weight from 48.26 to 10.05 carats (Fig. 286).

FIG. 285.—Vargas diamond, two-thirds natural size. (*Courtesy Harry Winston, Inc.*)

Excelsior, found in the Jagersfontein mine in 1893; weight uncut 995.3 carats. It was cut into twenty-one stones varying in weight from 70 carats to a fraction of a carat.

Great Mogul, 240 carats cut. This is the largest Indian diamond, and is said to have weighed 787 carats, but after being recut the weight was reduced to 240 carats. No information concerning this stone has been available since 1665, when it was seen in India by a French jeweler, Tavernier.

Jubilee, 245.3 carats cut. This is the third largest cut diamond. It was found in the Jagersfontein mine in 1895, and uncut weighed 650.8 carats.

Orloff, 194.8 carats cut; a rose-cut stone which formed the top of the Russian imperial scepter. It is said to have been stolen from a temple in Mysore, India, where it was one of the eyes of an idol.

Regent or *Pitt,* 136.9 carats cut; an Indian stone, discovered in 1701. It was owned for a time by William Pitt, governor of Fort St. George at Madras. He had it cut and sold it in 1717 to the Duc d'Orleans, regent of France. It was stolen during the French Revolution, but was later returned by the thieves.

Florentine, also known as the *Austrian* and the *Grand Duke of Tuscany,* 133.2 carats cut.   This stone belonged to the Austrian

Fig. 286.—Stones cut from the Vargas diamond.   *(Courtesy Harry Winston, Inc.)*

imperial family, and has an authentic history of two centuries. It is slightly yellowish.

Tiffany, 128.5 carats cut with 101 facets.   The Tiffany is a brilliant of a beautiful deep yellow color, discovered in the Kimberley mine, 1878. It is owned by Tiffany and Company of New York.

Star of the South, 125.5 carats cut; a Brazilian diamond, discovered in 1853.

Kohinoor, new cutting 106.1, old cutting 186.1 carats. The name Koh-i-noor means "mountain of light." History traces the stone back to 1304, in India. In 1850 it was presented to Queen Victoria in the name of the East India Company, and in 1862 it was recut as a shallow brilliant.

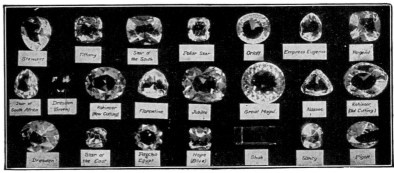

FIG. 287.—Photograph of glass models of famous large diamonds.

Hope, 44.5 carats; the largest blue diamond.

Dresden, 40 carats; a flawless apple-green diamond.

Liberator, the largest diamond ever found in Venezuela; 155 carats uncut. It was purchased by Harry Winston, Inc., in 1943, and cut into four stones ranging in weight from 39.8 to 1.44 carats.

Other large diamonds worthy of mention are the *Stewart,* 120 carats; *Nassak,* 89.5; *Shah,* 88; *Dresden* (English), 76.5; *Empress Eugenia,* 51; *Star of South Africa,* 46.5; *Polar Star,* 40; *Pasha of Egypt,* 40. Another large stone, weighing 1,680 carats, the *Braganza* of the Portuguese regalia, is reported to be colorless topaz.

In January, 1945, a diamond weighing 770 carats was found in the alluvials of Sierra Leone, West Africa. This is the largest diamond obtained thus far from alluvial deposits.

2. **Industrial Diamonds.**—Those diamonds which are not used as gems find wide application in industry because of their extreme hardness. They vary from well-formed crystals to irregular shapes and from compact masses to semi-porous aggregates. Some are

clear and transparent while others are opaque to black. In general, industrial stones are off-color and contain more flaws and inclusions than gem diamonds.

Industrial diamonds, in contrast to gemstones (p. 98), are consumed by use and consequently must be replaced. They constitute the bulk of the world's annual production of mined diamonds.

Industrial diamonds may be grouped as follows: (1) *fine industrials,* (2) *bort,* (3) *ballas,* and (4) *carbonado.*

1. *Fine Industrials.*—These stones are comparable to gem-quality diamonds except in color. They are used for the manufacture of wire drawing dies and shaped cutting tools.

2. *Bort.*—Through long usage bort, also called *bortz, boort, boart,* or *bowr,* has come to include irregularly shaped and badly flawed crystals and those with many inclusions (Fig. 288). Such diamonds are

Fig. 288.—Bort suitable for diamond drills.

wholly unsuited for gem purposes. The term *drilling bort* is restricted to small sound stones which average twenty or more to the carat and are used in diamond drill bits (Figs. 289 and 290). The term *crushing bort* is applied to the lowest grades of diamonds. The principal use of this type of bort is for crushing into grit or powder for the manufacture of bonded abrasive wheels. Bort is also used for glass cutting, sawing building stone, diamond-set tools, and other industrial purposes.

3. *Ballas* is the name given to spherical aggregates of many small diamond crystals arranged radially and more or less concentrically (Fig. 291). On account of the structure, these masses do not cleave easily. Ballas is extremely hard and very tough. It has many of the characteristics of carbonado and is therefore well adapted for drilling and industrial purposes. It is obtained principally from Brazil and the Jagersfontein mine, South Africa. Brazilian ballas is said to be tougher than the South African. Spherical white or grayish diamonds are often called ballas, although they should

be classified as bort on account of their cleavage. Because of its spherical shape, ballas is often called *shot bort.*

4. *Carbonado,* also called *black diamond* or *carbon,* is an opaque, black or gray, tough and compact variety of diamond (Fig.

FIG. 289.—Diamond-core drill bit.   FIG. 290.—Diamond blast-hole drill bit.

292). It has no cleavage. The specific gravity, 3.15 to 3.29, is lower than that of the diamond proper. Bahia, Brazil, is the chief source of carbonado. The largest piece ever found was somewhat heavier than the Cullinan diamond. Carbonado was formerly much used in diamond drills for deep boring and in diamond-set

FIG. 291.—Ballas, 110 carats, original size.   FIG. 292.—Carbonado. Brazil.

lathe tools for the truing of abrasive wheels and for other industrial purposes.

Special terms are in wide and uniform use for various types of diamonds, as *macles* for twinned crystals (p. 22), *cleavages* for fragments, and *flats* for distorted octahedrons which are triangular in outline (p. 21). *Rough* is a collective term applied to any large parcel of uncut stones. *Cuttables* are uncut stones which are suitable for gem purposes. Some cuttables are used in industrial tools and in physical apparatus used in the study of radioactivity and atomic energy.

Since the outbreak of the Second World War a better understanding of the properties of diamonds and a sounder technology in their uses have been developed, causing a greatly increased consumption. As a result, outlets have been established for the entire output of the mines, which should give greater stability to the diamond industry as a whole.

CORUNDUM

The precious stones, ruby and sapphire, are transparent, colored varieties of the mineral corundum. This mineral frequently occurs in good crystals, often large, which belong to the hexagonal system. The most common forms are the hexagonal prism, bipyramid, rhombohedron, and basal pinacoid (Fig. 293). The larger crystals may be rough or rounded, barrel shaped, and furrowed. Penetration twins sometimes occur, and polysynthetic twins are often noted, the twinning being parallel to the rhombohedron. Ruby and sapphire usually occur in crystals, but other varieties of corundum may be found as compact, granular, or platy masses.

The fracture is conchoidal. Corundum has no cleavage, but rhombohedral and basal partings occur. Fine parallel striations are characteristic of many crystals. As corundum crystallizes in the hexagonal system, this type of crystallization is revealed in the various patterns of the striations. The hardness is 9, which is next to that of the diamond, and therefore corundum is very durable. The specific gravity varies from 3.9 to 4.1.

Corundum is found in various colors. Crystals are often multicolored and may show zonal distribution of color (Fig. 253), which may correspond to the pattern of the striations. The mineral is transparent to opaque, and has a rather dull, greasy, or vitreous luster in the natural state, but is adamantine when cut. Gem varieties, which are transparent, may be colorless, red, blue, green, yellow, or violet, but common corundum is translucent to opaque and gray, bluish, brown, or black in color. When exposed to ultraviolet light some stones luminesce. By heat treatment some sapphires may be decolorized or made paler.

The indices of refraction are ω 1.768, ϵ 1.760. The optical character is negative, and the double refraction low, 0.008. The dispersion is weak, 0.018, and consequently there is very little fire. The ruby and sapphire therefore depend upon color for their appeal. Dichroism in corundum is strong. In ruby the colors

FIG. 293.—Crystals of natural corundum.

are dark red for o, pale red for e; in sapphire, blue for o, yellowish blue for e. To obtain the most pleasing colors (p. 76) the ruby and sapphire should be cut with the table parallel to the basal pinacoid. The ruby has a characteristic absorption spectrum (p. 79).

Corundum is Al_2O_3, aluminum oxide. The aluminum is often replaced by small amounts of chromium, titanium, or iron. The colors of the mineral may be due to these impurities; chromium causing the red color, titanium the blue, and iron the yellow. The more poorly crystallized varieties of corundum are often very impure.

Cut *en cabochon,* corundum may exhibit asterism; that is, a six-rayed star is observed, the rays being white regardless of the color of the stone (Fig. 74). This effect is due to inclusions or to a lattice-like structure within the mineral. Stones exhibiting such "stars" are called *star rubies* or *star sapphires.* Prior to September, 1947, they were not produced synthetically (p. 163). These synthetic stars are of good color. The rays are very sharp but do not always extend to the outer edge of the cut stone. The lower portion is generally transparent.

Common corundum and *emery* are used as abrasives. Common corundum consists of rather opaque crystals or masses with dull colors. Emery is a black, granular mixture of corundum with magnetite, hematite, quartz, and spinel.

Ruby and *sapphire* are the important gem varieties of corundum. The color of the *ruby* varies from a rose, through carmine, to a dark, somewhat purplish red, often called *pigeon's-blood red.*

This dark purplish red is the most desirable color exhibited by natural rubies. All precious corundum of a color other than red is called sapphire. The true *sapphire* is blue, the best tint being a velvety corn-flower blue, called *Kashmir blue*. The colorless stones are called *white sapphire,* the yellow ones *yellow* or *golden sapphire,* and the pale pink stones *pink sapphire*. Ruby and sapphire are cut step, cabochon, or brilliant.

The word *oriental* is often applied as a prefix to the names of other gems in naming varieties of corundum with the less popular colors: thus, *Oriental emerald* for green corundum, *Oriental topaz* for the yellow, and *Oriental amethyst* for the violet varieties, respectively. Such terms are misleading, and their use is to be avoided (p. 139).

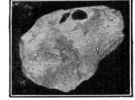

Fig. 294.—Corundum: Variety, ruby. India.

Ruby and sapphire occur both in placer deposits and *in situ*. Metamorphic rocks, such as metamorphosed limestones (Fig. 294), gneiss, and schist and igneous rocks, for example granite, nephelite-syenite, and peridotite, are the original sources of these stones. The minerals commonly associated with corundum are spinel, tourmaline, cyanite, magnetite, chlorite, and nephelite.

The methods of recovery of rubies and sapphires are rather primitive. The mines are simply open pits, and the gem-bearing sands and gravels are washed in much the same way as are the diamantiferous sands of Brazil.

The best rubies, including many with the esteemed pigeon's-blood red, are mined in upper Burma, in a district of which Mogok is the center. Here the stones occur in granular limestone and in sand, gravel, and soil, with the "balas ruby" or spinel, sapphire, zircon, and tourmaline. These mines have been worked since the fifteenth century. Although a great many rubies are found, few are large or of the best color. Important deposits occur near Bangkok, Thailand, where the rubies are associated with red spinel. Excellent sapphires come from these Siamese deposits, though the rubies from these mines are inferior to those from Burma. Kashmir, in northern India, has long been an extremely important locality for sapphires of gem quality. In Ceylon, also, many sapphires, but few rubies, are mined. Here the sapphires occur in gem-bearing gravels in the Balangoda, Rackwana, and Ratnapura districts. Other important sources of these stones are Afghanistan, Hindustan, China, the Ural Mountains, and Queensland.

In the United States fine rubies have been found in the crystalline rocks of North Carolina. Along the upper Missouri River, near Helena, Montana, sapphires and rubies are found *in situ*.

Rubies have always been highly prized. When cut, they are worth $100 to $1,500 per carat. Especially fine stones are priced much higher. Sapphires are less expensive. They range in price from $6 to $200 or more per carat. Star rubies and sapphires continue to be popular. Aside from their use as gems, rubies and sapphires have found application as jewels in the finer watches and as bearings in many scientific instruments. This is especially true of those from Montana, Ceylon, and Australia. Because of their improved quality and relative inexpensiveness, synthetic rubies and sapphires are now sold in large quantities for gem and industrial purposes (p. 166).

BERYL

The mineral beryl includes the emerald and aquamarine, as well as golden beryl and morganite. The emerald takes rank with the ruby as one of the most valuable gemstones.

Crystals of beryl belong to the hexagonal system and are sometimes of enormous size, exceeding a ton in weight. These mammoth crystals are invariably coarse and opaque and entirely unfit for use as gems. Beryl crystals are usually long, prismatic (Figs. 295 and 296), and very simple, consisting of prism and pinacoid. They are rarely tabular. Sometimes the crystals have highly modified terminations (Fig. 297).

Beryl has a distinct basal cleavage and a conchoidal to uneven fracture. The hardness is $7\frac{1}{2}$ to 8, and the stone is therefore durable. The specific gravity is 2.6 to 2.8. Common beryl is generally pale green, yellowish, or grayish white in color, and often mottled. Other varieties are blue, green, yellow, rose red, or colorless. The luster is vitreous. Beryl may be transparent to opaque.

Beryl is uniaxial and optically negative. The indices of refraction vary, ω 1.568 to 1.598, ε 1.564 to 1.590. The double refraction is low; the dispersion is 0.014. The refractivity and dispersion are both weak, so that the stone has little brilliancy and no fire. It is another stone which makes its appeal largely through its color and transparency. Dichroism is fairly distinct in the more deeply colored varieties.

The composition of beryl is rather complex, at least in comparison with that of diamond and corundum. It is a be-

FIG. 295.—Crystals of gem beryl.

FIG. 296.—Beryl in quartz. Acworth, New Hampshire.

FIG. 297.—Wooden model of a highly modified crystal of beryl.

ryllium aluminum silicate, with the formula $Be_3Al_2(SiO_3)_6$, or $3BeO.Al_2O_3.6SiO_2$. The beryllium is often replaced by small amounts of the alkalies, lithium, sodium, potassium, and caesium. The pink and colorless varieties especially are rich in these elements.

The following varieties of beryl are used as gemstones:

Emerald, which is the highly prized variety, is transparent to translucent and has an emerald-green color. The green color is thought to be due to a trace of chromium. As the red color of the ruby is also ascribed to the same element, it obviously must exist in different states of combination in the two minerals. Accordingly, in minerals and chemical compounds chromium may produce either a green or a red to violet color. The emerald has characteristic absorption bands (p. 79).

Aquamarine is transparent and usually blue to sea green in color. The color of many of these stones has been improved by heat treatment (p. 145).

Yellow or *golden beryl* has a beautiful golden-yellow color and is transparent.

Heliodor is a variety of yellow beryl from South-West Africa.

Morganite, also known as *vorobievite,* is a pink or rose-red beryl named after the late J. P. Morgan, who was a great lover and collector of gems. Some cut stones have been heat-treated and the color improved.

Goshenite is a very pure, colorless variety of beryl.

Of these varieties emerald and aquamarine are by far the most important.

Flawless emeralds of good color are extremely unusual. They are accordingly very valuable and may cost $1,000 to $10,000 per carat. The stones are usually variable in color and flawed. Owing to feathered inclusions, often called *silk,* they may have a mossy appearance. Emerald is generally cut step, but occasionally brilliant. Stones with many flaws are frequently cut *en cabochon* and engraved. Aquamarine and the other varieties of beryl are commonly given faceted cuts. Large aquamarine stones are not uncommon and are much less expensive than the emerald.

The emeralds of ancient times came largely from upper Egypt, where evidences of old workings are still to be seen. At present the best emeralds are obtained from the mines near Muzo and Chivor, Colombia. Here the stones are disseminated through a dark limestone, which is thought to have been metamorphosed by solutions from pegmatite intrusions (Fig. 298). Emeralds of lighter color but of good quality occur in an altered dolomitic marble near Bom Jesus dos Meiras, Bahia, Brazil. Emeralds are also found in mica schist at Tokovoja and Mursinka in the district of Sverdlovsk in the Ural Mountains, where they are associated with chrysoberyl and phenacite, which also are beryllium minerals. Small emeralds are found in schists in the Habachthal, Tyrol. Emeralds of good quality have been found in various parts of Australia. Occasionally emeralds are obtained from the crystalline rocks in North Carolina.

All varieties of beryl other than the emerald occur almost exclusively in granite pegmatites. Aquamarine, which is paler in color than the emerald, is, however, found in much larger and clearer crystals than the latter variety. Thus, an aquamarine crystal from Morambaya, Minas Geraes, Brazil, weighed 243 pounds and was transparent from end to end. The uncut crystal was sold for $25,000. Aquamarine and other gem varieties of beryl are found on the island of Elba, in Madagascar, in the Mourne Mountains of Ireland, the Ural Mountains, Maine, Con-

FIG. 298.—Chivor emerald mine, Colombia.

necticut, North Carolina, Colorado, and California, as well as in secondary deposits in Brazil, Ceylon, and India. The rose-red variety, morganite, is found in San Diego County, California, and in Madagascar. The stones from Madagascar are of a pure pink, while those from California incline to a salmon color. It is interesting to note that in both localities pink spodumene, called kunzite, and pink tourmaline or rubellite also occur with the pink beryl. Golden beryl is found in Bahia, Brazil, and also in Ceylon, Madagascar, Maine, and Connecticut. The goshenite variety is found at Goshen, Massachusetts, and also in Maine, Connecticut, and California.

Since 1930 small synthetic emeralds have been produced in the laboratory. They are not important commercially, and, because of characteristic properties, may be distinguished from natural emeralds (p. 165). Synthetic spinel, appropriately colored, is improperly sold as aquamarine (p. 165).   Doublets, triplets, and glass imitations have also been made (p. 171).

TOPAZ

In former times the name *topaz* was given to various yellow stones, especially to the yellowish variety of olivine now known as *chrysolite* and to yellow quartz properly designated as *citrine*. This practice has continued and led to the use of *Oriental topaz*

Fig. 299.—Wooden model of crystal of topaz.

Fig. 300.—Crystals of topaz.

for yellow sapphire, *smoky topaz* for smoky quartz, and to such terms as *Scotch topaz, false topaz,* or *Madeira topaz* for citrine and yellow quartz, the result of heat treatment (p. 143).   These are all misleading and should not be used.

Topaz belongs to the orthorhombic system, and its prismatic crystals are often rich in forms (Fig. 299).   Usually but one end of the crystal is terminated, the other being a cleavage plane (Fig. 300).   Topaz occurs also in granular or compact masses and in water-worn fragments.   The cleavage, parallel to the basal pinacoid, is perfect and easily obtained.   It is often clearly indicated by well-defined cracks.   In cutting topaz and in the wearing of the cut stone, great care must be exercised in order that the stone shall not break along cleavage planes.   The fracture is conchoidal to uneven.   Topaz is durable, having a hardness of 8.   Its specific gravity ranges from 3.4 to 3.6, according to the composition of the mineral, which is variable.

PLATE III

First row: 1 to 4, variously colored tourmalines, Brazil.
Second row: 1 to 5, variously colored tourmalines, Brazil.
Third row: 1, tourmaline, Brazil; 2, tourmaline cat's-eye, Brazil; 3, blue topaz, Brazil; 4, pink topaz, Brazil.
Fourth row: 1, pink topaz, Brazil; 2, yellow topaz, Brazil; 3, blue zircon, Indo-China; 4, zircon (hyacinth), Indo-China; 5, golden beryl, Brazil
Fifth row: 1, yellow beryl, Brazil; 2, pink beryl (morganite), Brazil; 3, aquamarine, Brazil; 4, emerald, Brazil; 5, emerald, Colombia.

Pure topaz is colorless, but owing to impurities of an unknown nature, the crystals are frequently colored. The colors include wine yellow, brownish, gray, and pale tints of blue, green, violet, and red. The yellow *precious topaz* is most often used as a gem. As already indicated (p. 143), yellow Brazilian topaz may be changed to a beautiful rose or pink color by heat. Pink topaz is extremely rare in nature. Pleochroism in topaz is weak. The mineral is usually transparent, and has a vitreous luster. Topaz is biaxial and positive in optical character. The three indices of refraction are α 1.619, β 1.620, γ 1.627. The double refraction is 0.008, and the dispersion 0.014. Colorless stones are attractive, especially when cut in the brilliant style. The step cut is also used.

Topaz is an aluminum silicate, containing fluorine and hydroxyl, which are present in varying proportions. The properties of topaz, such as specific gravity and indices of refraction, vary slightly with the change in composition from pure fluorine topaz, $Al_2F_2SiO_4$, to pure hydroxyl topaz, $Al_2(OH)_2SiO_4$. Fluorine usually predominates. Considerable amounts of impurities are frequently present, such as microscopic liquid or gaseous inclusions, especially liquid carbon dioxide.

Topaz occurs in gneisses, schists, granites, rhyolites, and pegmatites. It is characteristically formed by the action of gases containing fluorine and water vapor and emanating from igneous intrusions. Common mineral associates are tourmaline, quartz, fluorite, apatite, beryl, and the ores of tin and tungsten. The mineral, being durable and fairly heavy, is often found in placer deposits. The Ouro Preto district, Minas Geraes, Brazil, is the most important locality for gem topaz, which is found in various shades of yellow and in dark- and light-rose, ruby-red, and amethystine colors. Colorless crystals are common. Other important localities are the Ural Mountains, near Sverdlovsk, for green and blue topaz; Miask, in the Ilmen Mountains; the gold washings of the Sanarka River in the Government of Orenburg, Russia, for reddish crystals. Cairngorm, Banffshire, Scotland, and the Mourne Mountains of Ireland have furnished a considerable number of sky-blue topazes. Good crystals also occur in the tin mines of Saxony and Cornwall; in Ceylon, Japan, Mexico, and Tasmania; in the United States in the rhyolite rocks of the

Thomas Range of Utah; at Nathrop, Colorado; in the Ramona district, San Diego County, California; and in several localities in New England.

GARNET

Though the term garnet is often understood as referring to a single gem, in reality the name includes a number of closely

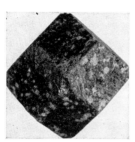

FIG.   301.—Garnet
(rhombic   dodecahedron).
Salida, Colorado.

related minerals.   Several chemically similar elements freely replace one another in the garnet group.   As a result, the properties of the group are variable, and consequently garnet gems may be quite different in appearance.

Garnets are in fact very attractive stones, but they are so abundant that they are not highly valued.   Red garnet is frequently sold under deceptive names, such as *Cape ruby* and *Arizona ruby,* and the green garnet from Russia is known as the *Uralian emerald.*   This undesirable practice has a tendency to increase the price of the gems masquerading under such titles (p. 139).

All varieties of garnet crystallize in the cubic system with very similar forms.   The rhombic dodecahedron (Fig. 301) and the

FIG. 302.

FIG. 303.—Garnet (tetragonal tris-octahedrons) in mica schist. Sunday River, Maine.

tetragonal trisoctahedron (Figs. 302 and 303), alone or in combination (Figs. 304 to 306), are the only commonly occurring forms.   Although the mineral is generally well crystallized, it may occur in compact granular aggregates, in rounded and disseminated glassy grains, or as water-worn pebbles. Garnet has an imperfect rhombic dodecahedral cleavage, and a conchoidal to uneven fracture. The hardness varies from 6½ to 7½, and the specific gravity from 3.4 to 4.3, depending upon the composition.

FIG. 304.—Wooden models showing combination of rhombic dodecahedron and tetragonal trisoctahedron.

FIG. 305.—Rhombic dodecahedral crystals of garnet.

Almost any color except blue may be observed in garnet. Red, brown, yellow, green, and black are the more common colors. It may also be colorless. Although the colors are largely due to the elements entering into the composition of the various members of the group, they may be attributed in part to impurities present in minute quantities. The lighter colored garnets are generally transparent to translucent; the dark-colored varieties, translucent to opaque. The luster is vitreous to resinous.

FIG. 306.—Crystal of garnet showing a combination of rhombic dodecahedron (large) and tetragonal trisoctahedron.

The index of refraction of gem garnets is as variable as the other properties, lying between 1.70 and 1.94. The dispersion ranges from 0.024 to 0.028 for most varieties. However, one variety, the demantoid or grass-green andradite, has a dispersion of 0.057, which is comparable to that of the diamond. Hence, when the color is not too dark, these garnets have considerable brilliancy and fire.

As garnets are isotropic, they do not show dichroism. This fact aids materially in differentiating red garnets from rubies, which possess similar indices of refraction and specific gravities.

The composition of the members of the garnet group is easily expressed by the generalized formula $M''_3M'''_2(SiO_4)_3$, in which M'' represents any of the bivalent metals magnesium, calcium, manganese, or iron and M''' a trivalent metal, aluminum, ferric iron, or chromium, for example, grossularite $Ca_3Al_2(SiO_4)_3$ or $3CaO.Al_2O_3.3SiO_2$ (see table below). A small amount of titanium may also be present. Thus, a garnet may contain all these bivalent and trivalent metals in almost any proportion, so long as the ratio between the bivalent and trivalent elements is 3 to 2. However, based upon composition, six varieties of garnet have been established. The composition of these varieties grades over into one another, and, consequently, also the various physical and optical properties. The composition of a garnet is hence commonly much more complex than that theoretically assigned to the variety to which it belongs. In the table below, the composition, specific gravity, and index of refraction n of each of the several varieties are given:

Variety	Composition	Specific gravity	Index of refraction n
Grossularite............	$Ca_3Al_2(SiO_4)_3$	3.5-3.7	1.735-1.763
Pyrope.................	$Mg_3Al_2(SiO_4)_3$	3.5-3.8	1.705-1.749
Spessartite..............	$Mn_3Al_2(SiO_4)_3$	4.1-4.3	1.794-1.814
Almandite..............	$Fe_3Al_2(SiO_4)_3$	3.9-4.2	1.766-1.830
Uvarovite..............	$Ca_3Cr_2(SiO_4)_3$	3.4-3.5	1.838
Andradite..............	$Ca_3Fe_2(SiO_4)_3$	3.7-3.8	1.865-1.940

The varieties of garnet will now be discussed, especially with regard to their use as gems.

Grossularite.—The lime-aluminum garnet is lighter colored than the other varieties; in fact, it is sometimes colorless. However, pale emerald green, rose red, or various shades of yellow and cinnamon brown are most commonly observed. The yellow- and cinnamon-colored stones are the ones frequently used as gems, under the names *cinnamon-stone, hessonite,* or *essonite.* The terms *hyacinth* and *jacinth,* the latter more properly applied to yellow or brown zircon, are also used for these stones. The green- and rose-colored varieties are rarely transparent enough for cutting. Hessonite has a peculiar granular structure, visible even in the cut stones. The green massive grossularite, often mottled green and white, from Buffelsfontein, Transvaal, is called *South African* or *Transvaal jade*. The mineral chromite is often associated with it.

Grossularite is characteristically found in metamorphosed, impure limestones, associated with vesuvianite, wollastonite, diopside, scapolite, and other lime silicates. Most of the hessonite is obtained from Ceylon, where it occurs with zircon in gravels.

Pyrope.—This is the most popular garnet, probably because it frequently has a beautiful ruby-red color, which is due to impurities. Pure pyrope would be colorless. Pyrope is the variety occurring with the diamond in South Africa, where it is sold as *Cape ruby* (p. 185). It is not often found in good crystals but usually occurs in grains or small irregular masses or as stream pebbles. The color varies from deep red to black, often with an undesirable tinge of yellow. *Rhodolite* is rose red or purple. Its composition and properties are intermediate between pyrope and almandite. The index of refraction is 1.760. It occurs in Macon County, North Carolina.

Pyrope occurs chiefly in basic igneous rocks, such as peridotite, and in the serpentines derived from them. Czecho-Slovakia, Saxony, South Africa, Arizona, and Colorado are important localities. Rose-cut pyrope is used in Bohemian jewelry. This type of garnet is commonly observed in antique brooches, necklaces, and so forth.

Spessartite.—This variety is not commonly used in jewelry, since ordinarily its color is an unpopular brown. The color may also be brownish red, orange red, or dark hyacinth red with a tinge of violet. It occurs in granite and quartzite and with topaz in rhyolite. Bavaria, Tyrol, Ceylon, Virginia, and Nevada are some of the localities for this variety.

Almandite.—The almandite garnet was known to the ancients. It includes the once popular *carbuncle*. The color of almandite varies from deep red and violet red through brownish red to almost black. The transparent red varieties are used as gems. However, most almandite is too dark and opaque for that purpose and accordingly on account of its superior hardness finds use as an abrasive. In artificial light almandite occasionally has an orange hue. The absorption spectrum is strong, and contains a pronounced band in the yellow, which accounts for the violet hue of some stones (p. 79). The cabochon cut is most used for the carbuncle, the darker stones often being cut in the hollow cabochon style, whereby a more attractive color is obtained. On some carbuncles a four-rayed cross of light is seen, constituting an interesting type of asterism.

Almandite is found in a variety of rocks, including gneiss, schist, granite, pegmatite, and other igneous rocks. Some localities for the gem variety of almandite are India; Ceylon, in gem gravels; South Australia; Minas Geraes, Brazil; Uruguay; Tyrol; various parts of the United States, especially Salida, Colorado; Gore Mountain, Warren County, New York; and Fort Wrangel, Alaska.

Uvarovite.—This is a rather uncommon emerald-green variety of garnet. Its color is due to the presence of chromium. The crystals are generally too small to be of value as gems. This variety is obtained principally from the Ural Mountains. It occurs at Orford and Wakefield, Quebec, and in eastern Finland.

Andradite.—Since the composition of andradite varies considerably, it is not surprising that it occurs in many colors—brownish red, brown, black, and various shades of yellow and green. *Topazolite,* as the name indicates, is a variety resembling topaz in yellow color and transparency. The use of this term should be discontinued. *Demantoid* is a grass-green variety, known erroneously as olivine. Demantoid is very brilliant, and has a high dispersion, which is unusual among colored stones. *Uralian emerald* is a misleading name often given to this variety. The black opaque andradite, called *melanite,* contains some titanium and has a very high index of refraction. It has been used as mourning jewelry. These garnets occur in nephelite-syenite, serpentine, chlorite schist, crystalline limestone, and stream beds. Demantoid is found in the Ural Mountains, in Saxony, and in Hungary. Topazolite occurs in the Piedmont region of Italy.

ZIRCON

Colorless zircon is next after the diamond in brilliancy and fire. The mineral also occurs in very pleasing colors. Although zircon as a gem has not been nearly so well known as its properties would warrant, it has become very popular during the last twenty-five years.

Zircon is tetragonal. The crystals are usually prismatic in habit (Figs. 307, 308, and 309). It is also found in rounded or angular lumps or grains. The cleavages, prismatic and pyramidal, are imperfect; the fracture, conchoidal. The hardness varies from one specimen to another, but is never far from 7½. The specific gravity has a wide range, 4.65 to 4.71.

FIG. 307.   FIG. 308.

FIGS. 307 and 308.—Wooden models of crystals of zircon.

FIG. 309.—Zircon in syenite. Ilmen Range, Ural Mountains.

The more usual colors are brown, brownish red, and gray; the less usual, yellow, green, blue, and colorless. The color is said to be due to iron and other constituents. Zircon is transparent to opaque, and has an adamantine luster. The indices of refraction ω 1.93 and ϵ 1.99, the double refraction 0.06, and the dispersion 0.048 are all high. Because of the strong double refraction the apparent doubling of the back facets should be quite readily observed when the stone is examined in several directions. The mineral is normally uniaxial and positive in optical character. Some crystals, however, show anomalous optical properties, being biaxial.

The variability in the character of zircon is noteworthy. In fact, three different types of the mineral are now recognized. These types, called *high, intermediate,* and *low zircons,* differ in specific gravity, hardness, optical properties, and behavior on heating. Some specimens are composed of all three types.

By Stevanovic, Spencer, Chudoba and Stackelberg, and Smith, a or α, b or β, c or γ are used to designate the low, high, and intermediate types, respectively, while Schlossmacher and Shipley apply a or α to the high, b or β to the intermediate, and c or γ to the low types. Because of this lack of uniformity in the use of the letters, it is preferable to designate the types merely as the high, intermediate, and low zircons and discard the letters.

High zircon, also called *normal zircon,* occurs with a uniform tetragonal crystal structure; hence, well-developed crystals are common (Figs. 307 and 308). The various physical and optical properties given above apply to this type.

Low zircon occurs as rolled pebbles and is without crystal form. It is usually amorphous, or nearly so, and hence isotropic. However, it may be slightly double refractive and even biaxial. Its specific gravity varies from 3.94 to 4.4. The hardness is 6 to 6½. The indices of refraction are lower than for the high type, namely, 1.78 to 1.84. In color the low type may be green or greenish brown. It is composed of amorphous silica, SiO_2, and amorphous or microcrystalline zirconium oxide, ZrO_2. This type is rare.

Intermediate zircon has properties which lie between those of the low and high types. Thus, the specific gravity varies from 4.1 to 4.65. The index of refraction is approximately 1.85. On heating to 1450°C. this type is converted to high zircon with slight changes in specific gravity, index of refraction, and double refraction.

Zircon, $ZrSiO_4$, is considered a silicate. It was formerly often interpreted as an oxide of zirconium and silicon. Usually a little iron is present, and a number of other elements are occasionally contained in the mineral. A rather constant impurity in zircon is the element hafnium. The varieties which contain uranium have a very characteristic absorption spectrum, consisting of a number of sharp, narrow bands throughout the spectrum. Fig. 150 shows the unit cell of zircon.

The gem varieties of zircon are as follows:

Hyacinth and *jacinth* are the terms applied to the clear, transparent yellow, orange, red, and brown varieties.

Jargon includes most of the other colors.

Matara or *matura diamond* is the name given to zircon from Matara, Ceylon, either naturally colorless or made so by subjecting colored stones to heat treatment. As these terms are misleading, they should not be used. These colorless stones should be called *white zircon.*

Blue zircon of gem quality has become very popular in recent years. These stones are obtained from the Mongka district, Indo-China. The attractive blue color is the result of heat treatment (p. 144).

Gem zircons are found principally in secondary deposits. The most important localities are the Mongka district, Indo-China, and Ceylon. Gem zircon also occurs in Burma, Tasmania, New South Wales, and New Zealand. Although the mineral occurs at various localities in Maine, New York, and North Carolina, stones of gem quality are not common.

OPAL

The opal was long in disfavor, for it had been considered a stone likely to bring misfortune and disaster upon its owner. In recent times this superstition has lost ground, and the opal has become much more popular. Some of the finer varieties are now highly valued. The ancients regarded opal as a very precious stone. Pliny ranked it next after the emerald, and describes it as embodying in one stone the colors of many gems.

Unlike most gem minerals, opal is amorphous and has no crystal form. Accordingly, it occurs as compact and irregular masses in veins and cavities. Some varieties are stalactitic or earthy. Opal has a good conchoidal fracture. It is fairly soft, $5\frac{1}{2}$ to $6\frac{1}{2}$, and therefore should not be exposed to undue wear. However, a worn and scratched stone can be restored by repolishing. Opal is light in weight, the specific gravity being 1.95 to 2.3.

The luster of opal is vitreous, dull, or greasy, and the mineral is transparent to opaque. The color varies greatly. Opal may be colorless, white, yellow, brown, red, pink, green, gray, blue, or black. A beautiful play of colors is to be observed, especially in the precious varieties. This is due to the interference of light, and must not be confused with the fire caused by dispersion (p. 55). It is a result of the breaking up of white light into its component colors within the mineral. This is caused either by minute cracks or, more probably, by the presence in the mineral of scattered patches in which the water content and consequently the refractivity differ from those of the body of the substance. Opal is formed from gelatinous silica, deposited in cracks and cavities from aqueous solution. In hardening, the silica loses some of its water and contracts, thus becoming opal. This contraction is likely to produce cracks, which may be later filled with successive deposits of opal with indices of refraction which differ materially from that of the mass. When these deposits or layers are thin enough, a play of colors is produced in the same way in which an oil film on water shows rather vivid colors.

Opal is isotropic, with an index of refraction of about 1.44 to 1.46, varying with the water content. Anomalous double refraction is not unusual.

The formula for opal is $SiO_2.xH_2O$; that is, it is hydrated silica. The content of water varies from 1 to 21 per cent. It usually ranges from 3 to 13 per cent, but in the precious opal the amount of water is generally 6 to 10 per cent. Specimens of opal should be immersed in water occasionally, otherwise, some are liable to crack. Impurities are not uncommon, as is the case with all amorphous minerals, which seem to have the faculty of absorbing foreign matter. Calcium, iron, magnesium, sodium, and aluminum compounds, as well as bitumen, are frequently present.

Precious opal includes the opals with a pleasing play of color or an attractive opalescence. These are cut cabochon, in order best to display this phenomenon. Stones with large areas of uniform color are the most desirable. Opal doublets are frequently sold (p. 172).

Common opal is translucent to opaque, and of many dull colors.

The following are varieties of precious opal:

White opals are those precious opals of a light color.

Black opals include the dark-gray, blue, and black types. This variety is very valuable.

Harlequin opals have patches of color which are rather uniform in size.

Lechosos opal is a variety showing a deep-green play of color.

Fire opal is a semi-transparent to transparent variety with an attractive yellow, orange, or red color. It may show a play of color.

Girasol has a blue-white sheen or opalescence.

Opal matrix is the term applied to cut stones consisting of opal in its matrix.

The following varieties of common opal have little or no play of color. Although they are not commonly cut as gems, they are nevertheless of interest:

Milk opal is milk white, yellowish, bluish, or greenish in color.

Resin opal is wax, honey, or ocher yellow in color, and has a resinous luster.

Agate opal is a banded opal.

Opal jasper is red, reddish brown, or brown, resembling jasper.

Prase opal is green in color.

Rose opal or *quinzite* is a beautiful pink variety.

Wood opal is pseudomorphous after wood (petrified wood) (Fig. 54), the woody structure being faithfully retained. Pseudomorphs of opal after bones and shells are also known (Fig. 55).

Hyalite is colorless and transparent, resembling drops of molten glass.

Hydrophane is cloudy, white, dehydrated opal, which becomes transparent when its pores are filled by immersion in water.

Moss opal, like moss agate, contains inclusions of manganese oxide, which resemble moss.

Opal is formed in a variety of ways, but most of it results from the decomposition of silicate minerals and volcanic glass by hot waters. The dissolved silica is subsequently deposited in cracks or crevices. This process takes place especially in recent erupted lavas. The early source of opal was Czerwenitza, near Košice, Czecho-Slovakia. Lately much precious opal of fine quality has been obtained from various localities in Australia: in New South Wales, at White Cliffs and at Lightning Ridge as black opal; in Queensland, blue opal from Bulla Creek and also from Barcoo River. Gracias á Dios, in Honduras, is another locality for precious opal. Fire opal is found at Querétaro and Zimapan, Mexico. Humboldt County, Nevada, has produced some fine black opals. Good opal has also been found in Latah County, Idaho. Common opal is widely distributed.

QUARTZ

Quartz is one of the most common minerals in the earth's crust. It occurs in nearly every type of rock, igneous, sedimentary, or metamorphic. It is found in formations of all geological ages. Quartz also occurs filling cracks and crevices, and it is the most abundant constituent of sands and gravels. It has been aptly called a "tramp" mineral. Many varieties are very attractive. In one form or another, quartz has been known from the earliest times. One of its varieties, flint, was employed in the manufac-

Fig. 310.—Quartz crystals—pyramidal, prismatic, long prismatic, tabular, skeletal.

ture of primitive weapons and for the production of a spark in the building of fires. Because of its useful and definitely recognized properties, quartz was undoubtedly one of the first minerals to be eagerly sought.

Quartz is hexagonal, and occurs in well-developed prismatic crystals (Figs. 310 to 313). The prism faces are generally horizontally striated. More rarely the crystals have a pyramidal development (Fig. 310). Over 140 different types of crystal faces have been observed on this mineral. The crystals are sometimes bent or twisted or otherwise greatly distorted. That quartz may occur in left- and right-handed crystals (Figs. 311 and 312) has already been indicated (p. 74). Twins are frequently observed. Figure 313 illustrates a very common type, in which the vertical axis is the axis of twinning. This twin may be considered as composed of two interpenetrating left-handed crystals. Other types of twins are not uncommon.

Quartz crystals frequently contain various inclusions, as follows: (1) solids, such as rutile, hematite, epidote, actinolite, and

PLATE IV

First row: 1, kunzite, Madagascar; 2, turquois, Persia; 3, turquois, California; 4, turquois, Africa.
Second row: 1, lapis lazuli, Afghanistan; 2, moonstone, Ceylon; 3, labradorite, Labrador; 4, amazonite, Colorado.
Third row: 1, 4, black opals, Australia; 2, 3, precious opals, Australia.
Fourth row: 1, fire opal, Mexico; 2, opal matrix, Australia; 3, smithsonite, Mexico; 4, chrysoprase, Germany.
Fifth row: 1, amethyst, Brazil; 2, amethyst, Uruguay; 3, smoky quartz, Switzerland; 4, citrine, Brazil; 5, citrine, Spain.

organic matter; (2) liquids, of which water and liquid carbon dioxide are the most common; (3) gases, mostly carbon dioxide.

Quartz has a distinct rhombohedral cleavage and a perfect conchoidal fracture which are made use of by the lapidary in the rough shaping, or knapping, of the specimens before cutting. The hardness is 7; hence, quartz gems are durable (p. 29). The specific gravity of pure quartz is 2.66, though the varieties range from 2.5 to 2.8.

FIG. 311.   FIG. 312.   FIG.   313.—
FIGS. 311 and 312.—Models of left-(311)   Model of twinned
and right-handed (312) crystals of quartz.   crystal of quartz.

Pure quartz is colorless; as the result of its impurities, the mineral is found in practically every color. Many of the varieties are based on differences in color. Various shades of gray, yellow, pink, red, blue, green, brown, purple, and black are to be noted. The colors are in many cases unstable, being destroyed by a low heat. They are also susceptible to change by the action of radiations, such as ultraviolet light and those of radium. The colors are generally attributed to traces of inorganic, or possibly organic, impurities. For some of the more unstable colorings the action of radioactive waters or minerals subsequent to the formation of the quartz, has been suggested as the cause of the color. The luster of quartz is vitreous. The mineral may be transparent, translucent, or opaque.

Quartz is uniaxial and optically positive. The indices of refraction are ω 1.544, ϵ 1.553. The double refraction, 0.009, and the dispersion, 0.013, are both low. It is optically active, rotating the plane of polarized light. Right-handed crystals rotate the plane of polarization to the right; left-handed crystals, to the left (p. 74). Because of the piezoelectric properties of quartz, properly oriented sections are used in radio and other electronic apparatus.

The composition of quartz is simply SiO_2, silicon dioxide. Some quartz is very pure. Quartz frequently contains mineral inclusions and other foreign matter. It is often pseudomorphous after other minerals or after wood, as in silicified or petrified wood. Quartz is usually considered a very resistant mineral, but in nature it may be replaced by other minerals, including even the very soft talc.

The varieties of quartz may be grouped into the following three large classes:

Crystalline varieties are vitreous, crystallized or crystalline, and more or less transparent.

Cryptocrystalline varieties are compact and homogeneous, with a crystalline structure which may be observed with the microscope.

Clastic varieties are those which are made up of fragments of quartz, often cemented into a coherent mass. These include sand and gravel and the rocks sandstone and quartzite.

The gem varieties of quartz belong to the first two groups. Those which are crystalline may be cut in faceted forms or cabochon, while those which are cryptocrystalline are cut cabochon, as cameos, and in large polished pieces.

Crystalline Varieties.—*Rock crystal* is pure, transparent, and water-clear quartz (Fig. 314). It is usually, but not always, well crystallized (Fig. 315). Cut into vases, crystal balls, and so on, it has long enjoyed considerable popularity (Fig. 316). Cut into beads and fancy shapes or fashioned to resemble the diamond, this variety of quartz is often sold as *rhinestone* and improperly as *Herkimer diamond, Lake George diamond, Mexican diamond, Alaska diamond,* or *Cornish diamond.* The large quantities of oscillating quartz plates, which are so important in radio and other electronic apparatus, are made from rock crystal (p. 51). This variety of quartz is among the most abundant of gem minerals. The following principal localities may be mentioned: Brazil, Japan, Madagascar, Switzerland, New York, and Arkansas.

Amethyst is a popular transparent variety of purple or violet quartz. It is usually well crystallized. The color varies a great deal in intensity, and is often unevenly distributed. The pigment is probably an iron compound. Under certain conditions the color of amethyst may be greatly improved by heat treatment (p. 144). It is very difficult, if not impossible, to detect stones that have been treated in this way. Under other conditions the original color is destroyed, the stone first becoming yellowish and finally colorless. Amethyst is slightly dichroic. Reddish-

FIG. 314.—Rock crystal. Dauphiné, France.

or purplish-violet amethyst of fine quality, known in the trade as *Siberian amethyst,* is considered the most valuable variety. This term was originally applied to stones obtained from the Ural Mountains, but now it indicates quality and not the source of the gem mineral. Although faceted cuts, such as the step or brilliant, are common, it may also be engraved or carved into attractive forms or shapes. Important localities are Brazil, Uruguay, Siberia, Ceylon, India, Madagascar, Persia, Mexico, Maine, New Hampshire, Pennsylvania, North Carolina, and the Lake Superior district.

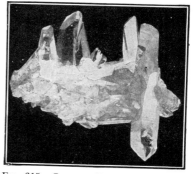

FIG. 315.—Quartz. Dauphiné, France.

Rose quartz is invariably massive, transparent to translucent, and of a rose-pink color, due to manganese. In the darker specimens there is a very slight dichroism. The mineral is often opalescent. It may show asterism. *Asteriated* or *star rose quartz* is rather common. The asterism is best seen in transmitted light. Rose quartz is cut cabochon or as unfaceted beads. *Bohemian ruby* is a misleading trade name for rose quartz. Japan, Madagascar, Bavaria, France, Brazil,

Maine, South Dakota, and California are important localities for rose quartz.

FIG. 316.—Chinese vase carved from rock crystal. *(Courtesy of American Museum of Natural History.)*

Smoky quartz is generally well crystallized and is smoky yellow to dark brown or black in color (Fig. 317). Smoky quartz is often called *cairngorm*. The black variety may be designated as *morion*. The use of *smoky topaz* for smoky quartz leads to deception and should be discontinued. Like amethyst, smoky quartz is easily decolorized by heat. The color may be due to the action of radium radiations. Smoky quartz is slightly dichroic. It is usually cut in the brilliant style, and is a great favorite in Scotland, where it is used in brooches, pins, and other ornaments. Important localities are Ceylon; the Alps; Cairngorm, Banffshire, Scotland; Paris, Maine; New Hampshire; and Pikes Peak, Colorado.

Citrine is yellow quartz. It resembles precious topaz in color and transparency (Fig. 318). Unfortunately it is known as *false topaz* and even sold simply as *topaz* (p. 139). It is usually found in crystals. The color is ascribed to ferric iron. The color of some varieties of quartz may be changed to that of citrine by heat treatment (p. 143). Much citrine comes from Brazil. Nearly all yellow quartz which is sold as citrine, false topaz, and so forth, has been heat-treated.

FIG. 317.—Smoky quartz with muscovite. Paris, Maine.

Milky quartz is translucent to opaque. It has a milky-white color. Milky quartz containing native gold is sometimes cut cabochon or with a flat surface and called *gold quartz*. California and Alaska supply this variety of quartz, which also occurs in other important gold-mining districts.

Siderite or *sapphire quartz* is a rare variety having an indigo or Berlin-blue color.

Aventurine quartz contains glistening scales of brightly colored minerals, such as hematite or chromium mica. It is usually yellow, brown, green, or red in color. Aventurine is found in Siberia, India, China, and Madagascar. An imitation aventurine, known as *goldstone* (p. 169), is extensively used in cheap jewelry.

Rutilated quartz or *sagenite*, more fancifully known as *Venus* or *Thetis hairstone*, is rock crystal containing long, fine, light-brown needles of rutile (Fig. 319). This variety is found in Madagascar, Switzerland, Brazil, Vermont, and North Carolina. Other minerals, such as hornblende, actinolite (Figs. 320 to 322), and goethite, may occur in quartz in a similar manner. Pale amethyst, penetrated by needles of goethite, is cut and sold as *Cupid's darts*. It is also called *onegite*, for Lake Onega, Russia, a locality for this variety.

Tiger's-eye is quartz which is pseudomorphous after crocidolite. It retains the fibrous structure of the original mineral, asbestos (Fig. 323). When cut cabochon this variety is strongly chatoyant. It is yellowish brown, bluish, or red in color. It is used in jewelry and for ornamental objects, such as paper weights and umbrella handles. Griqualand West, Union of South Africa, is the principal source of tiger's-eye.

Cat's-eye is chatoyant, containing parallel fibers of asbestos, and is grayish, brownish, or green in color. This variety somewhat resembles the more valuable chrysoberyl cat's-eye or cymophane (p. 232). Like that mineral, it is cut cabochon. Important localities are Ceylon, India, Bavaria, and Brazil.

Cryptocrystalline Varieties.—*Chalcedony* of gem quality is a transparent to translucent, light-colored, white, gray, brown, or blue form of quartz, with a waxy luster. It may occur in stalactitic (Fig. 324) or concretionary forms or as a lining of cavities. It was very popular in ancient times, and is frequently referred to in Biblical literature. Chalcedony is cut cabochon. Stones commonly sold as *blue* or *green chalcedony* have been given a uniform color artificially (p. 141). Chalcedony is widely distributed. Excellent specimens are obtained from Uruguay, Brazil, and the Lake Superior district.

The following varieties of cryptocrystalline quartz, through to jasper, are generally regarded as special types of chalcedony.

Carnelian or *sard* is a reddish chalcedony. It varies in color from a pale red to deep clear red and through brownish red to

FIG. 318.—Citrine cuvette.

FIG. 319.—Rutilated quartz. Alexander County, North Carolina.

FIG. 320.   FIG. 321.   FIG. 322.

FIGS. 320 and 321.—Quartz with inclusions; hornblende. FIG. 322.—Actinolite.

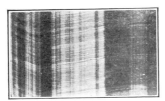

FIG. 323.—Tiger's-eye. Griqualand West, South Africa.

FIG. 324.—Chalcedony (stalactitic). Havana, Cuba.

yellow-brown. Ferric oxide causes the color. Carnelian is rather widely distributed. Stained and heat-treated agate from Brazil and Uruguay is frequently sold as carnelian.

Chrysoprase is a variety of chalcedony having an apple-green color due to a trace of nickel. It is obtained from Silesia, Oregon, and California.

Prase is translucent, with a dull leek-green or sage-green color. It was used by the ancients for engravings. Saxony is a locality for prase.

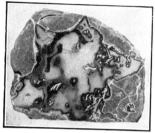
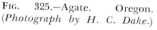
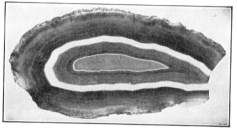

Fig. 325.—Agate. Oregon. (*Photograph by H. C. Dake.*)

Fig. 326.—Agate. Serra do Mar, Brazil.

Plasma has for its color some shade of green, often a dark grass green. It contains irregularly distributed white or yellowish spots. India and China furnish plasma of good quality.

The foregoing three green varieties grade imperceptibly into one another.

Heliotrope or *bloodstone* is a dark green chalcedony containing scattered spots of red jasper. It was frequently used in the early church as the material for engraved sacred objects, in which the red spots represented bloodstains, and was called *St. Stephen's stone.* Bloodstone is used in signet rings. It is found in India, Siberia, and the Hebrides.

Agate is one of the most popular cryptocrystalline varieties of quartz. It occurs in geodes in volcanic and sedimentary rocks and frequently as pebbles. It consists of chalcedony in which the color is irregularly distributed (Fig. 325). Usually the colors are disposed in curved parallel bands, which are more or less wavy. Such varieties are called *banded agates* (Figs. 326 to 329). Some specimens may be so cut that the differently colored bands are circularly or elliptically arranged so as to resemble an eye

(Fig. 330) and are then called *eye agates*. In *fortification agates* the bands are angular and so arranged as to simulate the outline of a fortification. The name *clouded agate* is self-explanatory. *Moss agate,* often called *Mocha stone* (Fig. 331), is a variety which

FIG. 327.—Agate. Czecho-Slovakia. (*Courtesy of National Museum, Praha.*)

contains dendritic inclusions of dark pigmenting matter. These resemble moss or ferns. *Agatized* or *petrified wood* is clouded agate pseudomorphous after wood.

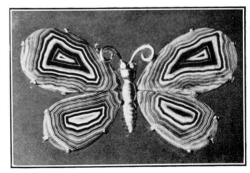

FIG. 328.—Agate. Serra do Mar, Brazil.

FIG. 329.—Agate ornament. Czecho-Slovakia. (*Courtesy of National Museum, Praha.*)

There are many other varieties, such as *tree, flower, plume, landscape,* or *scenic,* and *polka-dot agates.* These terms are self-explanatory. The colors of agate are white, brown, red, bluish, and so on. More often than not agates have been artificially

colored (p. 141). The different varieties of agate are most frequently cut with large plane or slightly curved surfaces such as
will best display the banding. Idar-Oberstein, Germany, and
Providence, Rhode Island, are the most important centers for
the cutting and polishing of agates (p. 110). Many agates are
cut and polished by professional and amateur lapidaries in the
United States. Uruguay, Brazil, Czecho-Slovakia, Oregon, Montana, Wyoming, Washington, California, and the Lake Superior
district are important localities for the occurrence of agate.

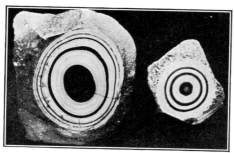

FIG. 330.—"Eye" agates.

Onyx is like agate, except that the colored bands are straight
and parallel (Fig. 332). The colors are generally white or black.
Onyx is used for cameos (Figs. 190 to 192).

Sardonyx consists of layers of sard or carnelian in combination
with white layers of chalcedony.

Jasper is an opaque red, yellow, brown, dark-green, or grayish-
blue cryptocrystalline quartz. It is generally impure. When the
colors are in broad bands or stripes, the name *riband jasper* is
applied. *Egyptian jasper* is a yellow to brown variety, irregularly
marked. *Swiss* or *German lapis* is an artificially colored jasper
(p. 142). The term *jasper-agate* is given to lighter colored agates
containing irregular particles of jasper.

Flint is translucent to opaque and gray, smoky, brown, or black
in color. It is usually found in nodules in limestone or chalk
beds, and frequently has a white coating upon the exterior of
the mass (Fig. 333). The conchoidal fracture is very conspicuous.
Flint was used very generally by primitive peoples for knives and
for arrowheads and spearheads. The chalk cliffs along the English Channel are a famous locality for flint.

FIG. 331.—Moss agate. Oregon. (*Photograph by H. C. Dake.*)

FIG. 332.—Onyx. Serra do Mar, Brazil.

FIG. 333.—Flint. Dover Cliffs, England.

Basanite is a velvet-black variety of quartz formerly used for determining the streak of alloys of precious metals. It was also called *touchstone*.

Hornstone and *chert* are rather impure and unattractive varieties of cryptocrystalline quartz. They are generally of a grayish color and resemble flint.

Clastic Varieties.—The clastic varieties of quartz include *sand, gravel, sandstone,* and *quartzite,* which are widely distributed. Some sands and gravels are important sources of gems. Sandstone and quartzite are used for building and decorative purposes. *Itacolumite* is unique in that it is a flexible sandstone. It is found in India, Brazil, and North Carolina.

JADE

The material known as jade includes two minerals of similar appearance, *nephrite* and *jadeite*. It is convenient to discuss them together, since a distinction is rarely made except by the mineralogist. Jade is placed above all other precious stones in China, and in the Orient it is carved into elaborate figures and designs (Figs. 334 and 335). The Chinese believe that jade embodies the five cardinal virtues, charity, modesty, courage, justice, and wisdom. Remedial qualities are also ascribed to it. Primitive peoples likewise regarded jade with esteem, and they fashioned it into ornaments and into axes and other implements. Such objects have been found in the Swiss lake dwellings and in France, Greece, Egypt, Asia Minor, New Zealand, Alaska, British Columbia, Mexico, Central America, and northern South America.

Nephrite is the more common form of jade. It is a monoclinic variety of amphibole. The mineral is compact and tough, and the fracture is splintery. The hardness is 6 to $6\frac{1}{2}$, and the specific gravity 2.9 to 3.1. The most common colors vary from bright to dark green, these being due to the presence of ferrous iron. Because of the oxidation of the iron, old ornaments of nephrite often possess a superficial brownish to reddish color. Nephrite may also be white, yellowish, reddish, or bluish. The color is often irregularly distributed. The terms *mutton-fat* and *spinach jade* are sometimes used for appropriately colored nephrite.

Nephrite has a glistening luster, and is translucent to opaque. It is pleochroic, and the index of refraction β is 1.62. The composition of nephrite is $Ca(Mg,Fe)_3(SiO_3)_4$; that is, it is a calcium, magnesium, and iron silicate.

Jadeite is a monoclinic member of the pyroxene group of minerals. It is rarer than nephrite. Like nephrite, it is tough and compact, and has a splintery fracture. In hardness it is 6½ to 7.

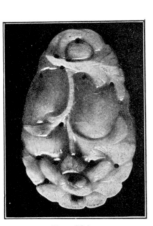 

FIG. 334.   FIG. 335.

FIGS. 334 and 335.—Carved Chinese jade.

The specific gravity is 3.3. A specific gravity determination will therefore serve to distinguish the two minerals. The color is white or greenish white to emerald green or, more rarely, brown, orange, red, or black. The luster is subvitreous to pearly. Jadeite is translucent to opaque. The mean index of refraction is 1.66. Jadeite is a sodium aluminum silicate, $NaAl(SiO_3)_2$. It fuses more readily than nephrite. *Chloromelanite* is a dark-green to nearly black variety of jadeite. *Imperial* or *gem jade* includes the semi-transparent varieties with colors that closely approximate that of gem emerald.

Nephrite occurs in various parts of China, in Turkestan, Siberia, New Zealand, and Alaska, and at Lander, Wyoming. Jadeite is found in upper Burma, Yünnan in southern China, Tibet, Mexico, and South America.

Certain greenish varieties of a number of other minerals have some resemblance to jade. Some of these are green grossularite from Buffelsfontein, Transvaal, often called *South African* or *Transvaal jade* (p. 211); californite, a green variety of vesuvianite, termed *vesuvianite jade* (p. 269); green serpentine from Rhode Island, New Zealand, and China, sometimes known as *bowenite* or *serpentine jade* (p. 263); artificially colored calcite onyx, improperly called *Mexican jade;* amazonite, a green microcline feldspar (p. 242); green aventurine (p. 223); saussurite, a tough white to greenish-gray variety of zoisite (p. 270); and massive greenish forms of pectolite and prehnite (p. 261). The physical and chemical properties of these minerals are such that they can be readily distinguished from the true jades, nephrite and jadeite.

CHRYSOBERYL

Two rather unusual gems are varieties of the mineral chrysoberyl. To one, *alexandrite,* belongs the striking property of hav-

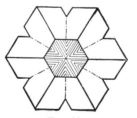

FIG. 336.

FIG. 337.—Chrysoberyl (twin). Haddam, Connecticut.

FIG. 338.

ing a different color in artificial light from that which it has in daylight; the other, *cat's-eye,* has an attractive chatoyancy.

Chrysoberyl is orthorhombic, and the usually striated crystals are often twinned into heart-shaped (Figs. 336 and 337) and pseudo-hexagonal (Fig. 338) forms. Crystal fragments and loose or rounded grains are also found. The mineral has a distinct pinacoidal cleavage and a conchoidal fracture. The hardness is $8\frac{1}{2}$, and chrysoberyl is therefore very durable. Its specific gravity is 3.5 to 3.8. The color is greenish white, greenish yellow, or asparagus to emerald green or, less often, yellow to brown. The luster is generally vitreous; in cat's-eye, it is silky. Chrysoberyl is transparent to translucent. Pleochroism is noted in the more deeply colored varieties. The indices of refraction are α 1.747, β 1.748, γ 1.757; the double refraction is 0.010, and the dispersion 0.015. The optical character is positive.

Chrysoberyl has been assumed to be beryllium aluminate, $Be(AlO_2)_2$, but it is now considered as a double oxide of beryllium and aluminum, $BeAl_2O_4$, or $BeO.Al_2O_3$. It may contain a little iron and chromium.

There are three gem varieties of chrysoberyl.

Chrysolite is a name given to the yellowish-green chrysoberyl, but more properly applied to olivine with the same color.

Cat's-eye or *cymophane* is a chatoyant, opalescent variety, with a silky luster and a greenish color. When it is cut cabochon, light appears to be concentrated in a line or band which extends across the surface of the stone. As the stone is turned, the position of the line changes, strikingly reminding one of a cat's eye. This is due to the more or less fibrous structure of the mineral. This variety is now very popular.

Alexandrite is interesting in more than one way. It was named in honor of Czar Alexander II of Russia, for it was first discovered in 1833, in the Ural Mountains, on the day on which his attainment to majority was celebrated, and the gem remained in vogue in Russia for some time. It is strongly pleochroic, showing the colors emerald green, columbine red, and orange yellow. This difference in color is easily visible to the unaided eye. A striking property of alexandrite is that it has an emerald-green color in daylight but in artificial light it appears columbine red. It has a strong absorption band in the yellow (p. 79), and this in conjunction with the difference in composition of sunlight and artificial light causes the foregoing phenomenon, which is further intensified by the strong pleochroism.

Cut cat's-eyes and alexandrites of high quality cost up to $400 per carat.

Although chrysoberyl has been made artificially, the product is of no commercial importance (p. 166). The alexandrite variety, however, has been rather successfully imitated by appropriately colored synthetic corundum and spinel (p. 165).

Certain solutions containing trivalent chromium have the same strikingly characteristic property of being blue green by daylight and red in artificial light. This strongly suggests chromium as the cause of the color, and analyses of alexandrite show a trace of that element. However, in the synthetic corundum, sold as alexandrite, vanadium is the pigment (p. 155). Vanadium and chromium are closely related elements, and some of the solutions of vanadium also have a color that varies according to the type of illumination, though the phenomenon is less marked than in the case of chromium. *Alexandrite cat's-eye* is the name given to chatoyant alexandrite from Ceylon.

Chrysoberyl occurs in gneiss, mica schist, granite, and stream deposits with such minerals as beryl, tourmaline, and apatite. Chrysolite is found in Brazil; Haddam, Connecticut; Greenfield, New York; and Norway and Stoneham, Maine. The cat's-eye variety is obtained from Ceylon, China, and Brazil. Alexandrite is found in Ceylon, the Ural Mountains, and Tasmania.

TOURMALINE

Tourmaline is rather unique in coloring, since a single crystal may be zoned in a variety of beautifully contrasting colors. In addition, the mineral shows strong dichroism, and can be cut in such a way that the colors due to this phenomenon may be seen, which adds still more to the attractiveness of the stone.

Tourmaline commonly occurs in well-developed, prismatic, vertically grooved or striated crystals of the hexagonal system (Figs. 339 to 341). These crystals generally exhibit a rounded triangular outline (Fig. 342). The vertical axis is polar; that is, different crystal forms are present at opposite ends, one termination being more obtuse than the other. This polar character is further evidenced by the electrical properties of the mineral (p. 50). Tourmaline occurs also in compact or disseminated masses and in radially divergent aggregates and also in loose, more or less rounded crystals in secondary deposits.

Tourmaline has no well-defined cleavage. The fracture is subconchoidal to uneven. The hardness is 7 to 7½, a little low for satisfactory use in rings, where the wear is great, though hard enough for brooches, pendants, and so forth. The specific gravity of the mineral is 3.0 to 3.2.

In color, tourmaline may be pitch black, brown, gray, yellow, green, red, pink, blue, or colorless. The mineral is transparent to opaque. The black and brown varieties are generally opaque, while the lighter colored stones are more or less transparent.

FIG. 339.   FIG. 340.

FIGS. 339 and 340.—Wooden models of crystals of tourmaline.

Tourmaline has a vitreous luster. *Tourmaline cat's-eye* possesses a marked chatoyancy.

The colors of the alkali tourmalines are frequently arranged in regular zones or bands. The zones may be horizontal, running

FIG. 341.—Tourma-
line in albite. Mesa
Grande, California.

FIG. 342.—General-
ized cross section of a
crystal of tourmaline.

across the length of the crystals (Fig. 343, the two outside speci-mens). Typical arrangements of color are as follows: green at one end and red at the other, with a narrow colorless zone between; green followed by yellow, red, and green again; or per-haps crimson or green tipped with black. The contacts between the zones are sharp, increasing the contrast in coloring. Again, the colors may be arranged in vertical, somewhat cylindrical zones, parallel to the prism faces of the crystal. In this case a cross section through the stone reveals the zonal character (Fig. 343, the central specimen, and Figs. 344 and 345). In Brazilian stones the core is generally red, with a marginal zone of green and an intermediate colorless band. This arrangement is reversed in the case of crystals from southern California, which are most often green inside and red outside. Stones from Madagascar frequently have numerous narrow zones in various shades. Sometimes both types of zoning are observed in a single crystal.

Tourmaline is optically negative. The indices of refraction of gem tourmaline vary: ω 1.648 to 1.655, ϵ 1.625 to 1.633. The double refraction is fairly high, and the dispersion 0.016. The strong dichroism is a prominent character. The ordinary ray is much more strongly absorbed than the extraordinary ray; therefore, to obtain the best color, the stone is usually cut with the table parallel to the vertical

FIG. 343.—Tourmaline crystals showing zonal distribution of color and spherical triangular outline. San Diego County, California.

axis (p. 76). Not only is the color brighter if the stone is so cut, but both of the dichroic colors may be seen as the stone is turned about in various directions, giving a very pleasing variation in color.

The composition of tourmaline is rather complex. Authorities differ somewhat as to the correctness of the formula, which is generally written $M'_{20}B_2Si_4O_{21}$, the mineral being a borosilicate. In this formula M' represents various combinations of hydrogen, fluorine, lithium, sodium, potassium, magnesium, calcium, manganese, iron, and aluminum. Depending upon the composition, lithium, iron, and magnesium tourmalines are recognized. It is chiefly the tourmaline rich in alkalies which is transparent and possesses the most attractive colors.

The varieties of tourmaline used as gems are *achroite,* colorless; *rubellite,* rose red or pink; *siberite,* purple; *indicolite,* dark blue; and green, blue, yellowish-green, and honey-yellow tourmalines.

The iron tourmaline, or *schorl,* is black; and the tourmaline rich in magnesia is brown.

The terms Brazilian emerald (green), Brazilian sapphire (blue), Brazilian peridot (yellowish green), and peridot of Ceylon (honey yellow) are all misleading and should not be used. These stones should be designated as *green, blue, yellowish-green,* and *honey-yellow tourmaline,* respectively. By heat treatment the color of some tourmalines may be improved. This is especially true of

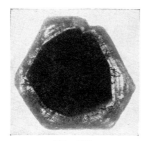 

Fig. 344.   Fig. 345.

Figs. 344 and 345.—Sections of tourmaline from Madagascar showing pronounced zonal distribution of color. Fig. 344, pink and green. Fig. 345, light and dark green.

the dark-blue stones from South-West Africa, which can be changed to an emerald green (p. 145).

In the cutting of tourmaline various styles are employed. The multi-colored stones are very attractive when cut in a long cabochon or step style. The brilliant and emerald cuts are also used for the mineral. Internal feathers and cracks are the flaws most common in tourmaline.

Tourmaline occurs in metamorphic rocks, such as gneiss, schist, and marble, and in pegmatites. It is in pegmatites that the gem varieties are principally found. Quartz, beryl, apatite, topaz, and fluorite are some of the associated minerals. Localities for the mineral are numerous. On the island of Elba are found pink, red, green, black, colorless, and zoned crystals. Magnificent tourmalines, in a great variety of colors and frequently zoned, are found at many localities in Madagascar (Figs. 344 and 345) and South-West Africa. Small yellow stones of gem quality are obtained from Ceylon. These were the first tourmalines to appear in Europe. Other important foreign localities are India; Burma, in alluvial deposits; Siberia; and Minas Geraes, Brazil. In the United States there are two widely separated regions famous for their beautifully colored tourmalines, in Maine, at Mount Mica, Mount Apatite, and Mount Rubellite, in the towns of Paris, Auburn, and Hebron, respectively; and the Mesa Grande district, in San Diego County, California. Other localities in this country are Chesterfield and Goshen, Massachusetts; Haddam, Connecticut; Gouverneur, DeKalb, and Pierrepont, New York; and Chester County, Pennsylvania.

OLIVINE

The mineralogist's olivine is better known to the jeweler as *peridot* and *chrysolite* or as the *evening emerald*. Olivine is used,

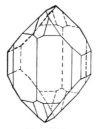

FIG. 346.

FIG. 347.—Olivine (green glassy grains). Near Balsam, North Carolina.

improperly, as a trade name for green garnet and other green stones.

Olivine belongs to the orthorhombic system. It occurs in crystals (Fig. 346), rounded and disseminated grains, granular masses (Fig. 347), and as water-worn pebbles (Fig. 348). The mineral has pinacoidal cleavages in two directions. The fracture is conchoidal. The hardness of olivine is not high for a gem, 6½ to 7. The specific gravity is 3.2 to 3.4 or even higher.

In color, olivine has less variety than the previously described minerals. Various shades of green and yellow, brown, reddish, grayish, and colorless comprise the list. The best color is a beautiful bottle green, which, however, is not observed so frequently as the other less desired shades. The olive-green variety is called *peridot;* the yellow to greenish-yellow stones have the name *chrysolite*. It is transparent to translucent. The luster of olivine in general is vitreous; on fractured surfaces, it is greasy.

Olivine is biaxial and optically positive. The determination of the double refraction, which is high, 0.37, is a reliable means of identification. This is readily done with the refractometer. The indices of refraction vary: α 1.653 to 1.681, β 1.670 to 1.706, γ 1.689 to 1.718. The stones with the higher indices have high specific gravities. The dispersion is 0.018. Pleochroism is weak in this mineral.

FIG. 348.—Waterworn pebbles of olivine. Fort Defiance, Arizona.

The composition of olivine is $(Mg,Fe)_2SiO_4$. As the iron content increases, the mineral becomes heavier and the color deepens.

The cuts generally employed are the step and the brilliant, but the cabochon is sometimes used. Being soft, the stone does not long retain a good polish or sharp edges when exposed to wear.

Olivine occurs in basic igneous rocks and in crystalline limestones. Olivine of gem quality occurs in meteorites. Most gem olivine is obtained from an island in the Red Sea, called St. John's or Zeberged, belonging to Egypt. Other localities are Burma, Ceylon, Queensland, Brazil, and the Navaho Indian country of Arizona and New Mexico, where it occurs as a constituent of sand. It is believed that much of the modern olivine has been recut from old jewelry.

SPINEL

As indicated by the names of some of its varieties, such as *ruby spinel, balas ruby,* and *rubicelle,* red spinel has often been confused with the ruby, especially since the two minerals are associated in gem gravels. Spinel has been called "mother of ruby," on account of this association, and many historic "rubies" were in all probability red spinels. Blue spinel may likewise be mistaken for sapphire. Actually the distinction between spinel and the ruby and sapphire is not difficult, since spinel is softer, lighter in weight, isotropic, and not pleochroic.

Spinel is cubic. Generally the crystals have an octahedral habit, and are often modified by the rhombic dodecahedron (Fig. 349). Contact twins, in which an octahedron face is the twinning plane, are common. These are known as *spinel twins* (Fig. 50). The mineral occurs as disseminated or loose crystals (Fig. 350) or as rounded grains.

The cleavage is imperfect octahedral; the fracture, conchoidal. In hardness, spinel is rather superior, the value being 8. The

FIG. 349.—Spinel (octahedron and rhombic dodecahedron) in calcite. Franklin Furnace, New Jersey. (See Fig. 19.)

FIG. 350.—Octahedral crystals of ruby spinel. Placer deposits. Ceylon.

specific gravity is 3.5 to 4.1, that of the gem varieties lying between 3.5 and 3.7.

The colors of spinel are red, orange, yellow, green, blue, violet, brown, and black, with many intermediate hues. Blue varieties have an absorption spectrum characteristic of cobalt, which is probably their pigment. The red and green varieties are thought to be colored by chromium and iron, respectively. The luster is vitreous splendent to dull, and the mineral is transparent to opaque. The index of refraction of most of the gem varieties varies from 1.72 to 1.75. The dispersion is about 0.020. Being cubic, spinel is isotropic.

Spinel has usually been assumed to be magnesium aluminate, $Mg(AlO_2)_2$. It is now considered as a double oxide of magnesium and aluminum, $MgAl_2O_4$ or $MgO.Al_2O_3$. The magnesium may be replaced in part by ferrous iron, zinc, manganese, or cobalt; the aluminum, by ferric iron or chromium.

The following terms have long been widely used for spinels of different colors: *ruby spinel,* deep red and transparent, the most popular gem variety; *balas ruby,* rose red to pink; *rubicelle,* yellow to orange red; *almandine,* violet and purple; *sapphirine,* blue spinel; *chlorospinel,* iron-bearing, of a grass-green color which is probably due to a trace of copper. These names are misleading, and cause much confusion with other gem minerals. Their use should be discontinued, and all gem spinel designated in terms of color, thus, *red spinel, pink spinel, blue spinel,* and so forth.

Synthetic spinels are now made in very attractive colors. They are sold under various names (p. 163).

Spinel occurs in contact metamorphic rocks, such as crystalline limestone, serpentine, and gneiss, and in gravels. Gem spinels are found as pebbles in the placers of Ceylon, Burma, and Thailand. Some are also supplied by India, Madagascar, Australia, Afghanistan, and Brazil. Some good gem material has been obtained from the limestones and serpentines of northern New Jersey and southeastern New York.

TURQUOIS

Because its distinctive blue color forms a very agreeable contrast to gold and silver settings, turquois has been popular since ancient times. The cabochon cut is employed for this stone.

Turquois is apparently amorphous, occurring in veins or crusts and as rounded masses, disseminated grains, or rounded pebbles. It was not until 1912, when minute crystals of turquois were found in Virginia, that the true, crystalline character of this mineral became known. It is triclinic. The fracture is conchoidal. Its hardness is 6; the specific gravity, 2.6 to 2.8. Turquois is usually opaque. The luster is somewhat waxy.

The color varies from greenish gray, yellowish green, apple green, and greenish blue to sky blue. Turquois with a uniform sky-blue color is most valued. Unfortunately the color is susceptible to a change to an undesirable green. The mineral is porous and easily becomes dirty and greasy. Perspiration has a bad effect on the color. Exposure to sunlight and heating causes the color to fade. It is said that a temporary restoration of the blue color can be effected by soaking the gem in ammonia, followed by an application of grease. The stone is sometimes dyed in blue solutions in an attempt to improve the color.

Since turquois is opaque, it is usually cut cabochon. The index of refraction β is 1.62.

Turquois has a complex formula: $H_5[Al(OH)_2]_6Cu(OH)(PO_4)_4$. It is, hence, a basic phosphate of copper and aluminum. Ferric iron may replace part of the aluminum. The blue color is due to copper. Ferric iron, if present, imparts a greenish shade.

Turquois matrix is the name applied to gems consisting of bits of turquois in the associated rock. The matrix is usually limonitic.

Bone or *fossil turquois,* also called *odontolite,* is mineralogically not a variety of true turquois. It consists of ivory, fossil bones or teeth, which have been colored blue either naturally or artificially. Odontolite may be distinguished from true turquois by its organic structure, which is best seen under the microscope. When rubbed, odontolite becomes electrified, while turquois does not. Odontolite is heavier than turquois. When heated, a disagreeable odor is emitted by odontolite. Aside from the substitution of odontolite, turquois is imitated in appropriately colored opaque glass, porcelain, and plaster of Paris.

Turquois is formed by deposition from solutions, and its most common associates are limonite, quartz, feldspar, and kaolin, of which the first is very characteristic. Fine turquois is found in volcanic rocks near Nishapur, in the province of Khurasan, Persia. *Egyptian turquois* is obtained from the Sinai peninsula. Other localities for turquois are New South Wales, Queensland, Victoria, and Turkestan. In the United States important deposits of turquois of fine quality occur at Los Cerillos, New Mexico; Turquois Mountain, Arizona; San Bernardino County, California; and Nye County, Nevada.

FELDSPAR

The minerals known as the *feldspars* are very important as major constituents of igneous rocks. Much feldspar is opaque and unattractive, but certain varieties are of gem quality.

Orthoclase is monoclinic, whereas the other feldspars are triclinic. These minerals occur in good crystals (Figs. 351 and 352) or as cleavage masses. Twinning is very common (Figs. 353 and

354). There are excellent cleavages in two directions. The hardness is 6 to 6½, and the specific gravity 2.5 to 2.8. Feldspars are colorless, white, pale yellow, green, or reddish. They have a vitreous to pearly luster, and are transparent to opaque. The index of refraction β of the gem varieties varies from 1.524 to 1.563 (pp. 294 and 305). The double refraction is low, ranging from 0.008 to 0.011. Dispersion in the feldspars is also low, albite having the value of 0.012. All feldspars are biaxial, albite and labradorite being optically positive, and the others negative.

FIG. 351.—Orthoclase. Lincoln County, Nevada.

FIG. 352.—Orthoclase: Variety, sanidine. Fort Bayard, New Mexico.

FIG. 353.   FIG. 354.

FIGS. 353 and 354.—Orthoclase (left and right Karlsbad twins). Fort Bayard, New Mexico.

The composition is as follows: *orthoclase,* monoclinic, and *microcline,* triclinic ($KAlSi_3O_8$), potassium aluminum silicate; *albite,* triclinic ($NaAlSi_3O_8$), sodium aluminum silicate; *anorthite,* triclinic ($CaAl_2Si_2O_8$), calcium aluminum silicate; *oligoclase,* and *labradorite,* also triclinic, are intermediate in composition between albite and anorthite, and with them form a continuous series, called the *plagioclase feldspars.* The feldspars occur in igneous and metamorphic rocks.

The common gem varieties of orthoclase are transparent to translucent. They are called *adularia* or, when opalescent, *moonstone.* Moonstone varieties of albite and oligoclase also occur. Moonstones are cut cabochon. They occur at St. Gothard, Switzerland, and in Elba, Ceylon, and Burma. An interesting transparent yellow orthoclase, which is very attractive when faceted, occurs in Madagascar.

The bright-green variety of microcline is called *amazonstone* or *amazonite* (Fig. 355). It is usually cut cabochon because of its pleasing color, which resembles that of jade. It is used in brooches and pendants. Localities are the Ural Mountains; Pennsylvania; Virginia; and Pikes Peak, Colorado.

Sunstone or *aventurine oligoclase* is of a reddish color, with bright-yellow or red reflections from included crystals of iron oxide. The principal localities are Norway and Siberia.

Labradorite is characterized by a beautiful play of colors (p. 46) in blue and green and less often in yellow, red, or gray. This attractive effect is perhaps caused by fine microscopic inclusions or by repeated twinning. The mineral takes its name from the most important locality, Labrador. A similar play of color is shown by *peristerite*, a variety of albite. Attractive peristerite occurs in Ontario and Quebec, Canada, and Madagascar.

FIG. 355.—Microcline: Variety, amazonstone. Pikes Peak, Colorado.

LAZURITE (Lapis lazuli)

This mineral is often called *lapis lazuli* or simply *lapis*. By ancient peoples it was known as sapphire. Lazurite has long been used for mosaics, inlaid work, vases, and other ornamental objects. It is also cut cabochon for jewelry. Beads of lazurite are popular at present. The mineral was formerly ground for use as a blue pigment called *ultramarine*, but artificial ultramarine has now replaced the natural pigment. The material used for gem and ornamental purposes is a mixture of a number of minerals, the most prominent constituent being lazurite, which gives it the deep-blue color. The others are hauynite, diopside, amphibole, mica, calcite, and pyrite. Lapis lazuli has a hardness of 5 to 5½. The specific gravity varies from 2.4 to 2.95; for the more homogeneous types, 2.4 to 2.5; for the material commonly used for gem purposes, 2.64 to 2.95. The higher specific gravity is due to the presence of larger amounts of pyrite. The mineral is deep blue, azure blue, Berlin blue, or greenish blue. The luster is vitreous to greasy. It is opaque to translucent. Lazurite has the formula $(Na_2,Ca)_2Al_2[Al(NaSO_4,NaS_3,Cl)](SiO_4)_3$, being a sodium, calcium, and aluminum sulfo- and chlorosilicate. The mineral is cubic and isotropic, with an index of refraction of about 1.50. The yellow metallic mineral pyrite is a characteristic disseminated associate of lazurite. Its presence adds to the attractiveness of the mineral and is an aid in its identification.

Lapis lazuli may be imitated by blue glass or by stained quartz or jasper (Swiss lapis, p. 142). Two other minerals, sodalite (p. 264) and lazulite (p. 259), have a similar appearance. Lazurite occurs in the province of Badakshan, Afghanistan; at the southern end of Lake Baikal, Siberia; in Ovalle, Chile; and in San Bernardino County, California.

ANATASE

Transparent brown anatase is occasionally cut for gem purposes. This mineral is also called *octahedrite*. It is tetragonal, the crystals being of an octahedral habit. The hardness is 5½ to 6; the specific gravity, 3.8 to 4.0. Anatase is brown to black, and varies from transparent to nearly opaque. The luster is adamantine. It has high indices of refraction, ω 2.554, ϵ 2.493, and a strong double refraction, 0.061. The mineral is optically negative. Anatase has the composition TiO_2, titanium oxide. Rutile, a mineral frequent as inclusions in quartz (p. 223), has the same formula. Transparent crystals of anatase occur in Burke County, North Carolina. Other important localities are Cornwall, England; France; Germany; Switzerland; and Brazil.

ANDALUSITE

This mineral occurs in large orthorhombic crystals. Its hardness is 7 to 7½, and the specific gravity is 3.1 to 3.2. Andalusite

Fig. 356.—Andalusite: Variety, chiastolite. Lancaster, Massachusetts.

may be gray, green, yellow-green, bottle green, brown, pink, red, or violet in color. Often the colors are mixed. It has a vitreous to dull luster, and is transparent to opaque. The pleochroism is sometimes strong in green and red, yellow, or brown. The indices of refraction are α 1.634, β 1.639, γ 1.643. Andalusite has a negative optical character. The composition of andalusite is Al_2SiO_5, aluminum silicate. Cut stones of brown or green andalusite are difficult to distinguish from tourmaline and apatite of the same color. Andalusite is usually cut in the step fashion. Important localities are the province of Andalusia, Spain, from which the mineral takes its name, and also Ceylon and Brazil.

Chiastolite is a variety of andalusite containing black carbonaceous inclusions. These usually have a definite arrangement, resembling a cross (Fig. 356). Chiastolite is cut cabochon.

APATITE

Attractive gems are cut from this mineral. There are several varieties of apatite, which differ widely in appearance, but the

FIG. 357.　　　　　　FIG. 358.

FIGS. 357 and 358.—Apatite crystals—prismatic, fused edges and corners, tabular.

material used for gem purposes is usually found in well-developed hexagonal crystals (Figs. 357 and 358). It has a hardness of 5 and hence is quite soft. The specific gravity is 3.1 to 3.2. Gem apatite may be colorless, yellow, green, pink, blue, purple, or violet. Blue-green apatite is called *moroxite,* and the yellow-green *asparagus stone.* The gem varieties are transparent. Apatite has a vitreous to greasy luster. The indices of refraction are ω 1.649, ϵ 1.644. The double refraction is 0.005, which is very low. The mineral has a negative optical character. Apatite has the formula $Ca_5(F,Cl)(PO_4)_3$, being a calcium fluoro- or chlorophosphate. It occurs in many rocks, but crystals are found principally in pegmatites and in other igneous and metamorphic rocks.

Gem localities are Ehrenfriedersdorf and Schlaggenwald, Germany; St. Gothard, Switzerland; Ceylon; Cerro de Mercado, Mexico; and Auburn, Maine.

AXINITE

This is not an important gem mineral. It occurs in wedge-shaped triclinic crystals. The hardness is 6½ to 7. It has a specific gravity of 3.3. Axinite is brown, yellow-brown, or violet. It has a vitreous luster, and is transparent to translucent. The indices of refraction are α 1.678, β 1.685, γ 1.688. Axinite has a negative optical character. It is a borosilicate of iron, calcium, and aluminum, with the formula $(Ca,Fe)_7Al_4B_2(SiO_4)_8$. The most important localities are Le Bourg d'Oisans, Dauphiné, France, and San Diego County, California.

AZURITE AND MALACHITE

These are two brightly colored minerals, blue and green, respectively. They are not very durable when used for personal

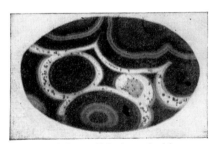

FIG. 359.—Polished malachite.   FIG. 360.—Malachite (polished). Rhodesia, Africa.

adornment, but are extensively employed in the fashioning of ornamental objects, for example, table tops and vases. Malachite, especially, is much used for this purpose. Malachite and azurmalachite find some use as pins, shirt buttons, and other similar articles.

Both azurite and malachite are monoclinic. Azurite is often well crystallized. Malachite, however, usually occurs in rounded masses with a radial fibrous or banded structure, which is very attractive in polished specimens (Figs. 359 to 361). Their hardness is 3½; their specific gravity, 3.7 to 4.0. Malachite is emerald green to grass green; azurite, light azure to deep blue. The streaks are lighter shades of the same colors. These minerals are translucent to opaque, with a silky, vitreous, adamantine, or dull luster. The indices of refraction of azurite are α 1.730, β 1.758, γ 1.838; for malachite α 1.655, β 1.875, γ 1.909. The double refraction is strong, 0.108 for azurite, 0.254 for malachite. Azurite

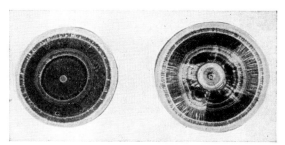

FIG. 361.—Polished sections of malachite with concentric structure. Bisbee, Arizona. (Natural size.)

is optically positive; malachite, negative. The formulas are azurite, $2CuCO_3.Cu(OH)_2$; malachite, $CuCO_3.Cu(OH)_2$, both being copper carbonates.

Malachite matrix is the term applied to polished specimens containing some of the gangue minerals. When azurite and malachite are intimately associated, as frequently is the case, the material is called *azurmalachite*. Azurite and malachite are the alteration products of other copper minerals. Azurite has a tendency to alter gradually into the more stable malachite. These minerals occur in the Ural Mountains; Rhodesia; Chile; Bisbee and Clifton, Arizona; the Belgian Congo; and Australia.

BENITOITE

This mineral was discovered in 1907, in San Benito County, California, the only known locality. Crystallographically, benitoite is of special interest, as it is a representative of the ditrigonal bipyramidal class of the hexagonal system. Previous to 1907 the existence of this class was a matter of mathematical deduction from the principles of symmetry, the validity of which was strikingly confirmed by the discovery of benitoite. Because of its deep-blue color it greatly resembles the sapphire, from which it is easily distinguished, however, through its inferior hardness and optical properties.

The hardness of benitoite is $6\frac{1}{2}$. Its specific gravity is 3.65. Benitoite has a pale- to deep-blue color, such as is caused by trivalent titanium. The luster is vitreous. Benitoite is transparent. It has strong pleochroism, white for the ordinary and blue for the extraordinary ray, so that the stone should be cut with the table parallel to the vertical axis. The indices of refraction are high, ω 1.757, and ϵ 1.804. The double refraction is strong, 0.047. It is optically positive. Benitoite is cut brilliant, sometimes cabochon. The formula for benitoite may be most simply given as $BaTiSi_3O_9$; that is, it is a silicate containing titanium and barium.

BERYLLONITE

This mineral is but little used as a gem. It is orthorhombic. The hardness is $5\frac{1}{2}$ to 6, and the specific gravity is 2.85. Beryllonite is transparent and colorless to pale yellow. It has a vitreous luster. The indices of refraction are α 1.552, β 1.558, γ 1.561. The mineral is optically negative. It is a sodium beryllium phosphate, $NaBePO_4$. Beryllonite is found in veins in granite at Stoneham, Maine. It is distinguished only with difficulty from other colorless gems with low indices of refraction.

BRAZILIANITE

This new gem mineral was described by F. H. Pough and E. P. Henderson in 1945. It occurs in large monoclinic crystals with a perfect side pinacoidal cleavage. The hardness is $5\frac{1}{2}$; the specific gravity, 2.94. It is translucent to transparent, has a vitreous luster, and is yellow-green in color. The indices of refraction are α 1.598, β 1.605, γ 1.617. The double refraction is 0.019. Brazilianite is optically positive. It is a sodium aluminum phosphate, $Na_2Al_6P_4O_{16}(OH)_8$. It occurs in altered pegmatite near

Conselheira Pena, Bahia, Brazil. In color brazilianite resembles chrysoberyl and yellow beryl, but is much softer than these minerals.

CALCITE

This is one of the most common minerals and occurs in a great diversity of crystal forms of the hexagonal system. It also occurs in extensive massive deposits, which are widely distributed.

The hardness of calcite is 3; the specific gravity, 2.72. The indices of refraction are ω 1.658, ϵ 1.486. The double refraction is strong, 0.172, and the mineral is optically negative. Calcite is calcium carbonate, $CaCO_3$, often very pure.

Three varieties of calcite are used for gem, ornamental, or decorative purposes.

Satin Spar.—This is a white, reddish, bluish, or greenish, fibrous calcite with a pronounced sheen or chatoyancy. It is transparent to translucent, and is frequently cut cabochon or as beads, especially in Europe. The term satin spar is also applied to fibrous gypsum (p. 256), calcium sulfate, $CaSO_4.2H_2O$, which is softer (hardness 2). These satin spars can be readily distinguished by their differences in hardness and composition. The calcite variety effervesces with dilute hydrochloric acid, while the gypsum satin spar does not.

Marble.—Compact masses of crystalline calcite, usually the result of the action of metamorphism on limestone (p. 97), are termed marble. There are many kinds of marble, which possess different colors, often irregularly distributed in streaks or patches. Marble takes a good polish and is extensively used for ornamental, decorative, or statuary purposes. The names given to the various marbles may indicate the source, character, or some peculiar characteristic, as *Vermont marble, shell marble,* or *brecciated marble.*

Mexican Onyx.—This is a translucent, banded variety of calcite. It generally possesses colors suitable for ornamental and decorative purposes, and is frequently called *onyx marble.* It is sometimes colored artificially, for example, green, and improperly sold as *Mexican jade.* Mexican onyx must not be confused with true onyx, a variety of quartz (p. 227), from which it is easily distinguished by the marked difference in hardness and composition.

CASSITERITE

Transparent cassiterite is rare but is sometimes used as a gem. It is tetragonal. The crystals are prismatic and pyramidal and

often twinned. Cassiterite also occurs in massive forms. The hardness is 6 to 7, the specific gravity, 6.8 to 7.1. It has a brown, reddish-brown, black, or yellow color. Cassiterite is transparent to opaque, with an adamantine luster. The in-

FIG. 362.—Cassiterite with fluorite. Saxony.

dices of refraction are ω 1.997, ϵ 2.093. It is optically positive. The double refraction is very strong, 0.096. Cassiterite is SnO_2, tin oxide. It is the chief ore of tin. Good crystals occur in Cornwall, England; Germany; and Bolivia (Fig. 362).

CHLORASTROLITE

This is a greenish, fibrous mineral occurring in small round or irregular aggregates in the basic igneous rocks in the vicinity

FIG. 363.—Chlorastrolite—"Green stone." Isle Royale, Lake Superior. (Two-thirds natural size.)

of Lake Superior. Especially fine specimens have been found on Isle Royale. The chlorastrolite weathers out along the shore of the lake and is found in smooth, rounded pebbles of various sizes. This mineral is closely related to prehnite (p. 261). It depends upon its chatoyancy and unique markings in white and dark green for its attractiveness (Fig. 363). Chlorastrolite is especially popular in the region around Lake Superior. The hardness is 5 to 6; the specific gravity, 3.2. The gem is cut cabochon, and worn in brooches, pins, or occasionally rings.

CHRYSOCOLLA

This is a colored copper mineral which is occasionally used for ornamental purposes or cut as charms or pendants. It is apparently amorphous, occurring in compact or earthy masses, veins, or crusts. The hardness is 2 to 4; the specific gravity, 2.0 to 2.2. The mineral occurs in various shades of green and blue. It is translucent to opaque, with a vitreous, greasy, or dull luster. The indices of refraction vary, ω 1.46$\pm$, ϵ 1.57$\pm$. Chrysocolla is optically positive. It is a hydrous copper silicate, with an indefinite composition. Chrysocolla is formed by the alteration of other copper minerals, and is found in the Ural Mountains, Chile, Arizona, and Nevada.

FIG. 364.—Cyanite (bladed). Litchfield, Connecticut.

CYANITE

The name of this mineral is also spelled *kyanite*. Cyanite occurs in bladed triclinic crystals (Fig. 364), the hardness of which varies greatly with direction, ranging from 4 to 7 (p. 29). The specific gravity is 3.5 to 3.7. This mineral is light to sky blue or white, gray, green, brown, or colorless. The color is usually irregularly distributed. Cyanite has a vitreous luster and is transparent to translucent. It is biaxial, with a negative optical character. The indices of refraction are α 1.712, β 1.720, γ 1.728. Cyanite has the formula Al_2SiO_5, aluminum silicate. In this respect it is identical with andalusite. Cyanite occurs in metamorphic rocks, commonly associated with staurolite and garnet. Important localities are St. Gothard, Switzerland; the

Tyrol; Brazil; India; Massachusetts; Pennsylvania; North Carolina. When clear and of good color cyanite may be cut to advantage.

DANBURITE

Crystals of this orthorhombic mineral, which may be colorless or yellow, resemble those of topaz. However, in contrast to topaz it lacks the basal cleavage; is softer, hardness 7; and is lighter in weight, specific gravity 3. The indices of refraction are α 1.630, β 1.633, γ 1.636. The composition is $CaB_2Si_2O_8$, calcium borosilicate. Danburite is not a common gem mineral. The principal localities are Danbury, Connecticut; Mogok, Burma; Japan; Madagascar; and Switzerland.

DATOLITE

This mineral occurs both in glassy monoclinic crystals, often with many faces, and in compact, opaque masses, with a dull luster, and resembling unglazed porcelain. The latter variety

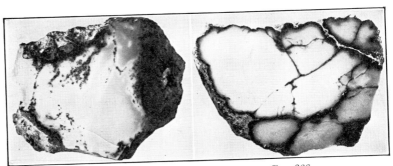

FIG. 365.   FIG. 366.

FIGS. 365 and 366.—Polished sections of massive datolite. Franklin mine, Lake Superior copper district. (One-third natural size.)

is found in the Lake Superior copper district, and frequently contains native copper inclusions (Fig. 365). The color of massive datolite is white, yellowish, reddish, greenish, or brownish, and often mottled. This material is very attractive when polished (Figs. 365 and 366) and is used for ornamental purposes, or cut cabochon for brooches or pins. Datolite has a hardness of 5 to 5½ and a specific gravity of 2.9 to 3.0. It is biaxial, and has a negative optical character. The indices of refraction are α 1.626, β 1.654, γ 1.670. The double refraction is strong, 0.044. Datolite is a calcium borosilicate, $Ca(B.OH)SiO_4$.

DIOPSIDE

Transparent diopside of a pleasing green color is sometimes used as a gem. It is monoclinic and occurs in well-developed crystals. There is a good prismatic cleavage, as well as a basal parting. The hardness is 5 to 6, and the specific gravity is 3.2 to 3.3. Diopside is light to dark green, colorless, gray, or yellow. The color is often zonally distributed (Fig. 367). It has a vitreous to resinous or dull luster, and is transparent to opaque. The index of refraction β varies from 1.671 to 1.708. Diopside has strong double refraction. It is biaxial and optically positive. The

FIG. 367.—Diopside with zonal distribution of color. Ala, Italy.

formula is $CaMg(SiO_3)_2$, calcium magnesium silicate. Other names are *malacolite* and *alalite*. Diopside occurs in metamorphosed limestones, much of the best material coming from the Ala Valley, Piedmont, Italy; the Tyrol; Renfrew County, Ontario; and New York. Diopside occurs as an associate of the diamond in the mines of South Africa and is sometimes cut as a gem. *Violan* is a variety with a fine blue color, from St. Marcel, Piedmont, Italy.

DIOPTASE

This beautiful green mineral, which strikingly resembles the emerald, is quite rare. It crystallizes in the hexagonal system and exhibits some uncommon crystal faces. It possesses a rhombohedral cleavage which often produces an internal pearly luster. The fracture is conchoidal to uneven. The hardness is 5; hence, the mineral is used to best advantage in pins and brooches. The specific gravity is 3.3. The indices of refraction are ω 1.655,

ϵ 1.708. It is a copper mineral, H_2CuSiO_4, and has been called *copper emerald*. Excellent crystals have been obtained from the Kirghiz Steppes, Russia; the French Congo; the Belgian Congo; Chile; and Clifton, Graham County, Arizona.

ENSTATITE, BRONZITE, AND HYPERSTHENE

These closely related minerals have occasionally been cut for gem purposes. Bronzite is a variety of enstatite. Bronzite, which is fibrous, has a pleasing chatoyant bronzy luster. Hypersthene is sometimes cut cabochon because of its metalloidal iridescence. The minerals are orthorhombic members of the pyroxene group and usually occur in fibrous, platy, or compact masses. They have prismatic and pinacoidal cleavages. The hardness is 5 to 6; the specific gravity, 3.1 to 3.5. In color they are grayish white, greenish, yellowish, and brown to black, enstatite being the lightest and hypersthene the darkest. The luster is vitreous, bronzy, or pearly. These minerals are translucent to opaque. For enstatite the index of refraction β varies from 1.653 to 1.670; for hypersthene, 1.678 to 1.728. Both are biaxial; enstatite is generally optically positive and hypersthene negative. The general formula for these minerals is $(Mg,Fe)_2(SiO_3)_2$. Hypersthene contains more iron than enstatite.

EPIDOTE

The distinctive pistachio-green color of epidote, also called *pistacite,* does not have a wide appeal, though the mineral is not

uncommonly cut. Epidote is monoclinic, occurring in excellent prismatic crystals (Fig. 368) or in fibrous aggregates or granular masses. It has a basal cleavage. The hardness is 6 to 7; the specific gravity, 3.3 to 3.5. Epidote is yellowish to blackish green, pistachio green, or more rarely colorless or brown. In manganiferous varieties the color may be red. (See Thulite, p. 270.) The luster is vitreous to resin-

FIG. 368.—Epidote.   Untersulzbach-thal, Tyrol.

ous. Epidote is transparent to opaque. The index of refraction β varies from 1.719 to 1.763. The double refraction and dispersion are both strong. The mineral is biaxial with a negative optical character. The pleochroism is marked, in yellow, green, and brown. The formula is $Ca_2(Al,Fe)_2(Al.OH)(SiO_4)_3$, calcium, iron, and aluminum silicate. Epidote occurs in metamorphic rocks. Localities yielding good crystals are Tyrol; Piedmont, Italy; Elba; Dauphiné, France; Arendal, Norway; and Prince of Wales Island, Alaska.

EUCLASE

Largely because of its rarity, euclase is not well known as a gem. It is monoclinic, occurring in prismatic crystals. Euclase has an excellent pinacoidal cleavage. The hardness is 7½; the specific gravity, 3.1. It is colorless when pure, but is usually pale green, sea green, or blue, resembling aquamarine. The luster is vitreous, and the mineral is transparent. Euclase is biaxial and optically positive. The indices are α 1.653, β 1.656, γ 1.673. It is a beryllium aluminum silicate, with the formula $Be(Al.OH)SiO_4$. It occurs in metamorphic rocks, with topaz, beryl, and chrysoberyl, the principal localities being the Ural Mountains and Minas Geraes, Brazil.

FLUORITE

This mineral, also known as *fluorspar*, occurs in excellent crystals of the cubic system (Fig. 369). These are frequently twinned

FIG. 369.—Fluorite. Cumberland, England.

FIG. 370.—Fluorite (penetration cubes). Durham, Weardale, England.

in the form of interpenetrating cubes (Fig. 370). It is also cleavable, granular, or fibrous. The cleavage is perfect octahedral (Fig. 371). The hardness is inferior, being only 4. The specific gravity is 3.1 to 3.2. It is the color which makes fluorite attractive, and, like quartz, this mineral exhibits nearly every hue, yellow, orange, green, blue, red, violet, pink, or brown. It may also be colorless. Frequently fluorite is mottled or multi-colored. Fluorite is transparent to opaque, has a vitreous luster, and is

FIG. 371.—Fluorite (octahedral cleavage). Near Rosiclare, Illinois.

FIG. 372.—Fluorite dish. Derbyshire, England. (Four-fifths natural size.)

often fluorescent and phosphorescent. It is isotropic, with an index of refraction of 1.434. The dispersion is very low, 0.006. The composition is CaF_2, calcium fluoride. Fluorite is much used for vases, paperweights, and other similar articles (Fig. 372). Because of its easy and perfect octahedral cleavage, it is easily shattered, and great care must be exercised in cutting and handling it. It occurs in veins and in pegmatites and other rocks. The best material is found in England, in Derbyshire, the source of the deep-purple and fibrous *blue john,* and in Cumberland, Cornwall, Devonshire, and Durham. Other localities are Australia, South-West Africa, New York, and Illinois.

GYPSUM

The satin spar and alabaster varieties of gypsum are of importance as ornamental stones. Satin spar is also used in cheap jewelry. Gypsum is monoclinic, with a perfect pinacoidal cleavage, yielding thin sheets. It is very soft, having a hardness of 2. The specific gravity is 2.2 to 2.4. It is usually colorless or white, and also gray, yellow, brown, reddish, or black. Gypsum is transparent to opaque. The luster is subvitreous, pearly, silky, or dull. Gypsum is biaxial and optically positive. The indices

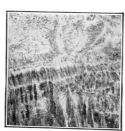

Fig. 373.—Gypsum (polished). Grand Rapids, Michigan.

Fig. 374.—Gypsum. Variety, satin spar. Montmartre, Paris, France.

of refraction are α 1.520, β 1.523, γ 1.530. The composition is $CaSO_4.2H_2O$, hydrated calcium sulfate.

Massive gypsum will take a good polish (Fig. 373). *Selenite* occurs in colorless, transparent crystals or cleavage masses. The crystals are often twinned, and may be very large. *Satin spar* is a chatoyant, fibrous variety with a silky luster (Fig. 374). This variety is cut cabochon (Fig. 375) or as beads, although

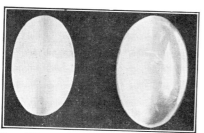

Fig. 375.—Gypsum. Variety, satin spar. Cut cabochon. (Natural size.)

Fig. 376.—Alabaster vase. Grand Rapids, Michigan. (One-third natural size.)

it is so very soft that it loses its polish and luster quickly. Important localities are England and Russia. Necklaces and trinkets of satin spar are cut, polished, and sold in considerable quantities at Niagara Falls, New York, and locally are called *Niagara spar* or *Falls spar*. *Alabaster* is a fine-grained, massive variety, usually snow white in color, easily carved and therefore used for statuary and decorative purposes or for many ornamental objects (Figs. 376 and 377). It is often colored artificially. Florence, Leghorn, and Milan, Italy; and Berlin, Germany, are important centers

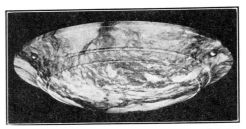

Fɪɢ. 377.—Alabaster bowl for indirect lighting fixture.

for the carving of alabaster objects. Alabaster of ornamental quality occurs in Michigan, Tennessee, Colorado, and Nova Scotia.

IOLITE

This stone is also known as *cordierite,* or *dichroite* because of its pleochroism. It is not much used as a gem, and when cut it is rarely faceted. The most interesting property is the very strong pleochroism in dark blue, light blue, and yellowish white. This variation of color in different directions is distinctly evident to the unaided eye. Iolite is orthorhombic, but is usually found in massive forms. The hardness is 7 to $7\frac{1}{2}$; the specific gravity, 2.6. The mineral has a dark smoky-blue to light-blue color. It is transparent to translucent, with a vitreous luster. Iolite greatly resembles quartz. It is biaxial and optically negative. The index of refraction β is variable, from 1.538 to 1.597. The double refraction is low, 0.008. The formula is $(Mg,Fe)_4Al_8(OH)_2(Si_2O_7)_5$, that is, magnesium, iron, and aluminum silicate. Iolite occurs in metamorphic rocks and stream gravels. Ceylon is the most important locality, and the gems from that country have sometimes been called *saphir d'eau* or "water sapphire."

LAZULITE

This mineral is sometimes mistaken for lazurite (p. 243), which it closely resembles in outward appearance, although quite different in composition. Lazulite is monoclinic, occurring in pyramidal crystals. It may also be massive or granular. It has a hardness of 5 to 6, and the specific gravity is 3.1. In color it is azure blue. The luster is vitreous. Lazulite is translucent to opaque. The indices of refraction are α 1.612, β 1.634, γ 1.643. The mineral is biaxial, and optically negative. It is pleochroic. In composition lazulite is a basic iron, magnesium, and aluminum phosphate, $(Fe,Mg)Al_2(OH)_2(PO_4)_2$. It occurs near Salzburg, Austria, and in North Carolina and Georgia.

MOLDAVITE

Several natural glasses are sufficiently important to warrant brief descriptions. They are moldavite or tektite, silica glass, and obsidian (p. 260). They are similar to ordinary glass, being amorphous and hence isotropic, transparent to translucent, and breaking with a conchoidal fracture and sharp edges.

Moldavite, also called *tektite,* resembles ordinary green bottle glass. This is a natural glass which is probably of meteoric origin. It is commonly bottle green to greenish brown in color, but may be nearly colorless or black and then opaque. The silica content varies from 70 to 77 per cent. The hardness is 5½, specific gravity 2.3 to 2.5, and index of refraction 1.48 to 1.52. It occurs as loose, rounded fragments on or near the surface in the Moldau River district in Moravia and also in Czecho-Slovakia, the East Indies, and Australia. This glass is sometimes called *bottle stone* or *water chrysolite.*

In the Libyan Desert lumps of natural and nearly pure *silica glass,* weighing up to 10 pounds, have been found. This glass consists of nearly 98 per cent silica. It is pale yellowish green in color. The index of refraction is 1.462, specific gravity 2.21, and hardness 6. The origin of this natural glass is uncertain. Because of its unfavorable optical properties, cut stones are not very attractive.

OBSIDIAN

When acid magmas or lava flows cool quickly, a volcanic glass, called obsidian, frequently is formed which contains 66 to 77 per cent of silica. Obsidian may be spotted or may show a striated structure. Under the microscope, minute crystals may be observed, due to devitrification, which sometimes produce a shimmer or chatoyancy.

The color of obsidian is variable. It is usually black, but is lighter in thin fragments; it also is red, brown, or greenish, and often is variegated. It is transparent to translucent. The index of refraction varies from 1.48 to 1.65; the specific gravity, from 2.3 to 3. The lower values apply to true obsidians, that is, to those formed from acid magmas or lavas, and the higher ones to those resulting from basic lava flows and properly called *tachylytes* (p. 95). The hardness is 5½.

Obsidians with attractive colors, such as leaf green, and those which are variegated or transparent are cut as gems. Primitive peoples have long used obsidian for ornamental purposes and for shaping into spear- and arrowheads and various implements. It is widely distributed. Important deposits of obsidian occur in Mexico, Greece, Iceland, California, Oregon, Yellowstone National Park, and Wyoming.

PHENACITE

Although brilliant, phenacite has little fire and is but little used as a gem. It occurs in well-formed hexagonal crystals. The hardness is 7½ to 8, and the specific gravity is 3.0. Phenacite is colorless, yellowish, or pale rose red. It is transparent to translucent with a vitreous luster. The mineral is uniaxial with a positive optical character. The indices are ω 1.654, ϵ 1.670. Phenacite has the formula Be_2SiO_4, beryllium silicate. It occurs in pegmatites and metamorphic rocks, and is very similar in appearance to quartz and topaz, which occur in the same rocks. Localities are near Sverdlovsk in the Ural Mountains; Minas Geraes, Brazil; Durango, Mexico; Stoneham, Maine; and Colorado.

PREHNITE

This mineral is sometimes used as a gem, especially when of an oil-green color. Prehnite is orthorhombic, but it is rarely found in distinct crystals, usually occurring in rounded masses. The hardness is 6 to 6½; the specific gravity, 2.8 to 3.0. Prehnite may be colorless or white, but it is generally light green, apple green, oil green, or yellowish green. It has a waxy vitreous luster, and is transparent to translucent. Prehnite is biaxial and optically positive. The indices are α 1.615, β 1.625, γ 1.645; double refraction is strong. The mineral is a calcium aluminum silicate with the formula $H_2Ca_2Al_2(SiO_4)_3$. It occurs in veins and cavities in the more basic igneous rocks, with datolite. Dauphiné, France; the Lake Superior district; and New Jersey are important localities. Chlorastrolite (p. 251) is a closely related gemstone.

RHODONITE

This pink or red mineral polishes well and is used as an ornamental stone, especially in Russia. It is occasionally cut cabochon for use in pins or as beads or buttons. Rhodonite is triclinic, occurring in crystals or compact masses. Its hardness is 5½ to 6½; its specific gravity, 3.4 to 3.7. In color it is rose red or pink. It may also be yellowish, greenish, or brownish, easily changing to black owing to a superficial alteration to manganese oxides. The luster is vitreous to pearly. Rhodonite is transparent to opaque. The mineral is biaxial and optically negative. The index of refraction β varies from 1.720 to 1.740. The formula is $MnSiO_3$, manganese silicate. This mineral is not uncommon. The material used for ornamental purposes is obtained principally from the Ural Mountains, in the neighborhood of Sverdlovsk, but some rhodonite from Franklin, New Jersey, has been cut for gem purposes.

RUTILE

Although very dark in color, rutile is used to a slight extent as a gem. *Rutilated quartz* (p. 223) is a gem variety of quartz containing slender needles of rutile. Rutile is tetragonal, occurring in prismatic crystals, which are often striated and twinned (Fig. 378). The hardness is 6 to 6½; the specific gravity, 4.2 to 4.3.

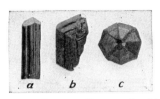

FIG. 378.—Rutile crystals. (*a*) Prismatic and striated. (*b*) Knee-shaped. (*c*) Rosette (eightling).

Its color is red-brown, blood red, or, in the variety *nigrine,* black. Rutile is opaque to transparent. It has a metallic adamantine luster, very high indices of refraction, ω 2.616 and ε 2.903, and strong double refraction, 0.287. Rutile is uniaxial and optically positive. It is titanium oxide, TiO_2 (see anatase, p. 244). Rutile occurs in Norway, Sweden, the Ural Mountains, Tyrol, Switzerland, France, and the United States; rutilated quartz in Madagascar, Switzerland, Brazil, Vermont, and North Carolina. Rutile is now made synthetically.

SEPIOLITE

Sepiolite, known in commerce as *meerschaum,* is easily carved and takes a fine polish. It was used extensively for pipe bowls and cigar holders. Sepiolite is monoclinic, but occurs only in earthy or compact nodular masses, with a conchoidal to earthy fracture (Fig. 379). The hardness is 2 to 2½; the specific gravity, 1 to 2. On account of its low specific gravity and its porosity, it may float upon water, and because of this fact, the mineral is called *meerschaum,* a German word, literally translated "sea foam." The color is white, yellowish,

FIG. 379.—Meerschaum. Grant County, New Mexico.

or grayish. The mineral is opaque and has a dull luster. It adheres to the tongue. Sepiolite is biaxial and optically negative. The indices of refraction are α 1.519, β 1.525±, γ 1.529. The formula is $H_4Mg_2Si_3O_{10}$, hydrated magnesium silicate. This mineral is derived from serpentine and magnesite, by their alteration.   Meerschaum is mined in Asia Minor, on the plains of Eskishehir.   Other localities are Greece, Spain, Moravia, Morocco, Pennsylvania, South Carolina, Utah, New Mexico, and California.

SERPENTINE

This mineral is employed for ornamental purposes, and is sometimes cut cabochon as a gem, though it is too soft for satisfactory use in this way.   Although it is monoclinic, serpentine is never found in crystals, but occurs in compact, fibrous, or platy

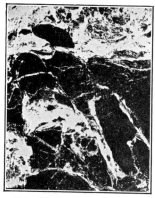

FIG. 380.—Serpentine. Variety, verd antique. Roxbury, Vermont.

FIG. 381.—Serpentine. Variety, asbestos. Near Globe, Arizona.

masses.   The hardness is $2\frac{1}{2}$ to 4; the specific gravity, 2.5 to 2.8. Serpentine occurs in various shades of green and is also yellowish, grayish, reddish, brownish, or black.   It is often spotted, clouded, or multi-colored.   The luster is dull, resinous, greasy, or waxy. It is translucent to opaque.   The feel is smooth to greasy.   The index of refraction β is variable, 1.512 to 1.550.   Serpentine is a hydrated magnesium silicate, $H_4Mg_3Si_2O_9$.   Iron and nickel may replace some magnesium.   This tends to give the mineral its characteristic green color.

Precious serpentine is translucent, massive, and of a uniform green or yellowish color.   *Bowenite* is a fine granular variety, green in color, and resembling jade (p. 231).   *Williamsite* has a blackish-green color.   *Verd antique* is a massive green serpentine, mottled or veined with white calcite, dolomite, or magnesite (Fig. 380). It is much employed as an ornamental stone for interior decoration. *Chrysotile* is a fibrous variety, and includes the asbestos used in the manufacture of heat-resisting materials (Fig. 381). Occasionally the fibrous serpentine is cut. Serpentine results from the alteration of other magnesian rocks or minerals. Localities are Sweden, Scotland, Silesia, Saxony, Rhode Island (bowenite), Vermont, Massachusetts, Pennsylvania (williamsite), and California.

SMITHSONITE

This mineral is usually rather unattractive in color. However, some specimens with a soft yellow, green, or blue color are cut cabochon, or are used for ornamentation. The mineral is hexagonal. Crystals are small and rough. Compact and stalactitic forms are more common. The hardness is 5; the specific gravity, 4.1 to 4.5. Smithsonite is colorless when pure, but it is usually gray or brown, sometimes white. It may also be yellow, owing to cadmium sulfide; pink, when cobaltiferous; and green or blue, owing to minute included particles of copper carbonates. Green smithsonite is sometimes cut and sold as *bonamite*. It has a vitreous to pearly luster, and is translucent to opaque. It is uniaxial and optically negative. The indices of refraction are ω 1.849, ϵ 1.621. The double refraction is high, 0.228. The formula is $ZnCO_3$, zinc carbonate. The mineral often contains small amounts of iron, manganese, cobalt, copper, and cadmium. Smithsonite is formed by the alteration of zinc sulfide, and much of it occurs in limestones and dolomites. The gem variety of smithsonite occurs at Laurium, Greece; Sardinia; Tsumeb, South-West Africa; Marion County, Arkansas; and Kelly, New Mexico.

SODALITE

Sodalite has a deep-blue color which is similar to that of lazurite, a mineral to which it is closely related (p. 243). Its properties vary but little from those of lazurite. Sodalite is cubic and hence isotropic. The hardness is 5 to 6, and the specific gravity varies from 2.2 to 2.4. The index of refraction is 1.483.

The composition of sodalite is sodium aluminum chlorosilicate, $Na_4Al_2(AlCl)(SiO_4)_3$. It is polished as an ornamental stone, or is sometimes cut cabochon. It is found in the Ural Mountains; on Mount Vesuvius; in Norway; in the provinces of Quebec and Ontario, Canada; and at Litchfield, Maine.

SPHALERITE

This common zinc sulfide, ZnS, occurs in excellent crystals of the cubic system, but is usually massive. Because of its easy and perfect rhombic dodecahedral cleavage, specimens, when being cut for gems, and even subsequently, must be handled with great care.

Sphalerite is relatively soft with a hardness of $3\frac{1}{2}$ to 4. The specific gravity is 3.9 to 4.0. The color varies greatly, from colorless, yellow, red, or green to black. Sphalerite is transparent to translucent, and has a resinous to adamantine luster. The index of refraction is very high, 2.37 for sodium light. The dispersion, 0.197, is unusually strong and is more than three times that of the diamond.

Even though sphalerite possesses many properties essential to gems, such as transparency, attractive colors, high index of refraction, and unusually strong dispersion, it is not much used as a gem, because of its softness and very easy cleavage. Moreover, material suitable for cutting is quite rare. Sphalerite is the chief ore of zinc and occurs in many localities.

SPODUMENE

Spodumene is ordinarily white, opaque, and unattractive, but two of its varieties are rather valuable as gems. These are *hiddenite,* with a yellow-green to emerald-green color, and *kunzite* (Fig. 382), with a delicate pink to lilac color. The colors may fade on exposure to light. Both varieties are transparent. Spodumene is monoclinic, occurring in crystals, sometimes of enormous dimensions (p. 12), and as tabular masses. It has perfect prismatic cleavage and pinacoidal parting. The hardness is 6 to 7; the specific gravity, 3.1 to 3.2. Spodumene in general is white, gray, green, pink, or, rarely, purple. The luster is vitreous to pearly. It is transparent to opaque. Spodumene is biaxial, and the optical character is positive. The indices of refraction are α 1.660, β 1.666, γ 1.676. The dispersion is 0.017. The colored varieties are pleochroic. The composition of spodumene is LiAl(SiO₃)₂, lithium aluminum silicate. On exposure to ultraviolet rays, X-rays, or radium, kunzite phosphoresces with an orange-pink light. Hiddenite is found at Stony Point, Alexander County, North Carolina, in pegmatites. The kunzite variety of spodumene occurs in pegmatites near Pala, California, and in Brazil and Madagascar. Yellowish, transparent crystals of spodumene come from Minas Geraes, Brazil.

FIG. 382.—Spodumene. Variety, kunzite. San Diego County, California.

STAUROLITE

This mineral is also known as *cross-stone* or *fairy-stone* because of the cross-shaped twins commonly formed by the crystals, which are orthorhombic (Fig. 383). It is of little value except as a curiosity. The twin crystals are polished and used as ornaments, as, for instance, crosses

FIG. 383.—Staurolite crystals. Simple; and plus- and X-shaped twins.

FIG. 384.   FIG. 385.

FIGS. 384 and 385.—Staurolite twin crystals, finished as watch charms.

worn by the clergy (Figs. 384 and 385). Their shape has caused the growth of legends assigning to them a supernatural origin. Staurolite has a hardness of 7 to 7½, which, owing to alteration, may be lower on the surface, and a specific gravity of 3.4 to 3.8. The color is usually reddish brown. The mineral is translucent to opaque, with a dull to vitreous luster. Staurolite is biaxial and optically positive. The indices of refraction are α 1.736, β 1.741, γ 1.746. The dispersion is 0.021. Staurolite shows some pleochroism. This mineral is an iron aluminum silicate,

FIG. 386.—Staurolite (dark) in paragonite schist. Tessin, Switzerland.

$HFeAl_5Si_2O_{13}$. It occurs in metamorphic rocks (Fig. 386), at St. Gothard, Switzerland, with cyanite; in Tyrol; in Brazil; and in Virginia (Figs. 383 to 385) and other eastern states.

STEATITE

The massive and sometimes quite impure variety of talc, $H_2Mg_3Si_4O_{12}$, is called steatite or *soapstone* because of its greasy or soapy feel. It is soft and readily cut with the knife and carved into images and ornaments. In color it is white to greenish or reddish, often streaked or mottled. The varieties that are translucent, at least at the thin edges, are preferred for carving purposes. The index of refraction varies from 1.54 to 1.59.

Agalmatolite is a term applied to some varieties of steatite and pinite. It is compact, has a waxy luster, and is grayish white, greenish, brownish, or reddish in color. It is easily carved into images or pagodas, and hence is often called *pagodite*.

The Chinese have long used these materials for carving purposes. Frequently the carved objects are waxed and polished to improve the luster.

THOMSONITE

When mottled in white, red, green, and yellow, thomsonite pebbles are frequently cut as gems. Eye markings—concentric bands of different colors—are especially popular. The mineral occurs in the basic igneous rocks of the Lake Superior district and, like chlorastrolite, is weathered out and is found as pebbles along the shores of the lake. The pebbles are cut cabochon and used in pins and brooches (Figs. 387 and 388). Their popularity is largely confined to the country about Lake Superior. Thomsonite is orthorhombic, occurring in crystals, compact masses, or spherical concretions. It has a hardness of 5 to 5½

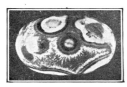

FIG. 387.—Thomsonite. Isle Royale, Lake Superior. (Natural size.)

FIG. 388.—Thomsonite. Isle Royale, Lake Superior. (Natural size.)

and a specific gravity of 2.3 to 2.4. The color is white, grayish, yellowish, brownish, and reddish; in the variety known as *lintonite* the color is greenish. Thomsonite is transparent to opaque, with a vitreous to pearly luster. Thomsonite is biaxial and optically positive. The index of refraction β varies from 1.513 to 1.531. It is a hydrated calcium, sodium, and aluminum silicate, $2(Ca,Na_2)Al_2(SiO_4)_2.5H_2O$.

TITANITE

Titanite or *sphene* makes a brilliant and attractive gem, but it is rather soft. It is usually faceted when cut. The mineral is monoclinic, the crystals often being wedge- or envelope-shaped

FIG. 389.—Titanite. Arendal, Norway.

(Fig. 389). It has a hardness of 5 to 5½ and a specific gravity of 3.4 to 3.6 When titanite is pure, its color is gray, but it is more often yellow, green, or brown. The luster is adamantine. The mineral is transparent to opaque. Titanite is biaxial, with a positive optical character. The indices of refraction are very high—α 1.900, β 1.907, γ 2.034. The double refraction is strong, 0.134, and the dispersion likewise is notable, 0.050. Because of the strong double refraction the apparent doubling of the back facets is readily observed. The formula is $CaTiSiO_5$, calcium titanium silicate. Titanite occurs in schists and limestone in Switzerland, at St. Gothard; in Ziller-thal, Tyrol, and many other European localities; in Madagascar; and in Maine, New York, and Pennsylvania.

VARISCITE

Being somewhat like turquois in appearance, variscite is some-times used in its place. The properties of the two minerals, however, are entirely different. Variscite is orthorhombic, and occurs in crusts, rounded nodules, or crystalline aggregates. It has a hardness of 4 to 5. The specific gravity is 2.5. The color, apple green to blue-green, is due to chromium or vanadium. The luster is vitreous, and the mineral is translucent to opaque. Variscite is biaxial and optically negative. The index of refrac-tion β varies from 1.571 to 1.584. Variscite is a hydrated alumi-num phosphate, $AlPO_4.2H_2O$.

Variscite occurs in shales or slates. Important localities are Lucin, Utah, and in Tooele and Utah counties in the same state. The name *utahlite* is given to the compact variety.

VESUVIANITE

Another name for this mineral is *idocrase*. A compact green variety is called *californite,* which resembles jade (p. 231). *Cyprine* is a blue variety, containing cop-per. Vesuvianite occurs in pris-matic tetragonal crystals (Fig. 390) and in compact masses. Its hardness is 6½; its specific grav-ity, 3.3 to 3.5. Vesuvianite oc-curs in various shades of yellow, green, or brown or, more rarely, blue, red, or nearly black. It is translucent, with a vitreous or greasy luster. Vesuvianite is uni-axial and usually negative in op-

Fig. 390.—Vesuvianite. (*a*) Wilui River, Siberia. (*b*) Achmatovsk, Russia.

tical character. The indices are approximately ω 1.713, ϵ 1.705. It has weak pleochroism. The composition is calcium aluminum silicate, $Ca_6[Al(OH,F)]Al_2(SiO_4)_5$. Cut stones resemble diopside and epidote, but they can be distinguished by their optical properties. Vesuvianite is a contact metamorphic mineral. Localities are Mount Vesuvius, from which the name is derived; Wilui River, Siberia, for the variety *wiluite;* Eger, Germany, for *egeran;* Telemarke, Norway, for *cyprine,* and California, from which the name *californite* is derived.

WILLEMITE

Although transparent willemite is not common, it has occasionally been cut in the brilliant style for use as a gem. Willemite is hexagonal, occurring in small crystals or granular masses. It has a hardness of 5 to 6, and the specific gravity is 3.9 to 4.3. The color is yellow, green, brown, or reddish or, more rarely, colorless, white, blue, or black. It is transparent to opaque, and has a greasy, vitreous luster. Willemite is uniaxial and optically positive. The indices of refraction are ω 1.691, ϵ 1.719. It is a zinc silicate, Zn_2SiO_4. Willemite of gem quality is found only at Franklin, New Jersey.

ZOISITE

This is a calcium aluminum silicate belonging to the epidote group. It crystallizes in the orthorhombic system. Its color is

FIG. 391.—Zoisite.   Variety, thulite.   Norway.

gray, greenish, or red. The other properties are practically the same as for epidote (p. 254). The index of refraction β is 1.703. The rose-red, strongly pleochroic variety, colored by manganese, is *thulite* (Fig. 391). It is used for ornamental objects or cut cabochon. Thulite occurs in Norway and in Piedmont, Italy.

CHROMITE

Chromite, which is black and opaque, somewhat resembles jet (p. 283), and is occasionally cut as beads. Chromite, however, is much heavier than jet, a fact which allows the two minerals to be readily distinguished. Chromite is cubic. It occurs granular or massive or in octahedral crystals. Its hardness is 5½; its specific gravity, 4.3 to 4.6. Chromite has an iron-black to brownish-black color. The streak is pale brown. Its luster is pitchy submetallic to metallic. The mineral is opaque. Chromite has the formula $(Fe,Cr)[(Cr,Fe)O_2]_2$, ferrite of iron containing chromium. Localities are New Zealand, New Caledonia, Rhodesia, Asiatic Turkey, Silesia, Cuba, Pennsylvania, and Maryland.

COBALTITE

Cobaltite is sometimes cut as a gem. It may resemble pyrite, but inclines toward a slightly pinkish rather than yellow color. Cobaltite is cubic and well crystallized. Its hardness is 5½; its specific gravity, 6.0 to 6.4. The color is silver-white, often with a reddish tinge. The mineral has a grayish-black streak, and is opaque, with a metallic luster. Its formula is $CoAsS$, cobalt and arsenic sulfide. Sweden; Norway; Cornwall, England; and the Cobalt district in Ontario are localities.

FIG. 392.—Gold in quartz. Tuolumne County, California.

GOLD

Native gold, alone as crystals or nuggets, or in white quartz (Fig. 392), is frequently worn in pins. Much of such material is obtained from California and Alaska, as well as from other gold-mining districts. Gold is cubic, but crystals are comparatively rare. It usually occurs in scales, grains, or nuggets. The hardness is 2½ to 3; the specific gravity, 16 to 19. In color and streak it is golden yellow. The luster is metallic. See Chapter XI.

HEMATITE

Cut cabochon or engraved, black hematite has at present a considerable vogue. This mineral is hexagonal, occurring in crystals or in compact, granular, fibrous, earthy, micaceous, or rounded masses (Fig. 393). The hardness is 5½ to 6½; the specific gravity, 4.9 to 5.3. Hematite has a black color when occurring in crystals and hard compact masses, but it is red in softer masses and when finely divided. The streak is cherry red. On this account a red

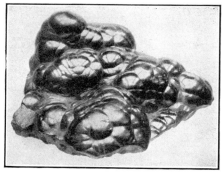

FIG. 393.—Hematite. Cumberland, England.

sludge is formed during the cutting process, and therefore lapidaries often call this mineral *bloodstone* (p. 225). Hematite is opaque, with a metallic splendent to dull luster. The formula is Fe_2O_3, ferric oxide. Much of the material cut for gem use is obtained from Cumberland, England. Other localities are Elba, Norway, Sweden, and the Lake Superior district.

PYRITE

Like hematite, pyrite is an iron mineral. It occurs in brilliant crystals of the cubic system (Fig. 394), which are frequently striated. The hardness is 6 to 6½; the specific gravity, 4.9 to 5.2. The mineral has a brass-yellow color and a greenish-black streak. The luster is bright metallic. Pyrite is iron sulfide, FeS_2. It is of widespread occurrence. Groups or clusters of small natural crystals are often mounted, uncut, in pins and other similar pieces of jewelry.

Marcasite has the same chemical composition as pyrite and resembles it in color, luster, and hardness. Marcasite crystallizes in the orthorhombic system. Its crystals differ markedly from those of pyrite. Specimens suitable for cutting are not so common as are those of pyrite. The cut material sold as marcasite is pyrite, steel, or other metal.

Turnov, Czecho-Slovakia, is a center for the cutting of pyrite for jewelry. Cutting is done by semi-automatic machines. The

FIG. 394.—Pyrite crystals. Octahedron, striated cube, cube and octahedron, pyritohedron.

pyrite is obtained from South Tuscany, Italy. Pyrite is also cut in the Jura Alps, France.

PEARL

Pearls are found within the shells of certain mollusks or shellfish. These animals are able to withdraw calcium carbonate from the water of the sea and use it in building their shells, which consist of three sections: (1) a horny organic substance called *conchiolin,* (2) prismatic crystals of calcium carbonate in the form of aragonite, and (3) the innermost section, very minute crystals of aragonite deposited in successive layers. The crystals in both sections are bonded with conchiolin and are perpendicular to the layers. The innermost section furnishes mother-of-pearl, which is used for cameos, called *shell cameos* (p. 109), and for buttons, knife handles, and so forth. If a foreign object, such as a minute parasitic organism, finds its way within the shell of the mollusk, the consequent irritation causes the animal to deposit a secretion about the offending object, so that gradually, layer by layer, a pearl is built up.

The composition of pearl is the same as that of mother-of-pearl but with concentric layers which give a radial arrangement to the aragonite crystals. Pearls have a hardness of 2½ to 3½ and a specific gravity of 2.5 to 2.7. Pearls are most often white or faintly yellowish or bluish, but they may be pink, yellow, purple, red, green, blue, brown, or black. They are translucent to opaque. The luster can be described only as pearly. Pearls may be iridescent, owing to the interference of light.

The best pearls are those which have a spherical form and which are also lustrous and iridescent, free from blemishes, and somewhat transparent. Fine black pearls are well thought of, but are not so valuable as the best grade of white ones. *Baroque pearls* are of irregular shape, but when of good color they are in demand. *Button pearls,* as the name implies, are flat beneath. *Blister pearls* are growths on the shells, stimulated by a parasite.

Being soft, pearls are easily scratched. The original luster, once lost, can rarely be restored, and then only by peeling off some of the outer layers of the pearl. Acids and perspiration also affect pearls. Even age alone causes them to deteriorate, since the organic conchiolin finally decays.

Pearls are obtained from many oysters and mussels, but most of them are furnished by members of the following families: Aviculidae, including the pearl oysters; Unionidae, fresh-water mussels; and Mytilidae. Pearl fisheries are operated along the coasts of India, Ceylon, the Persian Gulf, the Red Sea, Japan, Australia, the Sulu Archipelago northeast of Borneo, other Pacific islands, western Central America and Mexico, and the Caribbean Sea. Fresh-water mussels inhabit the streams of Europe, in Great Britain, Saxony, Czecho-Slovakia, and Bavaria; of North America, in Canada, Ohio, Indiana, Iowa, Arkansas, and Tennessee; and also of Japan and China.

Pearls are artificially cultivated by placing a small object inside the pearl oyster or mussel. The shellfish is then returned to the water and after a few years is again taken out, when the pearl which has formed about the introduced particle is removed. These are called *culture pearls.* In Japan a process has been employed, since 1920, by which the oysters are caused to grow pearls of spherical shape, resembling the finest natural pearls. A patch is cut from the mantle of an oyster. This is tied as a sac about a small, round object such as a bead of mother-of-pearl. The sac is then embedded in the tissues of another live oyster. After proper treatment of the wound, this oyster is returned to its bed. In the course of three or four years a fine pearl is formed. Such pearls are called *Mikimoto pearls,* after the inventor of the process. They are not easy to distinguish from natural pearls, because of the identical character of the outer layers of the two types. In cross section, however, and when studied under the microscope, it is observed that in the natural pearls the layers are all concentric around a nucleus, whereas in cultured pearls the concentric layers are superficial and enclose a larger nucleus with approximately parallel layers (Fig. 395).

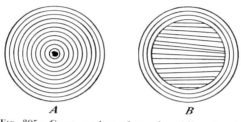

FIG. 395.—Cross section of pearls.   (*A*) natural,
(*B*) cultured.

The true origin of drilled pearls can be identified by optical methods using strong illumination, as embodied in the endoscope and pearloscope. X-ray methods are also employed and are applicable to drilled and undrilled pearls.

Pearls are imitated by hollow spheres of thin glass, which are coated with a preparation made from fish scales to give them a pearly luster. The glass sphere is then filled with white wax. A translucent white glass with a pearly luster is also used to imitate the natural gem.

CORAL

The composition of coral, like pearl, is principally calcium carbonate. This substance is secreted by small sea animals known as coral polyps, and is used by them in building up their skeletons. The variety most employed as a gem is the *precious* or *red coral.* In color it is red or pink. Its hardness is $3\frac{1}{2}$; its specific gravity, 2.6 to 2.7. The red coral is dredged from waters of moderate depth along the shores of the Mediterranean Sea—Tunis, Algeria, Morocco, Sardinia, Corsica, France, and near Naples. *Black coral*

has been obtained from the Persian Gulf and the Great Barrier
Reef of Australia.   Coral is used for necklaces, bracelets, rosaries,
and so on.

AMBER

Amber is a fossil resin which exuded from prehistoric conifer-
ous trees.   It generally occurs in loosely consolidated and geo-

FIG. 396.—Crude, sorted amber.   Palmnicken, Germany.

logically young deposits.   Most of the world's amber down
through the centuries has been obtained from the deposits along

FIG. 397.—Amber drop.

the southern coast of the Baltic Sea, west
and north of Königsberg, East Prussia.
But amber is also found in Rumania, Sic-
ily, and Burma.   Although the properties
of the amber from these various localities
are similar, there is sufficient variation to
warrant descriptions according to locality.

Baltic Sea Amber.—This is found in irregular amorphous masses, which vary
greatly in size from small pieces weighing
but a few grains to larger lumps of several
pounds in weight (Fig. 396).   Sometimes
more regularly formed masses called *drops*
or *tears* are found (Fig. 397).   The largest piece of amber found
thus far weighed about twenty pounds.

Amber often contains inclusions of a great variety of insects
(Figs. 398 to 400) and of plant remains, such as pine needles,

leaves, buds, and flowers. These inclusions are frequently very well preserved and are of scientific as well as popular interest. Minute crystals of pyrite may also be observed as inclusions.

Amber has a hardness of 2 to 2½; hence it is too hard to be scratched by the fingernail, but is scratched very easily and with

Fig. 398.   Fig. 399.

Figs. 398 and 399.—Amber with insect inclusions.

little pressure by the knife blade. It is amorphous and has a characteristic conchoidal fracture. Although it is brittle, it can be easily worked upon the lathe as well as carved (Fig. 402). Nearly all the varieties of amber take a good polish. The specific gravity is 1.0 to 1.1, and accordingly amber will float on a solution

Fig. 400.—Amber with insect inclusions.

consisting of four heaping teaspoonfuls of salt in a tumblerful of water (Fig. 66).

The characteristic color of amber is yellow, which may vary from almost colorless through the various shades to dark brown. It may also be whitish, greenish, reddish, bluish, or blackish, but these colors are rare. Light-colored amber may darken with age and become reddish or brownish red. The luster is greasy. Amber may be very clear and transparent, cloudy and translucent, or even quite opaque or opalescent. It may be fluorescent.

There are several varieties of amber:

1. *Clear.*—This variety is perfectly transparent and may be water white to yellow or brownish red in color.

2. *Fatty.*—This differs from the clear variety in that there is a slight turbidity due to the presence of air bubbles. In color and appearance it resembles goose or duck fat. The Germans call this variety *flohmig.*

3. *Bastard.*—This variety is quite cloudy and contains many small air bubbles.

4. *Bony or Osseous.*—This type looks like ivory or dried bone. It takes a good polish. It contains very many exceedingly minute air bubbles.

5. *Foamy or Frothy.*—This variety is chalk white and opaque. It does not polish well.

Some of the cloudy varieties may be clarified by careful heating in oil. During this process the oil penetrates into the interior and fills the small air spaces.

Being amorphous, amber is optically isotropic. The index of refraction is about 1.54; that of copal (p. 281) may be about the same, but it usually is slightly higher and varies more.

Amber is easily electrified by rubbing with a cloth and will attract bits of paper. It is a very poor conductor of heat and hence is warm to the touch. As it is a good insulator, amber is used in electrical and radio apparatus.

The composition of amber is very complex, for it is a mixture of several resins, succinic acid, and a volatile oil called *amber oil.* The mineralogical name *succinite* is sometimes applied to the amber from the Baltic Sea. The chemical composition is generally expressed by the formula $C_{40}H_{64}O_4$. Moreover, a small amount of hydrogen sulfide is always present.

Amber softens when heated to 170° to 200°C. and hence can be pressed. Material treated in this way is called *pressed amber* or *ambroid* (p. 145). In the temperature range from 280° to 375°C. amber melts, decomposes, and evolves white fumes with a characteristic aromatic odor. Amber ignites and burns in the flame of a match; hence it is called by the Germans *bernstein,* that is, "the stone that burns." If it is heated in a test tube, succinic acid will collect as a crystalline powder on the upper and colder portions of the tube. Owing to the presence of hydrogen sulfide in the fumes, filter paper moistened with a solution of lead acetate turns black when held in the tube. The residue remaining after driving off the volatile constituents at 280° to 375°C., which are principally succinic acid and amber oil, is

FIG. 401.—Amber mine, Palmnicken, Germany.

termed *colophony.* This residue dissolved in turpentine and linseed oil is called *amber varnish.* Amber is very slowly soluble in sulfuric ether and therefore may be readily distinguished from copal (p. 282).

The chief source of amber is in Samland, East Prussia, along the southern coast of the Baltic Sea, west and north of Königsberg. For centuries amber has been obtained from this district, where it is found disseminated in a greenish glauconite sand, called *blue earth,* which is overlain by beds of sand, lignite, clay, and soil. Palmnicken is the center of the mining operations. The principal plants for the preparation and manufacture of amber articles and products are located in Königsberg.

The amber-bearing bed is exposed along the Baltic coast in this district, and after storms, amber which has been washed out by wave action may be picked up on the shore. Material obtained from the sea in this way is called *sea-amber* or *sea-stone.* At Palmnicken, the amber deposit has been worked on a large scale as an open-pit mine (Fig. 401) by means of dredges and steam shovels. The overburden is first removed. The amber-bearing earth is then loaded into cars and trammed to the washing plant along the shore, where the amber is separated from the blue earth by powerful streams of water. This amber is called *pit-amber*. After being cleaned with sand and water in large revolving cylinders, it is sized and sorted. From 25 to 30 per cent of the material can be used as gem amber and for manufacture

into pressed amber. This material is shipped to Königsberg. The other material is heated in large retorts in the plant at Palmnicken, and succinic acid, amber oil, and the resin called colophony are obtained. Colophony is used extensively in the manufacture of the better grades of varnishes and lacquers.

At Königsberg the amber is further sorted and prepared for shipment to all parts of the

FIG. 402.—Jewel case with carved amber.

world, or is manufactured into the many diverse amber articles that are well known, such as beads, cigarette holders, pipestems, and jewel cases (Fig. 402). Pressed amber is also made at Königsberg (p. 145). Other important centers for the preparation of amber articles have been Danzig, Vienna, and Berlin. In East Prussia the mining and manufacturing of amber and its products have been a governmental monopoly.

Amber is also found along the Baltic Sea in Lithuania. This district is east of Samland. The deposits are similar to those which have just been described. Lithuania has been a minor producer of amber, for no important mines have been developed.

Rumanian Amber.—This amber, often termed *rumanite,* is generally brownish yellow to brown or, rarely, yellow in color. It is transparent and translucent and sometimes fluoresces. Specimens often possess many cracks but can be worked without shattering. Like true amber (succinite), Rumanian amber can be electrified by friction. Rumanite contains a somewhat larger percentage of sulfur, but less succinic acid, than the amber from the Baltic Sea. When heated it emits an aromatic odor. Hydrogen sulfide is also evolved. At 300°C. it melts without swelling up. The principal occurrence of this variety of amber is in the province of Buzău, Rumania.

Sicilian Amber.—In color, Sicilian amber is darker than that from the Baltic Sea in that red hues are more common. Thus, it is more apt to be reddish yellow or pale to dark red. Various shades of brown and yellow may, however, be observed. Like succinite, Sicilian amber fuses without swelling up. The fumes do not contain amber oil. They are also less irritating and do not cause coughing. The principal source of Sicilian amber, sometimes called *simetite,* is the district near the mouth of the Simeto River.

Burmese Amber.—The amber found in Burma is quite uniform in color. It is generally pale yellow, but reddish and dark-brown specimens are also known. The pale varieties may be transparent; the others, not. This amber, termed *burmite,* is slightly harder than succinite. It often has many cracks filled with calcite. The chief source is the valley of the Hukong, one of the upper tributaries of the Chindwin River. This district is also famous for its deposits of jadeite (p. 230). Although burmite is highly prized in Burma, India, and China, much Baltic Sea amber is shipped to these countries.

Imitations.—There are a number of imitations of amber on the market to which reference should be made. These include natural resins like *copal* and artificial materials such as *bakelite* and other plastics (p. 169), celluloid products, and glass. Of these imitations the first two are the most important. They are also more difficult to distinguish from amber than celluloid and glass imitations, which can usually be detected at sight.

Copal.—Copal is a natural resin very similar in appearance to amber. It occurs in rounded amorphous masses generally with a "goose-skin" surface (Fig. 403) and a conchoidal fracture. It is colorless, lemon yellow, or yellowish brown, and translucent to transparent. Although it is brittle, it can be turned on the lathe and carved like amber. The hardness, specific gravity, and index of refraction do not differ much from those of amber from the Baltic Sea. The chief sources of copal are Zanzibar, Mozambique, the East Indies, and Brazil. *Kauri copal* is obtained from New Zealand and New Caledonia. Copal is soluble in alcohol, ether, turpentine, and linseed oil. It is used in large quantities in the manufacture of varnishes and lacquers. The hardest varieties of copal are used for gem purposes.

Methods of Detection.—One of the best ways to differentiate between the natural resins and the various plastics is to determine the specific gravity. As the natural resins have a specific gravity but slightly greater than that of water, namely, 1.0 to 1.1, they will float on a solution of four teaspoonfuls of salt in a tumbler

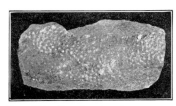

FIG. 403.—Copal showing goose-skin surface. Zanzibar.

of water. Bakelite and the other plastics, with the exception of the styrene resins (*styron*), on the other hand, have specific gravities of 1.20 to 1.60 and hence will sink when placed in the salt solution referred to above, as will also glass and celluloid products (p. 37). Since the specific gravity of the styrenes is 1.05 to 1.07, about the same as that of amber, these plastics will float on the salt solution.

The refractivity of the plastics varies from 1.46 to 1.70. With the exception of the styrenes, the plastics have specific gravities higher than that of the natural resins. Since the index of refraction of styrene, 1.59, is greater than that of the natural resins, the two groups of substances can be readily distinguished. See the table on page 171.

The resins that float on the salt solution are not all natural amber but also include pressed amber and copal. If the outer natural surface of the specimen has not been removed, copal can be easily recognized, for it has a characteristic "goose-skin" appearance (Fig. 403). If this is not to be observed, the ether test should be used, for when copal is placed in sulfuric ether in a closed vessel it swells up and partly dissolves in five or ten minutes, while there will be little or no action on amber and bakelite when they are treated in the same way. To carry out this test with cut and polished material without damage to it, a drop of ether may be placed on the surface of the specimen and allowed to evaporate. If the material is copal or pressed amber, a dull spot will be observed where the drop of ether was placed. Ether will evaporate from natural amber or bakelite without dulling the surface.

Bakelite and the other plastics may also be readily differentiated from amber and the natural resins by using a heated needle. When a hot needle is pressed against bakelite and the other thermosetting plastics, the surface of the material chars, while amber, the other natural resins, and the thermoplastics soften and allow the hot needle to penetrate.

From the chemical standpoint, amber and copal can be easily distinguished, because the former evolves hydrogen sulfide when heated, but the latter does not. Hence, if a strip of paper moistened with a solution of lead acetate turns black when held in the escaping fumes, the specimen being heated is amber; otherwise, it is copal.

In distinguishing between natural and pressed amber, one must depend largely upon the greater clarity and brilliancy of natural amber and the fact that pressed amber generally shows a fluidal structure when viewed in transmitted light. This is readily observed under the polarizing microscope, as is also the anomalous double refraction, which is due to the strained condition of the pressed amber. Bakelite can generally be distinguished from these materials because articles made of it tend to lose their clarity in a comparatively short time, that is, in two or three years. Moreover, yellow bakelite is apt to show with age a reddish layer that can be removed by grinding. When bakelite is used for cigarette holders or pipestems, a disagreeable taste generally develops in a year or two. Amber and pressed amber are more permanent with regard to clarity, color, and taste.

JET

Jet is a dense, compact, homogeneous, and coal-black variety of lignite or brown coal. It takes a good polish and is often used for ornaments and cheap jewelry, beads, and so forth. Jet has a conchoidal fracture. The hardness is 2 to 2½; the specific gravity, 1.1 to 1.4. It is tough, so that it can be worked upon the lathe. The chief center for jet articles is Whitby, Yorkshire, England, where local jet and some imported from Asturias and

Aragon, Spain, are used.   Anthracite coal from the Pennsylvania mines and Scotch cannel coal are both used in place of jet.   Black cryptocrystalline varieties of quartz sometimes artificially colored, as well as obsidian, glass, black bakelite (p. 169), and other plastics are often used in imitation of jet.

PART III

CLASSIFICATION OF GEM MATERIALS, ACCORDING TO VARIOUS PROPERTIES

TABLES I-XI

In Tables I to X, the gem minerals are classified according to crystal system, hardness, specific gravity, color, various physical and optical properties, and chemical composition.

A summary of all the important properties of each gem mineral is to be found in Table XI.

TABLE I.—CRYSTAL SYSTEM

Cubic System.—Diamond, garnet, spinel, lazurite, fluorite, sodalite, sphalerite, chromite, cobaltite, gold, pyrite.

Tetragonal System.—Zircon, anatase, cassiterite, rutile, vesuvianite.

Hexagonal System.—Corundum, beryl, quartz, tourmaline, apatite, benitoite, calcite, dioptase, phenacite, smithsonite, willemite, hematite.

Orthorhombic System.—Topaz, chrysoberyl, olivine, andalusite, beryllonite, danburite, enstatite, bronzite, hypersthene, iolite, prehnite, staurolite, thomsonite, variscite, zoisite.

Monoclinic System.—Nephrite, jadeite, azurite, malachite, brazilianite, datolite, diopside, epidote, euclase, gypsum, lazulite, orthoclase, sepiolite, serpentine, spodumene, steatite, titanite.

Triclinic System.—Turquois, axinite, cyanite, microcline, albite, oligoclase, labradorite, rhodonite.

Amorphous.—Opal, chrysocolla (apparently), obsidian, moldavite, amber, jet.

TABLE II.—HARDNESS

Diamond	10	Enstatite	5.5
Corundum	9	Hypersthene	5.5
Chrysoberyl	8.5	Obsidian	5.5
Topaz	8	Chromite	5.5
Spinel	8	Cobaltite	5.5
Beryl	7.5-8	Cyanite	4-7
Phenacite	7.5-8	Chlorastrolite	5-6
Zircon	7.5	Diopside	5-6
Euclase	7.5	Willemite	5-6
Tourmaline	7-7.5	Rhodonite	5-6
Andalusite	7-7.5	Lazulite	5-6
Iolite	7-7.5	Thomsonite	5-5.5
Staurolite	7-7.5	Titanite	5-5.5
Danburite	7	Datolite	5-5.5
Quartz	7	Lazurite	5-5.5
Garnet	6.5-7.5	Apatite	5
Olivine	6.5-7	Dioptase	5
Jadeite	6.5-7	Smithsonite	5
Axinite	6.5	Variscite	4-5
Benitoite	6.5	Fluorite	4
Nephrite	6.5	Sphalerite	3.5-4
Vesuvianite	6.5	Azurite	3.5
Cassiterite	6-7	Malachite	3.5
Epidote	6-7	Coral	3.5
Spodumene	6-7	Calcite	3
Prehnite	6-6.5	Serpentine	2.5-4
Feldspar	6-6.5	Pearl	2.5-3.5
Rutile	6-6.5	Chrysocolla	2-4
Pyrite	6-6.5	Gold	2.5-3
Turquois	6	Amber	2-2.5
Opal	5.5-6.5	Sepiolite	2-2.5
Hematite	5.5-6.5	Jet	2-2.5
Anatase	5.5-6	Gypsum	2
Beryllonite	5.5-6	Steatite	1.5-2.5
Brazilianite	5.5		

TABLE III.—SPECIFIC GRAVITY

Because of the variation in the specific gravity of minerals the values are given only to the first decimal place. The figures are either mean values or for pure specimens.

Gold	16-19	Enstatite	3.2
Cassiterite	6.9	Chlorastrolite	3.2
Cobaltite	6.2	Diopside	3.2
Hematite	5.2	Fluorite	3.2
Pyrite	5.0	Tourmaline	3.1
Chromite	4.5	Euclase	3.1
Zircon	4.0-4.8	Spodumene	3.1
Smithsonite	4.3	Lazulite	3.1
Spessartite	4.2	Danburite	3.0
Rutile	4.2	Phenacite	3.0
Almandite	4.1	Nephrite	3.0
Willemite	4.1	Brazilianite	2.9
Corundum	4.0	Datolite	2.9
Malachite	4.0	Prehnite	2.9
Sphalerite	4.0	Beryllonite	2.8
Andradite	3.8	Beryl	2.7
Anatase	3.8	Calcite	2.7
Azurite	3.8	Oligoclase	2.7
Pyrope	3.7	Labradorite	2.7
Chrysoberyl	3.7	Quartz	2.7
Staurolite	3.7	Turquois	2.7
Spinel	3.6	Steatite	2.7
Benitoite	3.6	Coral	2.7
Cyanite	3.6	Orthoclase	2.6
Rhodonite	3.6	Microcline	2.6
Diamond	3.5	Albite	2.6
Topaz	3.5	Iolite	2.6
Grossularite	3.5	Serpentine	2.6
Uvarovite	3.5	Pearl	2.6
Titanite	3.5	Lazurite	2.4-2.9
Hypersthene	3.4	Obsidian	2.3-2.6
Epidote	3.4	Variscite	2.5
Vesuvianite	3.4	Thomsonite	2.3
Olivine	3.3	Gypsum	2.3
Jadeite	3.3	Opal	1.9-2.3
Axinite	3.3	Chrysocolla	2.1
Dioptase	3.3	Sepiolite	1-2
Andalusite	3.2	Jet	1.1-1.4
Apatite	3.2	Amber	1.1

TABLE IV.—COLOR

In this table are included for the most part only those colors of gem minerals which are met with in cut stones.

Colorless

Diamond, corundum (white sapphire), beryl (goshenite), topaz, grossularite, tourmaline (achroite), zircon, opal, quartz (rock crystal), apatite, beryllonite, danburite, euclase, orthoclase (adularia), albite, oligoclase, phenacite, fluorite, gypsum (selenite), sphalerite.

White

White.—Opal, quartz (milky quartz, chalcedony, agate, onyx), thomsonite, datolite, gypsum (satin spar, alabaster), sepiolite, pearl, amber.

Greenish White.—Nephrite, jadeite, serpentine, garnet (grossularite).

Purple

Purple.—Rhodolite, spinel (almandine), quartz (amethyst), fluorite, pearl.

Lilac.—Spodumene (kunzite).

Violet

Corundum (Oriental amethyst), topaz, tourmaline, spinel (almandine), quartz (amethyst), andalusite, apatite, axinite, fluorite.

Blue

Violet Blue.—Lazurite, apatite, fluorite.

Dark Blue.—Tourmaline (indicolite), iolite, azurite.

Azure Blue.—Turquois, lazurite, sodalite, lazulite.

Sapphire Blue.—Corundum (sapphire), beryl, tourmaline, spinel (sapphirine), quartz (sapphire quartz), benitoite.

Sky Blue.—Beryl, turquois, odontolite, cyanite, fluorite.

Pale Blue.—Diamond, beryl, topaz, zircon, euclase, vesuvianite (cyprine), smithsonite, pearl.

Grayish Blue.—Opal, quartz (chalcedony, agate, jasper).

Greenish Blue.—Turquois, chrysocolla, fluorite, lazurite, beryl (aquamarine).

Green

Bluish Green.—Apatite, variscite, microcline (amazonstone), chrysocolla.

Dark Green.—Quartz (jasper), nephrite, chlorastrolite, diopside, dioptase, epidote, serpentine, garnet (grossularite).

Olive Green.—Olivine (peridot), enstatite, serpentine.

Emerald Green.—Beryl (emerald), grossularite, uvarovite, andradite (Uralian emerald), chrysoberyl (alexandrite), jadeite, dioptase, spodumene (hiddenite), malachite.

Grass Green.—Andradite (demantoid), spinel (chlorospinel), malachite.

Pistachio Green.—Epidote.

Bottle Green.—Olivine (peridot), andalusite, moldavite.

Oil Green.—Prehnite, serpentine.

Bright Green.—Corundum (Oriental emerald), tourmaline, quartz (plasma), cyanite, fluorite, serpentine.

Dull Green.—Quartz (cat's-eye, prase), nephrite, labradorite, obsidian, vesuvianite (californite), serpentine, garnet (grossularite).

Apple Green.—Quartz (chrysoprase), turquois, variscite, willemite, prehnite.

Sea Green.—Beryl (aquamarine), apatite, euclase.

TABLE IV.—COLOR (Continued)

Green (Continued)

Pale Green.—Diamond, topaz, zircon, opal, diopside, enstatite, euclase, thomsonite, titanite, datolite, smithsonite, pearl.

Brownish Green.—Andalusite, obsidian, moldavite.

Yellowish Green.—Tourmaline, olivine (chrysolite), chrysoberyl, andalusite, brazilianite, epidote, prehnite, spodumene (hiddenite).

Yellow

Greenish Yellow.—Olivine (chrysolite), chrysoberyl, willemite, serpentine, spodumene.

Golden Yellow.—Corundum (golden sapphire), beryl (golden beryl), spinel.

Bright Yellow.—Smithsonite.

Honey Yellow.—Tourmaline, amber.

Wine Yellow.—Topaz, grossularite, andradite (topazolite), fluorite.

Straw Yellow.—Titanite.

Pale Yellow.—Diamond, opal, beryllonite, orthoclase, phenacite, thomsonite, datolite, sepiolite, pearl.

Brownish Yellow.—Zircon (jacinth), tourmaline, quartz (citrine, tiger's-eye, jasper), axinite, staurolite, willemite, amber.

Orange

Orange.—Fluorite.

Reddish Orange.—Spinel (rubicelle), zircon (jacinth).

Red

Violet Red.—Almandite.

Scarlet Red.—Coral.

Crimson Red.—Fluorite.

Ruby Red.—Corundum (ruby), pyrope, spinel (ruby spinel).

Dark Red.—Spessartite, almandite.

Dull Red.—Quartz (carnelian, agate, jasper), obsidian, hematite.

Pale Red.—Opal, thomsonite, datolite, pearl.

Pink to Rose Red.—Diamond, corundum (pink sapphire), beryl (morganite), topaz, grossularite, tourmaline (rubellite), spinel (balas ruby), opal, quartz (rose quartz), andalusite, apatite, phenacite, spodumene (kunzite), fluorite, rhodonite, smithsonite, zoisite (thulite), pearl, coral.

Flesh Red.—Apatite, willemite.

Brownish Red.—Andradite, spessartite, almandite, zircon (jacinth), quartz (carnelian, agate), rutile, staurolite, amber.

Brown

Brown.—Andradite, anatase, cassiterite, hypersthene, thomsonite, titanite, vesuvianite, willemite, fluorite, amber.

Dull Brown.—Opal, quartz (cat's-eye, tiger's-eye, chalcedony, carnelian, agate, jasper, flint), obsidian.

Smoky Brown.—Quartz (smoky quartz).

Clove Brown.—Zircon (jacinth), axinite.

Cinnamon Brown.—Grossularite (cinnamon stone).

Yellowish Brown.—Topaz, tourmaline.

Pale Brown.—Datolite, pearl.

TABLE IV.—COLOR (*Continued*)

Gray

Opal, quartz (cat's-eye, chalcedony, flint), labradorite.

Black

Almandite, andradite (melanite), tourmaline (schorl), opal, quartz (morion, onyx, flint, basanite), anatase, cassiterite, obsidian, rutile (nigrine), sphalerite, chromite, hematite, pearl, jet.

Metallic Colors

Silver White.—Cobaltite.
Golden Yellow.—Gold.
Brass Yellow.—Pyrite (marcasite).

Banded and Mottled Colors

Banded Colors.—Tourmaline, quartz (agate, onyx, sardonyx, jasper), calcite (Mexican onyx), diopside.
Mottled Colors.—Quartz (jasper, agate), nephrite, jadeite, calcite (marble), chlorastrolite, cyanite, datolite, thomsonite, serpentine, steatite, azurmalachite.

Colored Streak

Blue.—Azurite.	*Brown.*—Chromite.
Green.—Malachite.	*Pale Brown.*—Rutile, cassiterite.
Pale Green.—Turquois.	*Black.*—Jet.
Golden Yellow.—Gold.	*Greenish Black.*—Pyrite.
Red.—Hematite.	*Grayish Black.*—Cobaltite.

TABLE V.—MISCELLANEOUS PHYSICAL PROPERTIES

Chatoyant.—Chrysoberyl (cat's-eye), quartz (tiger's-eye, cat's-eye), bronzite, calcite (satin spar), gypsum (satin spar), tourmaline, chlorastrolite.
Opalescent.—Opal, orthoclase, albite, oligoclase (moonstone).
Play of Color.—Opal, labradorite.
Asteriated.—Corundum (star ruby and sapphire), rose quartz, garnet.
Containing Inclusions.—Opal (moss opal), quartz (aventurine, rutilated quartz, moss agate), andalusite (chiastolite), oligoclase (sunstone), corundum, lazurite.

TABLE VI.—OPTICAL CHARACTER

Isotropic.—Diamond, garnet, opal, spinel, fluorite, lazurite, obsidian, sodalite, sphalerite, amber.
Uniaxial Positive.—Zircon, quartz, benitoite, cassiterite, dioptase, phenacite, rutile, willemite, chrysocolla.
Uniaxial Negative.—Corundum, beryl, tourmaline, anatase, apatite, calcite, smithsonite.
Biaxial Positive.—Topaz, olivine, chrysoberyl, turquois, brazilianite, diopside, enstatite, euclase, albite, labradorite, prehnite, spodumene, staurolite, thomsonite, titanite, azurite, gypsum, iolite, zoisite.
Biaxial Negative.—Andalusite, axinite, beryllonite, cyanite, danburite, hypersthene, epidote, orthoclase, microcline, oligoclase, iolite, vesuvianite, malachite, datolite, lazulite, steatite, rhodonite, serpentine.

TABLE VII.—INDICES OF REFRACTION, OPTICAL CHARACTER, AND BIREFRINGENCE

Gem mineral	Indices of refraction			Optical character	Bi-refringence
Rutile	ω 2.616	ε 2.903		+	0.287
Anatase	ω 2.554	ε 2.493		−	0.061
Diamond	n 2.417				
Sphalerite	n 2.37				
Cassiterite	ω 1.997	ε 2.093		+	0.096
Andradite	n 1.940 ↓				
Zircon	ω 1.931	ε 1.988		+	0.057
Titanite	β 1.907	α 1.900	γ 2.034	+	0.134
Malachite	β 1.875	α 1.655	γ 1.909	−	0.254
Andradite	n 1.865 ↑				
Smithsonite	ω 1.849	ε 1.621		−	0.228
Uvarovite	n 1.838				
Almandite	n 1.830 ↓				
Spessartite	n 1.814 ↓				
Spessartite	n 1.794 ↑				
Corundum	ω 1.768	ε 1.760		−	0.008
Almandite	n 1.766 ↑				
Epidote	β 1.763 ↓	α 1.729	γ 1.780	−	0.051
Azurite	β 1.758	α 1.730	γ 1.838	+	0.108
Benitoite	ω 1.757	ε 1.804		+	0.047
Spinel	n 1.75 ↓				
Pyrope	n 1.749 ↓				
Chrysoberyl	β 1.748	α 1.747	γ 1.757	+	0.010
Staurolite	β 1.741	α 1.736	γ 1.746	+	0.010
Rhodonite	β 1.740 ↓	α 1.733	γ 1.744	−	0.011
Grossularite	n 1.735				
Hypersthene	β 1.728 ↓	α 1.715	γ 1.731	−	0.016
Rhodonite	β 1.720 ↑	α 1.716	γ 1.728	+	0.012
Cyanite	β 1.720	α 1.712	γ 1.728	−	0.016
Epidote	β 1.719 ↑	α 1.716	γ 1.723	−	0.007
Spinel	n 1.718 ↑				
Vesuvianite	ω 1.713	ε 1.705		−	0.008
Diopside	β 1.708 ↓	α 1.702	γ 1.726	+	0.024
Olivine	β 1.706 ↓	α 1.681	γ 1.718	−	0.037
Pyrope	n 1.705 ↑				
Zoisite	β 1.703	α 1.700	γ 1.718	+	0.018
Axinite	β 1.692 ↓	α 1.684	γ 1.696	−	0.012
Willemite	ω 1.691	ε 1.719		+	0.028
Axinite	β 1.685 ↑	α 1.678	γ 1.688	−	0.010
Hypersthene	β 1.678 ↑	α 1.673	γ 1.683	±	0.010
Diopside	β 1.671 ↑	α 1.664	γ 1.694	+	0.030
Enstatite	β 1.670 ↓	α 1.660	γ 1.675	−	0.015
Olivine	β 1.670 ↑	α 1.653	γ 1.689	+	0.036
Spodumene	β 1.666	α 1.660	γ 1.676	+	0.016
Jadeite	β 1.659	α 1.654	γ 1.667	+	0.013
Calcite	ω 1.658	ε 1.486		−	0.172
Euclase	β 1.656	α 1.653	γ 1.673	+	0.020
Dioptase	ω 1.655	ε 1.708		+	0.053
Tourmaline	ω 1.655 ↓	ε 1.633		−	0.022
Phenacite	ω 1.654	ε 1.670		+	0.016
Datolite	β 1.654	α 1.626	γ 1.670	−	0.044
Enstatite	β 1.653 ↑	α 1.650	γ 1.658	+	0.008
Obsidian	n 1.65 ↓				
Apatite	ω 1.649	ε 1.644		−	0.005
Tourmaline	ω 1.648 ↑	ε 1.625		−	0.023
Andalusite	β 1.639	α 1.634	γ 1.643	−	0.009

TABLE VII.—INDICES OF REFRACTION, OPTICAL CHARACTER, AND BIREFRINGENCE
(*Continued*)

Gem mineral	Indices of refraction			Optical character	Bi-refringence
Lazulite	β 1.634	α 1.612	γ 1.643	−	0.031
Danburite	β 1.633	α 1.630	γ 1.636	−	0.006
Prehnite	β 1.625	α 1.615	γ 1.645	+	0.030
Topaz	β 1.620	α 1.619	γ 1.627	+	0.008
Turquois	β 1.62	α 1.61	γ 1.65	+	0.04
Nephrite	β 1.62	α 1.606	γ 1.632	−	0.026
Brazilianite	β 1.605	α 1.598	γ 1.617	+	0.019
Beryl	ω 1.598 ↓	ε 1.590		−	0.008
Iolite	β 1.597 ↓	α 1.592	γ 1.599	−	0.007
Steatite	n 1.59 ↓				
Variscite	β 1.584 ↓	α 1.566	γ 1.593	−	0.027
Variscite	β 1.571 ↑	α 1.554	γ 1.576	−	0.022
Beryl	ω 1.568 ↑	ε 1.564		−	0.004
Labradorite	β 1.563	α 1.559	γ 1.568	+	0.009
Beryllonite	β 1.558	α 1.552	γ 1.561	−	0.009
Serpentine	β 1.550 ↓	α 1.546	γ 1.557	+	0.011
Quartz	ω 1.544	ε 1.553		+	0.009
Oligoclase	β 1.543	α 1.539	γ 1.547	−	0.008
Steatite	n 1.54 ↑				
Amber	n 1.54±				
Iolite	β 1.538 ↑	α 1.534	γ 1.540	−	0.006
Thomsonite	β 1.531 ↓	α 1.528	γ 1.545	+	0.017
Albite	β 1.529	α 1.525	γ 1.536	+	0.011
Microcline	β 1.526	α 1.522	γ 1.530	−	0.008
Orthoclase	β 1.524	α 1.518	γ 1.526	−	0.008
Gypsum	β 1.523	α 1.520	γ 1.530	+	0.010
Sepiolite	β 1.525±	α 1.519	γ 1.529	−	0.010
Moldavite	n 1.52 ↓				
Thomsonite	β 1.513 ↑	α 1.511	γ 1.518	+	0.007
Serpentine	β 1.512 ↑	α 1.508	γ 1.522	+	0.014
Lazurite	n 1.50±				
Sodalite	n 1.483				
Moldavite	n 1.48 ↑				
Obsidian	n 1.48 ↑				
Chrysocolla	ω 1.46±	ε 1.57±			
Opal	n 1.46 ↓				
Opal	n 1.44 ↑				
Fluorite	n 1.434				

TABLE VIII.—DISPERSION

The values for the dispersion of the indices of refraction, as given in this table, have been obtained from several authorities, and for this reason the wave-lengths of light at which maximum and minimum values were measured are not uniform for all the gems. In each case, however, the dispersion recorded is that between the red and blue portions of the spectrum.

Sphalerite	0.197	Olivine	0.018
Diamond	0.063	Epidote	0.018
Andradite (demantoid)	0.057	Spodumene	0.017
Titanite	0.050	Tourmaline	0.016
Zircon	0.048	Chrysoberyl	0.015
Grossularite (hessonite)	0.028	Topaz	0.014
Pyrope	0.027	Beryl	0.014
Almandite	0.024	Quartz	0.013
Staurolite	0.021	Albite	0.012
Spinel	0.020	Fluorite	0.006
Corundum	0.018		

TABLE IX.—PLEOCHROISM

The following gem minerals are usually pleochroic in two or three shades of the color visible to the unaided eye or in that color and colorless, for example, ruby, pale yellowish red, and deep red.

Pleochroism strong to distinct: Corundum, tourmaline, benitoite, cyanite, dioptase, spodumene, malachite.

Pleochroism distinct to weak: Beryl, olivine, blue topaz, smoky quartz, amethyst, euclase, vesuvianite, azurite.

The following are pleochroic in two or three different colors, as indicated:

Gem mineral	Pleochroic colors
Chrysoberyl	Green, red, orange-yellow; strong
Andalusite	Colorless, yellow, red, or green; strong
Axinite	Green, brown, blue, or violet; strong
Epidote	Green, brown, yellow; strong
Emerald	Light green, dark green; distinct
Iolite	Yellow, blue; strong
Zoisite, thulite variety	Pink, yellow; strong
Anatase	Pale blue or yellowish, dark blue or orange; distinct
Hypersthene	Red, yellow, green; distinct
Staurolite	Red, brown, or yellow; distinct
Topaz, yellow and pink varieties	Yellow, pale pink to colorless; distinct to weak
Titanite	Red, yellow, greenish, or colorless; weak to distinct

Isotropic gems are of course non-pleochroic. Other gems not mentioned in this table are (*a*) non-pleochroic; (*b*) or only weakly pleochroic; (*c*) or being opaque do not readily reveal their pleochroic character.

TABLE X.—COMPOSITION

ELEMENTS

Diamond...................... C
Gold......................... Au

SULFIDES

Sphalerite.................... ZnS
Pyrite........................ FeS_2
Cobaltite..................... CoAsS

OXIDES AND HYDROXIDES

Quartz....................... SiO_2
Rutile........................ TiO_2
Anatase...................... TiO_2
Cassiterite................... SnO_2
Corundum.................... Al_2O_3
Hematite..................... Fe_2O_3
Opal......................... $SiO_2.xH_2O$

HALOIDS

Fluorite...................... CaF_2

CARBONATES

Calcite....................... $CaCO_3$
Smithsonite................... $ZnCO_3$
Malachite..................... $CuCO_3.Cu(OH)_2$
Azurite....................... $2CuCO_3.Cu(OH)_2$

SULFATES

Gypsum...................... $CaSO_4.2H_2O$

ALUMINATES

Spinel........................ $Mg(AlO_2)_2$
Chromite..................... $[Fe,Cr][(Cr,Fe)O_2]_2$
Chrysoberyl.................. $Be(AlO_2)_2$

PHOSPHATES

Beryllonite................... $NaBePO_4$
Brazilianite................... $Na_2Al_6P_4O_{16}(OH)_8$
Apatite....................... $Ca_5(F,Cl)(PO_4)_3$
Lazulite...................... $(Fe,Mg)Al_2(OH)_2(PO_4)_2$
Variscite..................... $AlPO_4.2H_2O$
Turquois..................... Basic copper aluminum phosphate.

SILICATES AND TITANATES

Staurolite.................... $HFeAl_5Si_2O_{13}$
Andalusite.................... Al_2SiO_5
Cyanite....................... Al_2SiO_5

TABLE X.—COMPOSITION (*Continued*)

SILICATES AND TITANATES (*Continued*)

Topaz	$Al_2(F,OH)_2SiO_4$
Datolite	$Ca(B.OH)SiO_4$
Danburite	$CaB_2Si_2O_8$
Euclase	$Be(Al.OH)SiO_4$
Tourmaline	$H_{20}B_2Si_4O_{21}$
Epidote	$Ca_2(Al,Fe)_2(Al.OH)(SiO_4)_3$
Zoisite	$Ca_2Al_2(Al.OH)(SiO_4)_3$
Vesuvianite	$Ca_6[Al(OH,F)]Al_2(SiO_4)_5$
Olivine	$(Mg,Fe)_2SiO_4$
Willemite	Zn_2SiO_4
Phenacite	Be_2SiO_4
Zircon	$ZrSiO_4$
Garnet	$M''_3M'''_2(SiO_4)_3$
Grossularite	$Ca_3Al_2(SiO_4)_3$
Pyrope	$Mg_3Al_2(SiO_4)_3$
Almandite	$Fe_3Al_2(SiO_4)_3$
Spessartite	$Mn_3Al_2(SiO_4)_3$
Andradite	$Ca_3Fe_2(SiO_4)_3$
Uvarovite	$Ca_3Cr_2(SiO_4)_3$
Chrysocolla	CuO, SiO_2, H_2O
Dioptase	H_2CuSiO_4
Prehnite	$H_2Ca_2Al_2(SiO_4)_3$
Axinite	$(Ca,Fe)_7Al_4B_2(SiO_4)_8$
Steatite	$H_2Mg_3Si_4O_{12}$
Serpentine	$H_4Mg_3Si_2O_9$
Sepiolite	$H_4Mg_2Si_3O_{10}$
Sodalite	$Na_4Al_2(Al.Cl)(SiO_4)_3$
Lazurite	$(Na_2,Ca)_2Al_2[Al(NaSO_4,NaS_3,Cl)](SiO_4)_2$
Enstatite	$Mg_2(SiO_3)_2$
Bronzite	$(Mg,Fe)_2(SiO_3)_2$
Hypersthene	$(Fe,Mg)_2(SiO_3)_2$
Diopside	$CaMg(SiO_3)_2$
Spodumene	$LiAl(SiO_3)_2$
Jadeite	$NaAl(SiO_3)_2$
Rhodonite	$Mn_2(SiO_3)_2$
Nephrite	$Ca(Mg,Fe)_3(SiO_3)_4$
Beryl	$Be_3Al_2(SiO_3)_6$
Iolite	$(Mg,Fe)_4Al_8(OH)_2(Si_2O_7)_5$
Orthoclase	$KAlSi_3O_8$
Microcline	$KAlSi_3O_8$
Albite	$NaAlSi_3O_8$ (*Ab*)
Anorthite	$CaAl_2Si_2O_8$ (*An*)
Oligoclase	Ab_9An_1 to Ab_7An_3
Labradorite	Ab_1An_1 to Ab_3An_7
Titanite	$CaTiSiO_5$
Benitoite	$BaTiSi_3O_9$
Thomsonite	$2(Ca,Na_2)Al_2(SiO_4)_2.5H_2O$

TABLE XI.—SUMMARY OF THE PROPERTIES OF THE GEM
FOR READY

Name, page reference, composition, and varieties	Color	Luster, transparency
AMBER *Fossil resin, succinite, rumanite, simetite, burmite* Hydrocarbon **276**	Yellow, also reddish, brownish, or whitish	Greasy Transparent to translucent
ANATASE TiO_2 **244**	Brown to black	Adamantine Transparent
ANDALUSITE Al_2SiO_5 *Chiastolite*, regular internal arrangement of dark inclusions **244**	Gray, green, yellow-green, bottle green, brown, pink, red, or violet	Vitreous to dull Transparent to opaque
APATITE $Ca_5(F,Cl)(PO_4)_3$ **245**	Green, pink, blue, purple, violet, or colorless	Vitreous to greasy Transparent
AXINITE $(Ca,Fe)_7Al_4B_2(SiO_4)_8$ **246**	Brown, yellow-brown, or violet	Vitreous Transparent
AZURITE $2CuCO_3.Cu(OH)_2$ **246**	Blue Blue streak	Vitreous to dull Translucent to opaque
BENITOITE $BaTiSi_3O_9$ **247**	Blue	Vitreous Transparent
BERYL $Be_3Al_2(SiO_3)_6$ *Emerald* .... *Aquamarine*........... *Golden beryl*........... *Heliodor*.............. *Morganite*............. *Goshenite*............. **202**	Emerald green Blue to sea green Yellow Yellow Pink to rose Colorless	Vitreous Transparent
BERYLLONITE $NaBePO_4$ **248**	Colorless to pale yellow	Vitreous Transparent
BRAZILIANITE $Na_2Al_6P_4O_{16}(OH)_8$ **248**	Yellow-green	Vitreous Translucent to transparent

MATERIALS DESCRIBED IN THE TEXT, ARRANGED ALPHABETICALLY
REFERENCE

Hardness (H.), specific gravity (S.G.)	Crystallization, structure, cleavage (C), and fracture (F)	Optical properties	Characteristics, occurrence, and principal localities
H. 2-2½ S.G. 1.0-1.1	Amorphous, irregular lumps F—Conchoidal	Isotropic n 1.54±	Electrified when rubbed. Melts at 280°C. Often contains inclusions —insects, vegetable remains, etc. Southern coast of Baltic Sea, Sicily, Rumania, Burma
H. 5½-6 S.G. 3.8-4.0	Tetragonal, only in crystals C—Pyramidal, basal perfect	Uniaxial; − ω 2.554 ϵ 2.493	With rutile. Crystals often resemble elongated octahedrons. Cornwall, England; France; Germany; Switzerland; Brazil
H. 7-7½ (often softer on surface.) S.G. 3.1-3.2	Orthorhombic, prismatic crystals	Biaxial; − α 1.634 β 1.639 γ 1.643	With cyanite, garnet, tourmaline, in metamorphic rocks. Andalusia, Spain; Ceylon; Brazil; Massachusetts
H. 5 S.G. 3.1-3.2	Hexagonal, prismatic, tabular crystals F—Conchoidal	Uniaxial; − ω 1.649 ϵ 1.644	With quartz, fluorite, tourmaline, in pegmatites and metamorphic rocks. Germany, Switzerland, Ceylon, Maine
H. 6½ S.G. 3.3	Triclinic, tabular crystals F—Conchoidal	Biaxial; − α 1.678 β 1.685 γ 1.688	Crystals sharp wedge-shaped. Dauphiné, France
H. 3½ S.G. 3.7-3.8	Monoclinic, tabular crystals, massive, fibrous	Biaxial; + α 1.730 β 1.758 γ 1.838	With malachite and other copper minerals. Ural Mountains, Rhodesia, Chile, Arizona
H. 6½ S.G. 3.6	Hexagonal, tabular crystals F—Conchoidal	Uniaxial; + ω 1.757 ϵ 1.804	Resembles sapphire. Strong dichroism: ϵ blue; ω white. San Benito County, California
H. 7½-8 S.G. 2.6-2.8	Hexagonal, prismatic crystals, massive F—Conchoidal	Uniaxial; − ω 1.568-1.598 ϵ 1.564-1.590 Dispersion 0.014	Generally in pegmatites, with quartz, topaz, tourmaline, chrysoberyl, garnet. *Emerald* in metamorphic rocks, Egypt, Colombia, Brazil, Urals, Tyrol, North Carolina. *Other varieties*, Brazil, Elba, Madagascar, Urals, Ireland, Ceylon, India, Maine, California
H. 5½-6 S.G. 2.85	Orthorhombic, highly modified crystals	Biaxial; − α 1.552 β 1.558 γ 1.561	In veins in granite, Stoneham, Maine
H. 5½ S.G. 2.9	Monoclinic C—Perfect pinacoidal	Biaxial; + α 1.598 β 1.605 γ 1.617	Well-formed crystals in pegmatite. Bahia, Brazil

TABLE XI.—SUMMARY OF THE PROPERTIES OF THE GEM

FOR READY

Name, page reference, composition, and varieties	Color	Luster, transparency

CALCITE
CaCO₃   Satin spar.................
          Marble....................
          Mexican onyx...............
249
	White, reddish, bluish, greenish, chatoyant
	Mottled
	Banded
		Translucent

CASSITERITE SnO₂ 250	Brown, reddish brown, black, or yellow	Adamantine Transparent to opaque
CHLORASTROLITE Silicate of calcium and aluminum 250	Green, with attractive white markings	Vitreous Translucent
CHROMITE (Fe,Cr)[(Cr,Fe)O₂]₂ 271	Iron black to brownish black Streak brown	Pitchy submetallic to metallic Opaque

CHRYSOBERYL
Be(AlO₂)₂   Chrysolite...............
          Cat's-eye.................
          Alexandrite...............
 	
231
	Yellowish green
	Green, chatoyant
	Emerald green in daylight, red by artificial light
		Vitreous or silky
		Transparent to translucent

CHRYSOCOLLA Hydrous copper silicate 251	Green and greenish blue	Vitreous, greasy, or dull Translucent to opaque
COBALTITE CoAsS 271	Silver white with a reddish tinge Streak black	Metallic Opaque
CORAL CaCO₃ Precious coral............... Black coral................. 275	Red Black	Dull Translucent

CORUNDUM
Al₂O₃   Ruby........................
          Sapphire....................
          White sapphire..............
          Golden sapphire.............
          Pink sapphire...............
          Green sapphire..............
          Yellow sapphire.............
          Violet sapphire.............
199   Star sapphire and star ruby......
	Rose to deep purplish red
	Blue
	Colorless
	Yellow
	Pink
	Green
	Yellow
	Violet
	Show asterism
		Adamantine when cut
		Transparent

DESCRIBED IN THE TEXT, ARRANGED ALPHABETICALLY
(*Continued*)

	Crystallization, structure, cleavage (C), and fracture (F)	Optical properties	Characteristics, occurrence, and principal localities
	Hexagonal, fibrous, compact massive	Uniaxial; − ω 1.658 ε 1.486 Strong double refraction	*Satin spar* in veins. *Marble*, metamorphosed limestone or dolomite. *Mexican onyx*, cave deposit
	tragonal; prismatic and pyramidal crystals, often winned	Uniaxial; + ω 1.997 ε 2.093	High specific gravity. In veins in granite, gneiss. With quartz, tourmaline, fluorite, apatite. Cornwall, England; Bolivia; Germany
	ys in rounded grains pebbles, fibrous		Weathers out of basic igneous rocks. Color unevenly distributed. Chatoyant. Lake Superior district
	; compact		With serpentine and chromium garnet. New Zealand, New Caledonia, Asiatic Turkey, Silesia, Pennsylvania, Maryland
	ombic; tabular shaped twins, or -hexagonal. rains. Cat's-eye is	Biaxial; + α 1.747 β 1.748 γ 1.757 Dispersion 0.015	Crystals striated. Pleochroism strong: green, red, and orange-yellow. Strong absorption band in yellow. In gneiss, mica schist, granite; with beryl, tourmaline, apatite. *Chrysolite* from Brazil; *cat's-eye*, Ceylon, China, Brazil; *alexandrite*, Urals, Ceylon
H. 2-4 S.G. 2.0-2.	masses; com- lal	Uniaxial; + ω 1.46± ε 1.57±	Enamel-like appearance. With other copper minerals. Urals, Arizona, Nevada, Chile
H. 5½ S.G. 6.0-6.4	Cubic; pyritohedrons		Sweden; Norway; Cornwall, England; Ontario
H. 3½ S.G. 2.6-2.7	Branching		Skeletons of small sea animals. From waters of moderate depth along shores of Mediterranean, Persian Gulf, Australia
H. 9 S.G. 3.9-4.1	Hexagonal; rough, barrel-shaped, or tabular crystals. Sometimes twinned. Conspicuous partings F—Conchoidal	Uniaxial; − ω 1.768 ε 1.760 Dispersion 0.018	Pleochroism strong. Darkest color through base. Cut cabochon may show asterism. Heat makes color paler. Phosphoresces with ultraviolet light. In placers, limestone, gneiss, schist, igneous rocks; with spinel, tourmaline. India, Burma, Ceylon, Siam, Urals, Montana, North Carolina

TABLE XI.—SUMMARY OF THE PROPERTIES OF THE GEM
FOR READY

Name, page reference, composition, and varieties	Color	Luster, transparency
CYANITE (kyanite) Al_2SiO_5 251	Light to sky blue, white, gray, green, brown, or colorless	Vitreous Transparent to translucent
DANBURITE $CaB_2Si_2O_8$ 252	Colorless, yellow	Vitreous Transparent to translucent
DATOLITE $Ca(B.OH)SiO_4$ 252	White, yellowish, reddish, greenish, brownish; mottled	Dull Transparent to opaque
DIAMOND C 181	Colorless, blue-white, yellow, brown, green, red, blue; pale	Adamantine Transparent
DIOPSIDE $CaMg(SiO_3)_2$ *Common* . . . . *Violan* 253	Green, yellow, colorless Blue	Vitreous to resinous Transparent
DIOPTASE H_2CuSiO_4 253	Emerald green	Vitreous
ENSTATITE $MgSiO_3$ **HYPERSTHENE** $(Fe,Mg)SiO_3$ 254	Grayish white, greenish, yellowish, brown, black; enstatite, light; hypersthene, dark	Vitreous, bronzy, or pearly Translucent to opaque
EPIDOTE $Ca_2(Al,Fe)_2(Al.OH)(SiO_4)_3$ 254	Yellowish to blackish or pistachio green; brown, red	Vitreous to resinous Transparent to opaque
EUCLASE $Be(Al.OH)SiO_4$ 255	Pale green or blue, colorless	Vitreous Transparent

MATERIALS DESCRIBED IN THE TEXT, ARRANGED ALPHABETICALLY
REFERENCE (*Continued*)

Hardness (H.), specific gravity (S.G.)	Crystallization, structure, cleavage (C), and fracture (F)	Optical properties	Characteristics, occurrence, and principal localities
H. 4-7, varying with direction S.G. 3.5-3.7	Triclinic; bladed crystals C—Perfect pinacoidal	Biaxial; — α 1.712 β 1.720 γ 1.728	Unevenly colored. Hardness varies with direction. In metamorphic rocks, with staurolite and garnet. Switzerland, Brazil, North Carolina
H. 7 S.G. 3	Orthorhombic, prismatic crystals F—Uneven to subconchoidal	Biaxial; — α 1.630 β 1.633 γ 1.636	Crystals resemble topaz. Danbury, Connecticut; Burma; Japan; Madagascar; Switzerland
H. 5-5½ S.G. 2.9-3.0	Monoclinic; compact F—Conchoidal	Biaxial; — α 1.626 β 1.654 γ 1.670	Resembles unglazed porcelain. With copper. In basic igneous rocks. Lake Superior district
H. 10 S.G. 3.5	Cubic; octahedrons, rounded, distorted; twinned C—Perfect octahedral	Isotropic n 2.417 Dispersion high, 0.063	Cold feel. Electrified on rubbing. Phosphoresces, fluoresces. Transparent to X-rays. With pyrope, gold; in placers and blue ground. South and West Africa, Belgian Congo, Brazil, India
H. 5-6 S.G. 3.2-3.3	Monoclinic, prismatic crystals C—Prismatic, basal parting	Biaxial; + β 1.671-1.708	Often zonally colored. In metamorphosed limestones. Piedmont, Italy; Tyrol; Renfrew County, Ontario; New York
H. 5 S.G. 3.3	Hexagonal; prismatic C—Perfect rhombohedral	Uniaxial; + ω 1.655 ϵ 1.708	Excellent crystals. French and Belgian Congo, Russia, Chile, Arizona
H. 5-6 S.G. 3.1-3.5	Orthorhombic; fibrous or lamellar masses C—Prismatic	Biaxial; *enstatite* +, β 1.653-1.670 *hypersthene* —, β 1.678-1.728	*Hypersthene* has metalloidal iridescence. South African *enstatite* sold as "green garnet." In basic igneous rocks
H. 6-7 S.G. 3.3-3.5	Monoclinic; excellent prismatic crystals C—Basal perfect	Biaxial; — β 1.719-1.763 Dispersion strong	Pleochroism marked. In metamorphic rocks. Tyrol; Piedmont, Italy; Elba; Dauphiné, France; Arendal, Norway; Prince of Wales Island, Alaska
H. 7½ S.G. 3.1	Monoclinic; prismatic crystals C—Pinacoidal	Biaxial; + α 1.653 β 1.656 γ 1.673	In metamorphic rocks with topaz, beryl, chrysoberyl. Brazil, Urals. Resembles aquamarine

TABLE XI.—SUMMARY OF THE PROPERTIES OF THE GEM

FOR READY

Name, page reference, composition, and varieties	Color	Luster, transparency
FELDSPAR $KAlSi_3O_8$, *orthoclase* and *microcline* $NaAlSi_3O_8$, *albite* $CaAl_2Si_2O_8$, *anorthite* *Oligoclase* and *labradorite* are intermediate between albite and anorthite 241	*Adularia*..Colorless *Moonstone*..Opalescent, white *Amazonstone*..Green *Sunstone* or *aventurine*.. Reddish *Labradorite*..Gray with marked play of colors *Yellow orthoclase*	Vitreous to pearly Transparent to opaque
FLUORITE CaF_2 255	Yellow, orange, green, blue, red, violet, pink, brown, colorless	Vitreous Transparent to translucent

GARNET
$M''_3M'''_2(SiO_4)_3$
  M'' M'''
  Ca Al *Grossularite, hessonite, South African jade*
  Mg Al *Pyrope*.....................
  Fe Al *Almandite, carbuncle*.........
          Rhodolite..................
  Ca Fe *Andradite*, includes:
          Topazolite...............
          Demantoid..............
          "Uralian emerald"........
    208   *Melanite*..................
	
	Yellow, brown, green
	
	Ruby red
	Deep red to black
	Rose red to purple (mixture of almandite and pyrope)
	
	Yellow
	Grass green
	Green
	Black
		Vitreous to resinous
		Light-colored varieties transparent; darker varieties opaque

GOLD Au 271	Golden yellow Streak golden yellow	Metallic Opaque
GYPSUM $CaSO_4.2H_2O$ *Satin spar*.............. *Alabaster*.............. 256	 White, chatoyant, fibrous, silky luster Snow white, fine-grained, opaque	Pearly, silky, or dull Transparent to opaque
HEMATITE Fe_2O_3 272	Black Streak red	Metallic splendent Opaque
IOLITE *Cordierite, dichroite* Magnesium, iron, aluminum silicate 258	Smoky blue to light blue	Vitreous Transparent to translucent

MATERIALS DESCRIBED IN THE TEXT, ARRANGED ALPHABETICALLY
REFERENCE (*Continued*)

Hardness (H.), specific gravity (S.G.)	Crystallization, structure, cleavage (C), and fracture (F)	Optical properties	Characteristics, occurrence, and principal localities
H. 6-6½ S.G. 2.5-2.8	Orthoclase monoclinic; others triclinic. Prismatic or tabular crystals and cleavage masses C—Perfect in two directions	Biaxial; *albite* and *labradorite* +; others — β 1.524-1.563 See p. 294	*Adularia* a variety of orthoclase; *moonstone*, of orthoclase, albite, and oligoclase; *amazonstone*, of microcline; *sunstone*, of oligoclase. *Adularia* and *moonstone:* Switzerland, Elba, Ceylon. *Amazonstone:* Urals, Pennsylvania, Colorado. *Labradorite:* Labrador. In pegmatites and metamorphic rocks
H.4 S.G. 3.1-3.2	Cubic; cubical crystals; also cleavage masses or fibrous C—Perfect octahedral	Isotropic n 1.434 Dispersion 0.006	Crystals frequently twinned. In veins and pegmatites; England most important
H. 6½-7½ S.G. 3.4-4.3 *Grossularite* 3.5-3.7 *Pyrope* 3.5-3.8 *Spessartite* 4.1-4.8 *Almandite* 3.9-4.2 *Andradite* 3.7-3.8	Cubic; good crystals; dodecahedron and tetragonal trisoctahedron; also as pebbles F—Conchoidal	Isotropic n 1.705-1.940 *Grossularite* 1.735 *Pyrope* 1.705 *Spessartite* 1.800 *Almandite* 1.830 *Andradite* 1.895 See pp. 210 and 293 Dispersion 0.024-0.028, for *demantoid* 0.057	*Grossularite:* in metamorphosed limestones, with vesuvianite, diopside; with zircon in placers; Ceylon, South Africa. *Pyrope:* rounded grains in peridotite and serpentine; South Africa, Czecho-Slovakia, Arizona. *Almandite:* in metamorphic and igneous rocks, with staurolite, cyanite, andalusite; widespread. *Rhodolite:* North Carolina. *Andradite:* in igneous and metamorphic rocks; Urals, Saxony
H. 2½-3 S.G. 16-19	Cubic; small crystals, or nuggets, or disseminated in quartz		In quartz veins or placers. California, Alaska, other gold-mining districts
H. 2 S.G. 2.2-2.4	Monoclinic; tabular crystals, cleavage masses, fibrous, granular C—Perfect pinacoidal	Biaxial; + α 1.520 β 1.523 γ 1.530	In limestones, shales. *Satin spar:* England; Niagara Falls, New York. *Alabaster:* Leghorn, Italy; Grand Rapids, Michigan
H. 5½-6½ S.G. 4.9-5.3	Hexagonal; tabular crystals, compact		Elba, Norway, Sweden, England, Lake Superior district
H. 7-7½ S.G. 2.6	Orthorhombic; massive C—Pinacoidal F—Conchoidal	Biaxial; — β 1.538-1.597	Pleochroism very strong in light and dark blue and yellowish white. In metamorphic rocks, gravels. Ceylon

TABLE XI.—SUMMARY OF THE PROPERTIES OF THE GEM
FOR READY

Name, page reference, composition, and varieties	Color	Luster, transparency
JADE *Nephrite*............$Ca(Mg,Fe)_3(SiO_3)_4$ *Jadeite*..................$NaAl(SiO_3)_2$ 229	White to leaf green, emerald green, or dark green	Subvitreous to pearly Translucent to opaque
JET Largely carbon, with hydrogen, oxygen 283	"Jet" black	Resinous Opaque
LAZULITE $(Fe,Mg)Al_2(OH)_2(PO_4)_2$ 259	Azure blue	Vitreous Translucent to opaque
LAZURITE *Lapis lazuli* Complex silicate 243	Deep blue, azure blue, Berlin blue, greenish blue	Vitreous to greasy Opaque to translucent
MALACHITE $CuCO_3.Cu(OH)_2$ 246	Emerald green, grass green Streak green	Silky or dull Opaque
MOLDAVITE *Tektite*................ 259	Green	Vitreous Transparent to translucent
OBSIDIAN *Volcanic glass*........... 260	Black, red, brown, greenish	
OLIVINE $(Mg,Fe)_2SiO_4$ *Peridot*............... *Chrysolite*............. 237	Bottle green, olive green Yellow to greenish yellow	Vitreous to greasy Transparent
OPAL $SiO_2.xH_2O$ *Gem opal*................ includes: *White opal*............... *Black opal*............... *Harlequin opal*.......... *Lechosos opal*............ *Fire opal*................ *Girasol*.................. *Opal matrix*.............. 215	Good play of colors Light-colored Dark gray, blue, black Uniform patches of color Green play of colors Yellow, red Blue white: opalescent Opal in its matrix	Vitreous to greasy Transparent to translucent

Materials Described in the Text, Arranged Alphabetically
Reference (*Continued*)

Hardness (H.), specific gravity (S.G.)	Crystallization, structure, cleavage (C), and fracture (F)	Optical properties	Characteristics, occurrence, and principal localities
H. 6½-7 S.G. *Nephrite* 3.0 *Jadeite* 3.3	Monoclinic; always massive, compact F—Splintery	*Nephrite;* biaxial − α 1.606 β 1.620 γ 1.632 *Jadeite;* biaxial + α 1.654 β 1.659 γ 1.667	Tough. Color often irregularly distributed. *Nephrite:* China, Turkestan, Siberia, New Zealand. *Jadeite:* Burma, Yunnan, Tibet, Mexico, South America
H. 2-2½ S.G. 1.1-1.4	Amorphous; compact F—Conchoidal		Tough. Takes good polish. Jet is a variety of brown coal (lignite). England, Spain, France, Germany, United States
H. 5-6 S.G. 3.1	Monoclinic, pyramidal crystals, also massive	Biaxial; − α 1.612 β 1.634 γ 1.643	Pleochroic. In quartz, slate, with corundum, and rutile. Austria, Georgia, North Carolina
H. 5-5½ S.G. 2.4-2.95	Cubic; compact	Isotropic *n* 1.50±	Lapis lazuli is a mixture of lazurite and other minerals, including pyrite. In metamorphosed limestone. Afghanistan, Siberia, Chile
H. 3½ S.G. 3.9-4.0	Monoclinic; fibrous, banded F—Conchoidal, splintery	Biaxial; − α 1.655 β 1.875 γ 1.909	*Malachite matrix* contains gangue. Alteration product of other copper minerals, with azurite. Urals, Rhodesia, Chile, Arizona
H. 5½ S.G. 2.3-2.6	Amorphous F—Conchoidal, with sharp edges	Isotropic *Moldavite* *n* 1.48-1.52 *Obsidian* *n* 1.48-1.65	Natural glasses of variable properties. *Obsidian* is of volcanic origin. *Moldavite*, of unknown origin; Czecho-Slovakia, Moravia, Australia, Libyan Desert
H. 6½-7 S.G. 3.2-3.4	Orthorhombic; prismatic crystals, granular masses, pebbles F—Conchoidal	Biaxial; + α 1.653 β 1.670 γ 1.689 Dispersion 0.018	In basic igneous rocks, limestones, with spinel, pyrope. St. John's Island, Red Sea; Burma; Ceylon; Queensland; Brazil; Navaho country of Arizona and New Mexico
H. 5½-6½ S.G. 1.95-2.3	Amorphous; compact masses F—Conchoidal, good	Isotropic *n* 1.44-1.46	Amount of water variable. In veins and cavities, deposited from hot waters. Czecho-Slovakia, Australia, Honduras, Mexico, Nevada, Idaho

TABLE XI.—SUMMARY OF THE PROPERTIES OF THE GEM
FOR READY

Name, page reference, composition, and varieties	Color	Luster, transparency

PEARL
$CaCO_3$ and organic matter
  Gem pearls.......spherical
  Baroque pearls....irregular in shape
  Button pearls.....flat
  Blister pearls.....growths on shells
  Mother-of-pearl...inner layer of pearl
    oyster shells
273
	White, pink, yellow, purple, red, green, blue, brown, black	Pearly
		Translucent to opaque

PHENACITE Be_2SiO_4 260	Colorless, yellowish, or pale rose red	Vitreous Transparent
PREHNITE $H_2Ca_2Al_2(SiO_4)_3$ 261	Light green, apple green, oil green, or yellowish green	Waxy vitreous Transparent to translucent
PYRITE FeS_2 272	Brass yellow Streak greenish black	Metallic Opaque

QUARTZ
SiO_2

Vitreous to greasy
Transparent to opaque

Crystalline varieties	*Cryptocrystalline varieties*
Vitreous, crystallized or crystalline, transparent to translucent	Less glassy than phanerocrystalline varieties; compact, homogeneous, microscopically crystalline

Crystalline varieties

Vitreous, crystallized or crystalline, transparent to translucent

  Rock crystal......Colorless
  Amethyst.........Purple, violet
  Rose quartz.......Pink, rose red
  Smoky quartz.....Smoky brown
  Citrine...........Yellow
  Milky quartz.....White
  Gold quartz.......Milky quartz with native gold
  Siderite..........Berlin blue

  Aventurine.......Yellow, brown, green, or red, containing glistening scales
  Rutilated quartz...Contains fine needles of rutile
  Tiger's-eye.......Fibrous, chatoyant; brown, blue, red

(Continued on page 310.)

218

Cryptocrystalline varieties

Less glassy than phanerocrystalline varieties; compact, homogeneous, microscopically crystalline

  Chalcedony.......Light colored
  Carnelian........Red
  Chrysoprase......Apple green
  Prase............Dull leek or sage green
  Plasma..........Green with white or yellowish spots
  Bloodstone.......Dark green with red spots
  Fortification agate.Angular bands
  Moss agate.......With dark dendritic inclusions
  Agate............Banded; curved bands
  Eye agate........Circular bands resembling an eye
  Agatized wood....Distinct woody structure
  Onyx............Banded; horizontal bands
  Sardonyx........Alternately red and white bands
  Jasper...........Opaque, red, yellow, brown, dark green, grayish blue

(Continued on page 310.)

MATERIALS DESCRIBED IN THE TEXT, ARRANGED ALPHABETICALLY
REFERENCE (*Continued*)

Hardness (H.), specific gravity (S.G.)	Crystallization, structure, cleavage (C), and fracture (F)	Optical properties	Characteristics, occurrence, and principal localities
H. 2½-3½ S.G. 2.5-2.7	Orthorhombic $CaCO_3$ (aragonite) with amorphous organic matter (conchiolin)		Best pearls round or pear-shaped. Soft, affected by acids, perspiration. Formed about foreign particles within shells of pearl oysters and mussels. In *culture pearls* growth is artificially stimulated. Warm seas of Orient (pearl oysters) and streams of Europe and United States (mussels)
H. 7½-8 S.G. 3.0	Hexagonal; well-formed crystals F—Conchoidal	Uniaxial; + ω 1.654 ϵ 1.670	Like quartz and topaz in appearance. Associated with them in pegmatites and metamorphic rocks. Urals; Minas Geraes, Brazil; Durango, Mexico; Stoneham, Maine
H. 6-6½ S.G. 2.8-3.0	Orthorhombic; in rounded masses, internal radial fibrous structure	Biaxial; + α 1.615 β 1.625 γ 1.645	In veins and cavities in basic igneous rocks, with datolite. Dauphiné, France; Lake Superior district; New Jersey
H. 6-6½ S.G. 4.9-5.2	Cubic; brilliant crystals, cubes, octahedrons, pyritohedrons, frequently striated		Widespread in occurence, in all kinds of rocks. Clusters, small natural crystals used uncut. Cut material sold as *marcasite* is usually pyrite
H. 7 S.G. 2.66	Hexagonal; prismatic crystals, horizontally striated, well-developed, often twisted or distorted, right- and left-handed, often twinned. Massive forms in veins and cavities, nodular, or compact F—Pronounced conchoidal (Continued on page 311.)	Uniaxial; + ω 1.544 ϵ 1.553 Dispersion 0.013 Right-handed crystals rotate plane of polarization of light to right (clockwise), left-handed crystals to the left (counterclockwise)	Occurs everywhere in all types of rocks *Agate:* Idar-Oberstein, Germany; Czecho-Slovakia; Uruguay; Lake Superior district; Oregon *Amethyst:* Ceylon, India, Siberia, Uruguay, Brazil, Maine, North Carolina, Lake Superior district *Aventurine:* Siberia, China, Madagascar *Bloodstone:* India, Siberia *Cat's-eye:* Ceylon, India, Germany, Brazil *Chalcedony:* Uruguay, Brazil, Lake Superior district *Chrysoprase:* Silesia, Oregon *Citrine:* Brazil *Gold quartz:* California, Alaska *Prase:* Saxony *Rock crystal:* Japan, Madagascar, Switzerland, Brazil, New York, Arkansas *Rose quartz:* Japan, Madagascar, Bavaria, France, Brazil, Maine, South Dakota

TABLE XI.—SUMMARY OF THE PROPERTIES OF THE GEM

FOR READY

Name, page reference, composition, and varieties	Color	Luster, transparency

QUARTZ (*Continued*)

Crystalline varieties		
Cat's-eye.........Fibrous, chatoyant; gray, brown, green	*Cryptocrystalline varieties*	
	Riband jasper....Banded	
	Egyptian jasper...Yellow to brown, irregularly marked	
218		

RHODONITE $MnSiO_3$ 261	Rose red, pink	Vitreous to pearly Opaque
RUTILE TiO_2 *Rutilated quartz*.............. 261	Red-brown, blood red, black Fine rutile needles in quartz	Metallic adamantine Opaque to transparent
SEPIOLITE $H_4Mg_2Si_3O_{10}$ *Meerschaum*.......... 262	White, yellowish, grayish	Dull Opaque
SERPENTINE $H_4Mg_3Si_2O_9$ *Precious serpentine*....... *Bowenite*............... *Williamsite*............. *Verd antique*.......... 263	Green or yellow Green, resembling jade Blackish green Mottled green and white	Dull, resinous, greasy, or waxy Translucent to opaque
SMITHSONITE $ZnCO_3$ 264	White, yellow, green, or blue	Vitreous to pearly Translucent to opaque
SODALITE Complex silicate 264	Deep blue, similar to that of lazurite	Vitreous to greasy Translucent
SPHALERITE ZnS 265	Colorless, yellow, red, green, black	Resinous to adamantine Transparent to translucent
SPINEL $Mg(AlO_2)_2$ *Ruby spinel*.............. *Balas ruby*.............. *Rubicelle*............... *Almandine*.............. *Sapphirine*............. 238 *Chlorospinel*.............	Deep red Rose red to pink Yellow, orange-red Violet, purple Blue Grass green	Vitreous Transparent

MATERIALS DESCRIBED IN THE TEXT, ARRANGED ALPHABETICALLY
REFERENCE (*Continued*)

Hardness (H.), specific gravity (S.G.)	Crystallization, structure, cleavage (C), and fracture (F)	Optical properties	Characteristics, occurrence, and principal localities
			Rutilated quartz: Madagascar, Brazil, Switzerland, Vermont *Smoky quartz:* Scotland, Switzerland, Maine, Colorado *Tiger's-eye:* South Africa
H. 5.5-6.5 S.G. 3.4-3.7	Triclinic; crystals or compact masses C—Prismatic	Biaxial; − β 1.720-1.740	Sverdlovsk, Ural Mountains; Franklin, New Jersey
H. 6-6½ S.G. 4.2-4.3	Tetragonal; prismatic, vertically striated, often twinned crystals	Uniaxial; + ω 2.616 ε 2.903	Norway, Sweden, Urals, Tyrol, Switzerland, France, Madagascar, Brazil, Vermont, North Carolina
H. 2-2½ S.G. 1-2	Monoclinic; always in earthy or nodular masses	Biaxial; − α 1.519 β 1.525± γ 1.529	May float on water because of porosity. Formed by alteration of serpentine and magnesite. Asia Minor, Greece, Spain, Moravia, Morocco
H. 2½-4 S.G. 2.5-2.8	Monoclinic; always massive F—Conchoidal, splintery	Biaxial; + β 1.512-1.550	Often spotted, clouded, or multicolored. Smooth, greasy feel. With pyrope. Sweden, Scotland, Silesia, Saxony, Rhode Island (*bowenite*), Vermont (*verd antique*), Massachusetts, Pennsylvania (*williamsite*), California. Results from alteration of other magnesian rocks and minerals
H. 5 S.G. 4.1-4.5	Hexagonal; compact, banded, stalactitic F—Splintery	Uniaxial; − ω 1.849 ε 1.621	Formed by alteration of zinc sulfide in limestone, dolomite. Laurium, Greece; Sardinia; Kelly, New Mexico; South Africa
H. 5-6 S.G. 2.2-2.4	Cubic; massive F—Conchoidal	Isotropic n 1.483	In igneous rocks. Urals; Mount Vesuvius; Norway; Ontario; Quebec; Litchfield, Maine
H. 3½ S.G. 3.9-4	Cubic, excellent tetrahedral crystals C—Perfect rhombic dodecahedral	Isotropic n 2.37 Dispersion 0.197	Very common mineral in zinc and lead deposits. Gem quality rare. Spain, Mexico
H. 8 S.G. 3.5-3.7	Cubic; octahedral crystals, twinned, also in grains C—Octahedral F—Conchoidal	Isotropic n 1.718-1.75 Dispersion 0.020	In limestones and placers with ruby. Ceylon, Burma, Siam, India, Madagascar, Australia, Afghanistan, Brazil, New Jersey, New York

TABLE XI.—SUMMARY OF THE PROPERTIES OF THE GEM
FOR READY

Name, page reference, composition, and varieties	Color	Luster, transparency
SPODUMENE LiAl(SiO$_3$)$_2$ *Kunzite*................. *Hiddenite*.............. 265	Pink to lilac Yellow green to emerald green	Transparent Vitreous
STAUROLITE HFeAl$_5$Si$_2$O$_{13}$ *Cross-stone, fairy-stone*... 266	Reddish brown	Vitreous to dull Translucent to opaque
STEATITE H$_2$Mg$_3$Si$_4$O$_{12}$ *Agalmatolite*........... 267	White, greenish, reddish Grayish white, greenish, brownish, reddish	Greasy Translucent
THOMSONITE 2(Ca,Na$_2$)Al$_2$(SiO$_4$)$_2$.5H$_2$O 267	White, red, green, and yellow; mottled	Vitreous to pearly Opaque
TITANITE CaTiSiO$_5$ *Sphene*................... 268	Yellow, green, brown, gray	Adamantine Transparent
TOPAZ Al$_2$(F,OH)$_2$SiO$_4$ *Precious topaz*........ 206	Pale blue, green, violet, or red Wine yellow	Vitreous Transparent
TOURMALINE Complex borosilicate *Achroite*.................... *Rubellite*.................... *Brazilian emerald*............ *Brazilian sapphire*........... *Brazilian peridot*............ *Peridot of Ceylon*............. *Siberite*..................... *Indicolite*................... 233	 Colorless Rose red Green Blue Yellowish green Honey yellow Violet Dark blue	Vitreous Transparent

MATERIALS DESCRIBED IN THE TEXT, ARRANGED ALPHABETICALLY
REFERENCE (*Continued*)

Hardness (H.), specific gravity (S.G.)	Crystallization, structure, cleavage (C), and fracture (F)	Optical properties	Characteristics, occurrence, and principal localities
H. 6-7 S.G. 3.1-3.2	Monoclinic; long prismatic crystals F—Prismatic	Biaxial; + α 1.660 β 1.666 γ 1.676 Dispersion 0.017	Somewhat pleochroic. Kunzite is strongly phosphorescent under radiations, with an orange-pink color. *Kunzite:* in pegmatites, with tourmaline, beryl; Madagascar; Pala, California. *Hiddenite:* in kaolin veins; North Carolina
H. 7-7½ S.G. 3.4-3.8	Orthorhombic; in cross-shaped twins	Biaxial; + α 1.736 β 1.741 γ 1.746 Dispersion 0.021	Some pleochroism. In metamorphic rocks, with cyanite, garnet, tourmaline. Tyrol, Switzerland, Brazil, Virginia
H. 1.5-2.5 S.G. 2.7	Massive, mottled, variegated	n 1.54-1.59	Alteration product. Composition varies. Widely distributed
H. 5-5½ S.G. 2.3-2.4	Orthorhombic; spherical concretions, rounded pebbles, radial fibrous	Biaxial; + β 1.513-1.531	"Eye markings" popular. Pebbles weathered out of basic igneous rocks along shores of Lake Superior
H. 5-5½ S.G. 3.4-3.6	Monoclinic; wedge-shaped crystals F—Conchoidal.	Biaxial; + α 1.900 β 1.907 γ 2.034 Dispersion 0.050	In schists and limestones, St. Gothard, Switzerland; Zillerthal, Tyrol; Madagascar; Maine; New York; Pennsylvania
H. 8 S.G. 3.4-3.6	Orthorhombic; prismatic crystals rich in forms, also massive C—Perfect basal F—Conchoidal	Biaxial; + α 1.619 β 1.620 γ 1.627 Dispersion 0.014	Pink topaz often artificially produced by heating yellow topaz. Occurs in gneiss, schist, granite, pegmatite; with tourmaline, quartz, apatite, fluorite, beryl. Urals, Scotland, Ireland, Brazil, Germany, Cornwall, Ceylon, Japan, Mexico, Utah, Colorado, Maine
H. 7-7½ S.G. 3.0-3.2	Hexagonal; prismatic, vertically striated crystals, with a rounded triangular outline F—Subconchoidal	Uniaxial; − ω 1.648-1.655 ϵ 1.625-1.633 Dispersion 0.016	Vertical axis polar. Electrified on rubbing. Often zonally colored. Strong dichroism, ω more strongly absorbed than ϵ. Gem tourmaline rich in alkalies. In pegmatites, with quartz, beryl, apatite, topaz, fluorite. Ceylon, Madagascar, South-West Africa, Siberia, Elba, Brazil, Maine, southern California

TABLE XI.—SUMMARY OF THE PROPERTIES OF THE GEM

FOR READY

Name, page reference, composition, and varieties	Color	Luster, transparency

TURQUOIS
Basic phosphate of copper and aluminum
    Turquois matrix..............
    Odontolite, fossil turquois.......
 	
    240
	Sky blue, greenish blue, apple green
	Turquois in its limonitic matrix
	Fossil ivory or bone colored by vivianite. Not true turquois
		Waxy
		Opaque

VARISCITE $AlPO_4.2H_2O$ *Utahlite*............... 269	Apple green to blue green Compact	Vitreous Translucent to opaque

VESUVIANITE
Calcium aluminum silicate
    Cyprine....................
    Californite..................
    269
	Yellow, green, brown
	
	Blue
	Green, compact
		Vitreous to greasy
		Translucent

WILLEMITE Zn_2SiO_4 270	Yellow, green, brown, reddish	Greasy vitreous Transparent

ZIRCON *Hyacinth, jacinth*............
$ZrSiO_4$ *Jargon*....................
 	
    Matara diamond.............
 	
    Blue zircon.................
    212
	Yellow, orange, red, brown
	Other colors than the above (colorless, gray, smoky)
	Colorless, either natural or produced artificially. Also green
	Blue
		Adamantine
		Transparent

ZOISITE $Ca_2Al_2(Al.OH)(SiO_4)_3$ *Thulite*......... 270	Rose red	Vitreous Transparent to translucent

MATERIALS DESCRIBED IN THE TEXT, ARRANGED ALPHABETICALLY
REFERENCE (*Continued*)

Hardness (H.), specific gravity (S.G.)	Crystallization, structure, cleavage (C), and fracture (F)	Optical properties	Characteristics, occurrence, and principal localities
H. 6 S.G. 2.6-2.8	Apparently amorphous; in veins, crusts, rounded masses F—Conchoidal	Biaxial; + β 1.62	Color unstable. Matrix usually limonitic. Formed by deposition from solutions. Persia, Sinai Peninsula, Turkestan, Australia, New Mexico, Arizona, California, Nevada
H. 4-5 S.G. 2.5	Orthorhombic; crusts, nodules, crystalline aggregates F—Conchoidal	Biaxial; − β 1.571-1.584	In shales and slates. Utah
H. 6½ S.G. 3.3-3.5	Tetragonal; prismatic crystals, compact	Uniaxial; − ω 1.713 ϵ 1.705	Weak pleochroism. In contact metamorphic deposits, with garnet, tourmaline, epidote. Mount Vesuvius; Wilui River, Siberia; Eger, Germany; California
H. 5-6 S.G. 3.9-4.3	Hexagonal; small crystals, massive	Uniaxial; + ω 1.691 ϵ 1.719	Franklin, New Jersey
H. 7½ S.G. 4.0-4.8	Tetragonal; prismatic crystals, lumps C—Imperfect F—Conchoidal	Uniaxial; + ω 1.931 ϵ 1.988 May be isotropic or biaxial, p. 213 Dispersion 0.048	Uranium varieties have a number of of sharp, narrow absorption bands. Pale-brown stones can be decolorized by heat (*Matara diamond*) or colored blue (*starlite*). In alluvial deposits. Ceylon; Australia; Expailly, France; Ilmen Mountains, Russia; Indo-China
H. 6-6½ S.G. 3.3-3.4	Orthorhombic; disseminated prismatic crystals	Biaxial; + α 1.700 β 1.703 γ 1.718	Strongly pleochroic. Norway, Italy

SELECTED BIBLIOGRAPHY

GENERAL

ANDERSON, B. W.: "Gem Testing for Jewellers," Heywood and Company, Ltd., London, 1942.

BAUER, M. H., and K. SCHLOSSMACHER: "Edelsteinkunde" (2 vols.), 3d ed., Tauchnitz, Leipzig, 1928-1932.

EPPLER, A., and W. F. EPPLER: "Edelsteine und Schmucksteine," Wilhelm Diebener, Leipzig, 1934.

ESCARD, J.: "Les pierres précieuses," Dunod, Paris, 1914.

FARRINGTON, O. C.: "Gems and Gem Minerals," A. W. Mumford, Chicago, 1903.

FOSHAG, WILLIAM F.: "Gems and Gem Minerals, Part II, Minerals from Earth and Sky," Smithsonian Institution, Washington, D. C., 1929.

KUNZ, G. F.: "Gems and Precious Stones of North America," Scientific Publishing Company, New York, 1890.

LIDDICOAT, R. T., JR.: "Handbook of Gem Identification," Gemological Institute of America, Los Angeles, 1947.

MERRILL, G. P., M. W. MOODEY, and E. T. WHERRY: "Handbook and Descriptive Catalogue of the Collection of Gems and Precious Stones in the United States National Museum," *Bulletin* 118, Government Printing Office, Washington, D. C., 1922.

SMITH, G. F. HERBERT: "Gemstones," 9th (rewritten) ed., Methuen & Co., Ltd., London, 1940.

SPENCER, L. J.: "A Key to Precious Stones," Blackie & Son, Ltd., Glasgow, 1936.

———: "Precious Stones" (English translation of Bauer's "Edelsteinkunde"), London, 1904.

WEBSTER, R.: "Practical Gemmology," N.A.G. Press, Ltd., London, 1940.

——— and V. V. HINTON: "Introductory Gemology," Gemological Institute of America, Los Angeles, 1945.

WHITLOCK, H. P.: "The Story of the Gems," Lee Furman, Inc., Publisher, New York, 1936.

ART OF CUTTING

BAXTER, W. T.: "Jewelry, Gem Cutting, and Metalcraft," 1st ed., Whittlesey House, McGraw-Hill Book Company, Inc., New York, 1938.

DAKE, H. C., and R. M. PEARL: "The Art of Gem Cutting," 3d ed., Mineralogist Publishing Company, Portland, Ore., 1945.

HOWARD, J. H.: "Revised Lapidary Handbook," J. Harry Howard, Greenville, S. C., 1946.

CRYSTALLOGRAPHY AND MINERALOGY

DANA, E. S.: "A Textbook of Mineralogy," 4th ed., revised by W. E. Ford, John Wiley & Sons, Inc., New York, 1932.

HURLBUT, C. S., JR.: "Dana's Manual of Mineralogy," John Wiley & Sons, Inc., New York, 1941.

KRAUS, E. H., W. F. HUNT, and L. S. RAMSDELL: "Mineralogy," 3d ed., McGraw-Hill Book Company, Inc., New York, 1936.

WAHLSTROM, E. E.: "Optical Crystallography," John Wiley & Sons, Inc., New York, 1943.

WINCHELL, A. N.: "Elements of Optical Mineralogy," 5th ed., John Wiley & Sons, Inc., New York, and Chapman & Hall, Ltd., London, 1937.

DIAMOND

AUSTIN, A. C., M. MERCER, and R. M. SHIPLEY: "The Story of Diamonds," Gemological Institute of America, Los Angeles, 1941.

BALL, S. H.: "The Diamond Industry." Annual Review, Jewelers' Circular-Keystone, New York.

CROOKES, W.: "Diamonds," Harper & Brothers, New York, 1909.

EPPLER, W. F.: "Der Diamant und seine Bearbeitung," Wilhelm Diebener, Leipzig, 1933.

FERSMANN, A., and V. GOLDSCHMIDT: "Der Diamant," 2 vols., C. Winter's Buchhandlung, Heidelberg, 1911.

GRODZINSKI, P.: "Diamant-Werkzeuge," Verlag von M. Krayn, Berlin, 1936.

———: "Diamond and Gem Stone Industrial Production," N.A.G. Press, Ltd., London, 1942.

SUTTON, J. R.: "Diamond: A Descriptive Treatise," Thomas Murby and Company, London, 1928.

TOLKOWSKY, M.: "Diamond Design," E. and F. N. Spon, Ltd., London and Spon and Chamberlain, New York, 1919.

WADE, F. B.: "Diamonds: A Study of the Factors That Govern Their Value," G. P. Putnam's Sons, New York, 1916.

WAGNER, P. A.: "The Diamond Fields of Southern Africa," The Transvaal Leader (Johannesburg), 1914.

WILLIAMS, A. F.: "The Genesis of the Diamond," 2 vols., Ernest Benn, Ltd., London, 1932.

WILLIAMS, G. F.: "The Diamond Mines of South Africa," 2 vols., B. F. Buck and Company, New York, 1905.

DICTIONARIES

"The Jewelers' Dictionary," Jewelers' Circular-Keystone, New York, 1945.

SHIPLEY, R. M., and others: "Dictionary of Gems and Gemology," 2d ed., Gemological Institute of America, Los Angeles, 1945.

STATISTICS

BALL, S. H.: "The Diamond Industry." Annual Review, Jewelers' Circular-Keystone, New York.

———: "Gem Stones." Annual Review, *Minerals Yearbook,* Government Printing Office, Washington, D. C.

ROUSH, G. A.: "Precious and Semi-precious Stones." Annual Review, *The Mineral Industry,* McGraw-Hill Book Company, Inc., New York.

SYNTHETIC GEMS

ESCARD, J.: "Les pierres précieuses," Dunod, Paris, 1914.

KRAUSS, F.: "Synthetische Edelsteine," Georg Stilke, Berlin, 1928.

MICHEL, H.: "Die Künstlichen Edelsteine," Wilhelm Diebener, Leipzig, 1926.

———: "Nachahmungen und Verfälschungen der Edelsteine und Perlen und ihre Erkennung," Ulr. Masers Buchhandlung, Graz, 1926.

PARSONS, C. H.: "Experiments on the Artificial Production of the Diamond," *Philosophical Transactions of the Royal Society (London)*, ser. A, vol. 220, pp. 67-107, 1919.

For other references, see Chapter X.

MISCELLANEOUS

ANDRÉE, K.: "Bernstein Forschungen (Amber Studies)," Walter de Gruyter & Company, Berlin, 1929-1939.

CATELLE, W. R.: "The Pearl: Its Story, Its Charm, and Its Value," J. B. Lippincott Company, Philadelphia, 1907.

DAKE, H. C., F. L. FLEENER, and B. H. WILSON: "Quartz Family Minerals," Whittlesey House, McGraw-Hill Book Company, Inc., New York, 1938.

DAKIN, W. J.: "Pearls," G. P. Putnam's Sons, New York, 1913.

GOETTE, J.: "Jade Lore," Reynal & Hitchcock, Inc., New York, 1937.

KUNZ, G. F.: "The Curious Lore of Precious Stones," J. B. Lippincott Company, Philadelphia, 1913.

———: "The Magic of Jewels and Charms," J. B. Lippincott Company, Philadelphia, 1915.

———: "Shakespeare and Precious Stones," J. B. Lippincott Company, Philadelphia, 1916.

——— and C. H. STEVENSON: "The Book of the Pearl: The History, Art, Science, and Industry of the Queen of Gems," D. Appleton-Century Company, Inc., New York, 1908.

NOTT, S. C.: "Chinese Jade throughout the Ages," B. T. Batsford, Ltd., London, 1936.

WILLIAMSON, G. C.: "The Book of Amber," Ernest Benn, Ltd., London, 1932.

JOURNALS

The American Mineralogist, Mineralogical Society of America, Ann Arbor, Mich.

Die Deutsche Goldschmiede-Zeitung, Wilhelm Diebener, Leipzig.

The Gemmologist, N.A.G. Press, Ltd., London.

Gems and Gemology, Gemological Institute of America (United States and Canada) Los Angeles.

Industrial Diamond Review, N.A.G. Press, Ltd., London.

The Jewelers' Circular-Keystone, Chilton Press, New York.

The Journal of Gemmology, Gemmological Association of Great Britain, London.

The Mineralogist, The Mineralogist Publishing Company, Portland, Ore.

National Jeweler, Chicago.

INDEX

Names of gem minerals and gem materials described or referred to in the text are printed in **boldface type,** synonyms and names of varieties in *italics,* and general subjects in light-face type. When there is more than one reference, the important one is printed in **boldface type.**

A

Absorption, selective, 75
Absorption spectra, 79
Achroite, **235,** 312
Acid rocks, 95
Adamantine luster, **47**
Adamas, 184
Adularia, 242, 304
Agalmatolite, **267,** 312
Agate, 110, 127, **225,** 308
  Lake Superior Fire, 169
  staining, **140,** 142
  varieties of, 225-227
Agatized wood, 226
Alabaster, 142, 256, **258,** 304
Alalite, 253
Albite, 20, **242,** 304
Alexandrite, 156, 166, **231,** 300
  cat's-eye, 231, 233
  synthetic, 165
Allochromatic, 41
Allotropic forms, 90
Alloys, of gold, silver, and platinum, 174, 176
Alluvial deposits, **94,** 97, 184, 190, 196
Almandine, **240,** 310
Almandite, **211,** 304
Amateur lapidaries, 110, 131
Amazonite, 242
Amazonstone, **242,** 304
Amber, 37, 50, 145, **276,** 298
  Baltic Sea, 276
  Burmese, 281
  imitations of, 282
  methods of detection of, 282
  pressed, **145,** 278, 282, 283

Amber, *Rumanian,* 280
  Sicilian, 281
  varieties of, 278-281
Ambroid, **145,** 278
Amethyst, **220,** 308
  heat treatment of, 144
  oriental, 201
Amorphous, definition of, 25
Analyzer, 65
Anatase, 244, 298
Andalusite, 43, **244,** 298
Andradite, **212,** 304
Angle, critical, **55,** 59, 60, 104, 105
Angstrom unit, 55
Anisotropic substances, 15, **63**
Anorthite, 242, 304
Apatite, 245, 298
Aquamarine, 45, **204,** 205, 298
  heat treatment of, 145
  Oriental, 139
  "synthetic," 165, 205
Aragonite, 273
Artificial coloring or staining, 140
Artificial gems, 146-167
Asparagus stone, 245
Asterism, **46,** 146, 200, 221
  in gems (table), 292
Aventurine glass, 169
  oligoclase, **243,** 304
  quartz, 223, 308
Axes, crystal, 12
  optic, 15, **64,** 70-72, 75, 153, 161 162
  twinning, 22
Axinite, 246, 298
Azurite, 246, 298
Azurmalachite, **247,** 298

321

B

Baguette cut, 106
Bakelite, 37, **169,** 282, 283
Balance, chemical, 34
  Jolly, 37
  Krätschmar, 39
  Westphal, 36
Balas ruby, 139, **238, 310**
Ballas, 197
Baroque pearls, 274, 308
Basalt, 96
Basanite, 229
Base, 102
Basic rock, **95,** 97
Beads, boring of, 133
Beauty in gems, 4
Beceka mines, 191
Becke's method, 58
Beetle, 171
Benitoite, 247, 298
Bernstein, 279
Beryl, 92, **202,** 298
  golden, **204,** 298
Beryllonite, 248, 298
Bezel, 101
Biaxial gems, table of, 292
Biaxial substances, 15, **64,** 71
Bipyramids, 17-21
Birefringence, 64
  of gem minerals (table), 293
Birne, 151
Bisectrix, 72
Blister pearls, 274, 308
Bloodstone, **225,** 272, 308
Blue ground, 185, 279
Blue john, 256
Blue-white diamonds, 124
Boart, 197
Bohemian ruby, 221
Bonamite, 264
Bone turquois, 241
Boring of beads, 133
Bort, 118, **197**
Bortz, 197
Bottle stone, 259
Boule, **151**-154, 157, 160, 163
  orientation of, **153,** 161
Bowenite, 231, 263, **310**

Bowr, 197
Bragg angle, 84
Bragg method, 84
Brazilianite, 248, 298
Breccia, **96,** 249
Brilliancy of gems, 4, 103, **104**
Brilliant cut, 100, **101,** 104
Brilliants, 100, 168
Brillianteerer, 117
Brittleness, 33
Bronzite, 254
Bruting, 115
Bubbles, gas, 157, **159,** 168
Bulfontein diamond mine, **187,** 190
Bullet cut, 106
Burmite, **281,** 298
Button pearls, 274, 308

C

Cabochon cut, 99
Cairngorm, 222
Calcite, 25, 26, 63, 68, 93, 94, **249,** 30θ
Californite, **269,** 314
Cameo, **108,** 133
Cape, silver, 124
  top, 124
Cape grade of diamonds, 124
Cape ruby, 139, 185, 208, **211**
Carat, **135,** 174
Carbonado, 197, **198**
Carbuncle, **211,** 304
Carnelian, **223,** 308
Cassiterite, 250, 300
Cat's-eye, 46
  chrysoberyl, 231, 233, 300
  quartz, **223,** 310
  tourmaline, 234
Cell, unit, 83
Celluloid, 170
Chalcedony, **223-229,** 308
Chaton, 168
Chatoyancy, 46
  in gems (table), 292
Chemical properties, 89, 296
Chert, 229
Chevee, 108
Chiastolite, 43, **245,** 298
Chips, diamond, 112
Chlorastrolite, 250, 300

Chloromelanite, 230
Chlorospinel, **240**, 310
Chromite, 211, **271**, 300
Chrysoberyl, 231, 300
  synthetic, 166
Chrysocolla, 251, 300
Chrysolite, 232, **237**, 259, 300, 306
Chrysoprase, **225,** 308
Chrysotile, 264
Cinnamon-stone, 210
Citrine, 143, 206, **222,** 308
Cleavage, 31
  false, 33
Cleaving of diamond, 31, **111**
Clerici solution, 37
Cobaltite, 271, 300
Colloids, 25
Colophony, 279
Color, 4, **41**
  and cutting of gems, 42, 44, 76, 161
  interference, 69
  play of, **46,** 292
  size and, 45
Color description, 43
Color grades of diamonds, 124
Color table of gems, 290-292
Coloring, artificial, **140,** 145
Combination of crystal forms, 16
Composition of gem minerals (table),
  296, 297
Compound, chemical, 88, **89**
Compound crystals, 21
Compounds, diamond, 186
Conchiolin, 273
Conchoidal fracture, **33,** 169
Conglomerate, 96
Contact twins, 22
  metamorphism, 91
Copal, 281, 282
Coral, 275, 300
Cordierite, 77, **258,** 304
Corundum, 104, **199,** 300
  heat treatment of, 144
  synthetic, 150-163
Cracks, internal, 157, **159**
Critical angle, **55,** 59, 60, 68, 104, 105
Crocidolite, 223
Crookes, Sir William, 147
Cross-stone, **266,** 312

Crossed nicols, 68
Crown, 101, 125
Cryptocrystalline, **25,** 220, 223
Crystal, 220
Crystal, attached, 92
  compound, 21
  definition of, **11,** 26, 81
  disseminated, 92
  distorted, 20
  size of, 12
  terminated, 92
  top, 124
  twinned, 22
Crystal aggregates, 26
Crystal angles, constancy of, 11
Crystal axis, 12
Crystal forms, 15
Crystal grade of diamonds, 124
Crystal structure, **81-88,** 112, 120
Crystal systems, **12,** 287
Crystalline aggregates, 25
Crystalloids, 26
Cube, 16
Cube faces, hardness of, 29, 120
Cubic system, 12, 14, **16**
Culet, 100
Cullinan diamond, 32, 190, **192**
Culture pearls, 274
Cupid's darts, 223
Curvette, 109
Cushion cut, 108
Cut-corner-triangle cut, 106
Cuttables, diamond, 183, **199**
Cutters, gem, 109, **128**
Cutting, 99
  of diamonds, 110, 115
  electrical, 120
  of gems, 99-134
Cuvette, **109,** 133
Cyanite, 251, 302
Cyclic twins, 22
Cymophane, 233
Cyprine, **269,** 314

D

Danburite, 156, 165, **252,** 302
Datolite, 252, 302
DeBeers Consolidated Mines, Ltd., 186

DeBeers mine, 190
Demantoid, **212**, 304
Dendritic, 43, 226
Density, 33, 289
Diamolite, 124
Diamond, 4, 21, 29, 32, 81, 104, 112, **181**, 302
Diamond cutters, 109
Diamond cutting, 104, 109, 110, **115**
  centers of, 169
  electrical, 120
  gauges for, 117, 136
  machines for, 123
Diamond dust, **114**, 118
Diamond lapper, 117
Diamond point, 121, 135
Diamond trigons, 181
Diamonds, artificial, 147
  atoms in, distribution of, 120
  ballas, 197
  black, 198
  bort, 118, **197**
  brillianteerer of, **117**
  carbonado, 198
  cleaving of, 31, 110, **111**
  color grading of, 124
  cut, make of, 125
  distorted, 21
  evaluation of, 124, 189
  famous, 192
  fancy, 124
  flaws in, 111, 125
  four-point, 121
  gem, 183, **191**
  hardness of, 29, 114, **119**
  imitation, *Alaska,* 220
    Cornish, 220
    glass, 168
    Herkimer, 220
    Lake George, 220
    Matara, 143, **214**, 314
    Matura, 143, **214**, 314
    Mexican, 220
  industrial, 184, **196**
  inspection of, 110
  occurrence and recovery of, 184
  polishing of, 110, **117**
  radiated, 145
  sand, 108
  sawing of, 111, **112**

Diamonds, sawing of, electrical, 115
  synthetic, 147
  three-point, 121
  treated, 145, 146
  two-point, 121
Diamondscope, 126
Diaphaneity, 48
Dichroism, **76**, 162, 295
Dichroite, **258**, 304
Dichroscope, 77
Diggings, 185
Dikes, 96
Dimorphous substances, 90
Diopside, 92, **253**, 302
Dioptase, **253**, 302
Dispersion, **53**, 105
  of gem minerals (table), 295
Distorted crystals, 21
Dodecahedral sawing grain, **115**
Dodecahedron, 16
  hardness of, 29, **120**
Domes, 19-21
Dop, 116, 120, 122
Double refraction, 15, **62**, 64
Doublet, 140, **171**
  imitation, 173
  opal, 172
Drill bit, diamond, 197
Durability, **4**, 28, 29
Dust, diamond, **114**, 118
Dutoitspan mine, 190

E

"Edge up," 124
Egeran, 270
Eight cut, 106
Electricity, frictional, **50**, 278
  piezo-, 50
  pyro-, 50
Elements, chemical, 88, 89
Emerald, 92, 104, **203**, 298
  "Brazilian," 165, **236**, 312
  copper, 254
  evening, 237
  oriental, 201
  soldered, 173
  synthetic, **165**, 205
  Uralian, 208, 212
Emerald cut, 106

Emery, 200
Enantiomorphism, **74**
Endoscope, 275
Engraving of gems, 133
Enstatite, 254, 302
Epaulet cut, 106
Epidote, 254, 302
Erb and Gray refractometer, 62
Essonite, **210,** 304
Euclase, 255, 302
Evaluation of diamonds, 124, 189
Extinction, 69, 71
Extraordinary ray, 63
Extrusive rocks, 95

F

"Face up," 124
Faceted cuts, 100-108
  machine for, 132
Facets, inclination of, 103, 104
  names of, 102
Fairy stone, 22, **266,** 312
False topaz, 139, 206, **222**
Fancy diamonds, 124, 182
Fashion in gems, 5
Feathers, 161, 204
Feldspar, 241, 304
Figure, interference, 70-72, **75**
File, jeweler's, 28
Fineness, of metals, 174
Fire, in gems, 4, **54,** 105
Fire opal, 217
Fish-eye, 103
Flats, **21,** 199
Flaws in diamonds, **111,** 125
Flint, 227
Fluorescence, 49
  in diamonds, 124
Fluorite, 74, 255, 304
Fluorspar, 255
Foil, 168
Forms, allotropic, **90**
  crystal, 15
  false, 23
Formation of gem minerals, **91**
Fossil resin, **276,** 298
  turquois, **241,** 314
Fracture, 33
  of glass, 168

Frémy and Feil, **150**
Full cut, 108
Fusion, formation from, **91**

G

Gangue, 93
Garnet, 171, 208, 304
Gauges, for diamond cutters, 117
  gem, 136
Gels, 25
Gem minerals, formation of, 91
  number of, 6
  qualifications of, 3
  synthetic, 3, **146-167**
Gemmology, **7**
Geode, 93
Geographical occurrence of gems, 97
Geological occurrence of gems, 97
German lapis, 142, 227
Gilt, 175
Girasol, **217,** 306
Girdle, 28, 101, 126
Girdling, 115
Glacial drift, diamonds in, 190
Glass, 168, 259, 260
  index of refraction of, 168
  silica, 259
  specific gravity of, 168
  volcanic, 259, 260
Gliding, **23, 33**
Glossiness, 44
Gneiss, 96, 97
Gold, 271, 304
Gold alloys, 174
Gold quartz, **222,** 308
Goldstone, 169, 223
Goshenite, **204,** 298
Grading of diamonds, **124,** 189
Grain, polishing, 112, 119
  sawing, 114
  unit of weight, 137
Greaser, diamond, 188
Greenstone, 250
Grossularite, **210,** 304
Gypsum, 142, 256, 304

H

Half-brilliant cut, 106
Half-moon cut, 106

Hannay, J. B., 149
Hardness, comparative table of, 30
  definition of, 26
  determination of, 26-31
  of gem minerals (table), 288
  Mohs scale of, 26
  pencils, 27
  points, 27
  variation in, **29**, 114, 119
  wheel, 28
Harlequin opal, **216**, 306
Heat, 49, 91, 142
  conduction of, **49**, 169, 183, 278
Heat treatment of gems, 140, **142**
Heavy liquids, 37
Heliodor, **204**, 298
Heliotrope, 225
Hematite, 272, 304
Hessonite, **210,** 304
Hexagon cut, 106
Hexagonal system, 13, **14,** 15
Hexahedron, 16
Hexahedron faces, hardness of, 29, 120
Hiddenite, **265,** 312
Hornstone, 229
Hue of color, 44
Hyacinth, garnet, 210
  zircon, **214,** 314
Hyalite, 217
Hydrophane, 217
Hypersthene, 254, 302

I

Iceland spar, 63, 68, 77
Idar-Oberstein, gem cutting at, 109, 110,
  127-134
  staining agates at, 141
Idiochromatic, 41
Idocrase, 269
Igmerald, 166
Igneous rocks, 95
Imitation gems, 140, **167-171**
Immersion method, 57
Imperfections in diamond, 110-113, 125
In situ deposits, 94
Inclination of facets, 103, 104
Inclined extinction, 71
Inclusions, **35,** 125, 159, 161, 204, 223,
  292

Index, determination of, 56-62
  of gem minerals (table), 293
  of glass, 168
  of liquids, 57
  of refraction, 53
Indicolite, **235,** 312
Intaglio, **109,** 133
Intensity of color, 45
Interference colors, 69
Interference figure, 70-72, 75
Interference of light, 46
Intrusive rock, 95
Iolite, 258, 304
Iridium, 175
Isotropic gems, table of, 292
Isotropic substances, 14, **63,** 69
Itacolumite, 229

J

Jacinth, garnet, 210
  zircon, **214,** 314
Jade, **229,** 306
  Mexican, 231, **249**
  serpentine, 231, **263,** 304
  South African, **211,** 231
  Transvaal, **211,** 231
  vesuvianite, 231, **269**
Jadeite, 229, 306
Jaeger grade of diamonds, 124
Jaegerstontein mine, 190
Jargon, **214,** 314
Jasper, **227,** 308
  varieties of, 227
Jet, 283, 306
Jolly balance, 37
Jonker diamond, 111, 115, 118, **193**

K

Karat, **136,** 174
Kashmir blue sapphire, 201
Kauri copal, 282
Keystone cut, 106
Kimberley mine, 185, 190
Kimberlite, 185
Kite cut, 106
Klein's solution, 37
Knots, 23
Krätschmar balance, 39

Kundt's method, 50
Kunzite, 156, **265,** 312
Kyanite (*see* Cyanite)

L

Labradorite, 242, 304
Lap, 118, 130
 (*See also* Skeif)
Lapidary, 109, 127, **130**
Lapidary stick, 130
Lapidist, 109, 130
Lapis lazuli, **243,** 306
 German, 142, 227
 Swiss, 142, 227
Lapper, 117
Laue diagram, 84
Laue method, 83
Lazulite, 244, **259,** 306
Lazurite, 243, 259, 264, 306
Lechosos opal, **216,** 306
Lentil cut, 99
Leveridge gauge, 136
Light, monochromatic, 54
 polarized, 65
 wave-length of, 55
Lintonite, 268
Lisbon cut, 105
Lozenge cut, 106
Lucite, 170
Lumarith, 170
Luminescence, 49
Lumpy diamond, 103
Luster, 4, **47**

M

Macle, **22,** 198
Madeira topaz, 206
Magma, 91, 95
Make of cut gem, 125
Malachite, 246, 306
 matrix, 247
Malacolite, 253
Man and minerals, 1
Manufactured gems, 140-176
Marble, 25, 97, **249,** 300
Marcasite, 169, **273**
Marquise cut, 106
Matara diamond, 143, 212, **214,** 314

Matrix, malachite, 247
 opal, **217,** 306
 turquois, **241,** 314
Matura (see Matara)
Mechanical dop, 122
Meerschaum, **262,** 310
Melanite, **212,** 304
Melee, **108,** 113
Metallic gem minerals, 179, 271-273
 luster, 47
Metals used for gem mountings, 174
Metamorphic processes, 91
Metamorphic rocks and minerals, 96 97
Mexican, jade, 231, **249**
 onyx, **249,** 300
Michaud, 147
Microcline, 242, 304
Micron, 55
Microscope, polarizing, 65
Mikimoto pearls, 273
Milky quartz, **222,** 308
Millimicron, 55
Mine cut, old, 101
Mineral, definition of, 3
Mineralizers, 91
Mocha stone, 226
Mohs scale of hardness, 26
Moissan, 147
Moldavite, 259, 306
Monochromatic light, 54
Monoclinic system, 14, **19**
Moonstone, **242,** 304
Morganite, **204,** 29
Morion, 222
Moroxite, 245
Moss agate, **226,** 308
Moss opal, 217
Mother-of-pearl, **273,** 308
Mountings, metals used for, 174
 special, 140, **146**
Multifacet cut, 105
Mutton fat jade, 229

N

Naming of gems, 138
Naturals, 102, 126
Navette, 106
Negative, optically, 64
Nephrite, 229, 306

Nicol prism, 67
Nicols, crossed and parallel, 68
Nigrine, 262
Noble, Sir Arthur, 147
Non-metallic luster, 47

O

Obsidian, 260, 284, 306
Occurrence of gem minerals, geographic, 97
  geological, 97
Octahedrite, 244
Octahedron, 16
Octahedron faces, hardness of, 29, 114, **120**
Odontolite, **241, 314**
Old English cut, 106
Oligoclase, 242, 304
Olivine, 237, 306
Onegite, 223
Onyx, 109, **227,** 308
  blue, 142
  Mexican, 249
Opal, 4, **215,** 306
  varieties of, 216
Opal doublet, 172
Opalescence, 46
Opalescent gem minerals (table), 292
Optic axis, 15, **64,** 70-72, 75
Optical groups, 63
Optical properties, 14, **52-80**
  of gem minerals (tables), 292-295
Ordinary ray, 63
Organic gem materials, 179
Oriental amethyst, 201
  aquamarine, 139
  emerald, 201
  topaz, **201,** 206
Orientation of cut stones, 76, 157, 161
Ornamental objects, 134, 179
Orthoclase, 242, 304
Orthorhombic system, 13, 14, **19**
Osmium, 176

P

P.K., 125
Padparadschah sapphire, 156
Pagodite, 267

Palladium, 176
Parallel extinction, **69, 73**
Parallel groups, 22
Parallel nicols, 68
Parallel polarized light, 68
Parsons, C. H., 149
Parting, 33
Paste, 168, **173**
Pavilion, 102, 125
Pearl, 273, 308
  culture, 274
  grain, 137
  varieties of, **274**
Pegmatites, 95, 97
Pencil, hardness, 27
Penetration twins, 22
Penfield's solution, 37
Pentagon cut, 106
Perfection of diamonds, 125
Peridot, **237,** 306
  "*Brazilian,*" **236,** 312
  "*of Ceylon,*" **236,** 312
Peridotite, 96
Peristerite, 243
Petrified shells, 23
Petrified wood, 23, **217,** 226
Phenacite, 260, 308
Phlogopite, 47
Phosphorescence, 49
Physical properties, 25-51
  of gem minerals (tables), 289-292
Piezoelectricity, 50
Pigeon's-blood ruby, 200
Pinacoid, 20
  basal, 18, 76, 162
Pinking of topaz, **143, 207**
Piqué (P.K.), 125
Pistacite, 254
Placer deposits, 94
Plagioclase feldspars, 242
Plasma, **225,** 308
Plastics, **169,** 282, 284
Platinum, 175
Play of color, **46,** 292
Pleochroism, 75-78
  of gems (table), 295
Plexiglass, 170
Plutonic rocks, 95
Point, four-, three-, two-, **121**
  hardness, 27

Point, unit of weight, 135
Polariscope, Shipley, 73
Polarization, circular, 74
Polarized light, 65
  convergent, 68
  parallel, 68
Polarizer, 65
Polaroid, 67
Polishing, of diamonds, 117-124
  of gems, 99-134
Polymorphous substances, 90
Polysynthetic twins, 22
Portability of gems, 6
Portuguese cut, 106
Positive, optically, 64
Prase opal, 217
Prase quartz, **225**, 308
Precious stone, 2, **29**, 179
Prehnite, 261, 308
Premier diamond mine, 188, 190, 192
Premier grade of diamonds, 124
Pressed amber, **145**, 280, 283
Pressure, 91, 96
  treatment of gems by, 140, **145**
Primary deposits, 94
Prism, 17-21
  Nicol, 67
Production of gems, statistics for, 98
Properties of gems, chemical, 89
  optical, 52-80
  physical, 25-51
Pseudomorph, 23
Pycnometer, 35
Pyralin, 170
Pyrite, 243, 272, 308
Pyroelectricity, 50
Pyrope, **211**, 304

Q

Quartz, 22, **218,** 308
  circular polarization of, 75
  treated, 140-143
  varieties of, **220-229** 308, 310
Quartzite, 97, **229**
Quinzite, 217

R

Radium treatment, 140, **145**
Rarity of gems, 5

Rayner refractometer, 62
Reconstructed gems, 147
Rector's solution, 37
Reflection of light, 52
  total, **55**, 105
Refraction, double, 15, **62**
  index of, 53
    determination of, 56-62
  of light, 52
  single, 14, **62**
Refractive index of gems (table), 293-294
Refractive liquids, 57
Refractometer, 59-62
Refractometer method, 59
Regional metamorphism, 93
Relief, 57
Resin, fossil, **276**, 298
Resinous luster, 47
Rhinestone, 168, 220
Rhodium, 176
Rhodolite, **211**, 304
Rhodonite, 261, 310
Rhombohedron, 18
Rock crystal, 104, **220**, 308
Rocks, description of, 94-97
Rods, synthetic, 153
Rhorbach's solution, 37
Rose cut, 100
  opal, 217
  quartz, **221**, 308
Rounding, 115
Royat, France, 110, 129, 130
Rozircon, 165
Rubellite, 139, **235**, 312
Rubicelle, 139, **238**, 310
Ruby, 104, **200**, 300
  American, 139
  Arizona, 139, **208**
  balas, 139, **238**, 310
  Bohemian, 139, **221**
  Brazilian, 139
  California, 139
  Cape, 139, 185, 208, **211**
  Colorado, 139
  dichroism and cutting of, **76**
  heat treatment of, 144
  Montana, 139
  pigeon's-blood, 200
  reconstructed, 147

Ruby, Rocky Mountain, 139
  Siberian, 139
  spinel, 238, 310
  star, 47, 146, 163, 200, 300
  synthetic, distinguishing characteris-
    tics of, 157-163
    manufacture of, 150-163
    properties of, 156
    value and uses of, 166
Rumanite, 280, 298
Ruthenium, 176
Rutilated quartz, 223, 261, 308, 310
Rutile, 23, 261, 310
Rutile inclusions in rubies, 158, 159

S

Sagenite, 223
St. Stephen's stone, 225
Sand, diamond, 108
Sandstone, 96, 229
Saphir d'eau, 258
Sapphire, 42, 104, 200, 300
  "Brazilian," 236, 312
  heat treatment of, 144
  quartz, 222
  star, 47, 146, 163, 200, 300
  synthetic, distinguishing characteris-
    tics of, 157-163
    manufacture of, 150-163
    properties of, 156
    value and uses of, 166
  varieties of, 200, 300
Sapphirine, 240, 310
Sard, 223
Sardonyx, 227, 308
Satin spar, 46, 257, 304
  calcite, 249, 300
  gypsum, 257, 304
Sawed top, 103
Sawing diamonds, 112
  electrical, 115
Sawing grain, 114
Scaife, 118
Scale of hardness, Mohs, 26
Scalenohedron, 18
Schists, 96, 97
Schorl, 236
Scientific gems, 147
Scotch topaz, 206, 308

Secondary deposits, 94, 185
Sedimentary rocks, 96
Selenite, 257
Semi-precious gems, 29, 179
Sepiolite, 262, 310
Serpentine, 93, 97, 263, 310
  jade, 231, 263
Shale, 96
Sharp, diamond, 112
Shell, cameo, 273
  opalized, 23
  petrified, 23
Siberian amethyst, 221
Siberite, 235, 312
Siderite, 222, 308
Silica glass, 259
Silk, in emerald, 204
Silver alloys, 176
Simetite, 281, 298
Single cut, 106
Single refraction, 14, 62
Size, of crystals, 12
  of cut gems, 134
Skeif, 118
Slate, 97
Smith refractometer, 60, 61
Smithsonite, 264, 310
Smoky quartz, 222, 308
Smoky topaz, 206, 222
Soapstone, 267
Sodalite, 244, 264, 310
Solder dop, 122
Solution, formation from, 91, 93
South African diamond mines, 184-190
South African jade, 211, 231, 304
Space lattice, 81
Spanish topaz, 139, 143, 206
Spar, Falls, 258
  Niagara, 258
  satin, 249, 257
Specific gravity, definition of, 33
  determination of, 33-41
  of gems (table), 289
  of glass, 168
Spectroscope, 79
Spectrum, 54
  absorption, 79
Spessartite, 211, 304
Sphalerite, 93, 265, 310
Sphene, 268, 312

Spinach jade, 229
Spinel, 104, **238,** 310
  ruby, **238,** 310
  synthetic, 150, **163**
Split brilliant cut, 106
Spodumene, 12, **265,** 312
Spread, 103
Square cut, 106
Staining gems, **140,** 146
Star cut, 106
Star rubies and sapphires, 47, 146, **200,** 300
Star rose quartz, 221
Starlite, 139, **143**
Staurolite, 266, 312
Steatite, 267, 312
Step cut, 108
Sterling silver, 176
Strain, 69, 161, 283
Strass, 168
Streak, 46
  of gems (table), 292
Striations, twinning, 23
Structure, amorphous, 25
  crystal, 81
  crystalline, 3, 25
  of minerals, 25
Structure lines in synthetic corundum, 157
Styron, **111,** 282
Succinite, **278,** 298
Sunstone, **243,** 304
Suspension method, 36
Swindled stones, 104
Swiss lapis, **142,** 227, 244
Symmetrical extinction, 69
Synthetics, 3, **146-167**
  alexandrite, 155, 165
  aquamarine, 165
  chrysoberyl, 166
  corundum, 146, **150-163**
  diamond, 147
  emerald, 165
  ruby, 146, **150-163,** 166
  rutile, 166
  sapphire, 150-163
  spinel, 150, 163
  zircon, 165
Synthetic materials, value and uses, 166

T

Table, 100
  cut, 100, 108
Tektite, **259,** 306
Tenacity, 33
Tennite, 170
Terminated crystals, doubly, 92
  singly, 92
Tetragonal system, 13, 14, **18**
  trisoctahedron, 16
Tetrahedron, 16
Thermoluminescence, 39
Thetis hairstone, 223
Thomsonite, 42, **267,** 312
Thoulet's solution, 37
Thulite, **270,** 314
Tiger's-eye, 24, 46, **223,** 308
Titanite, 92, **268,** 312
Tone of color, 45
Topaz, 104, **206,** 222, 312
  false, 139, 143, 206, **222**
  gold, 143
  Madeira, 143, **206**
  oriental, **201,** 206
  precious, **207,** 312
  Scotch, 206
  smoky, 206, **222**
  Spanish, 139, 143
Topazolite, **212,** 304
Total reflection, **55,** 105
Touchstone, 229
Toughness, 33
Tourmaline, 42, 104, **233,** 312
  dichroism of, 76
  heat treatment of, 145
  varieties of, **235,** 312
Translucent mineral, 48
Transparency, 4, 44, **48**
Transvaal jade, 211
Trap brilliant cut, 106
Trap cut, 108
Trapeze cut, 106
Treated gems, 140
Triangle cut, 106
Triboluminescence, 39
Trichroism, 77, 295
Triclinic system, 14, **19**
Trigons, diamond, 181

Trimorphous substances, 90
Triplets, 140, **173**
Trisoctahedron, tetragonal, 16
Tully refractometer, 60
Turquois, 240, 314
  bone, 241
  Egyptian 241
  fossil, **241,** 314
  matrix, **241,** 314
Twentieth century cut, 105
Twins, 22

U

Ultramarine, 243
Uniaxial substances, 15, **64,** 69, 292
Unit cell, 83
Uralian emerald, **208,** 212, 304
Utahlite, **269,** 314
Uvarovite, 212

V

Value of diamonds, 124
Vargas diamond, 194
Variscite, 269, 314
Vein, 92
Venus hairstone, 43, **223**
Verd antique, **263,** 310
Verneuil process, **150,** 163
V. S. I., 125
V.V.S.I., 125
Vesuvianite, 269, 314
  jade, 231, **269**
Vinylite, **171**
Violan, **253,** 302
Vitreous luster, 47
Vogue, 5
Volcanic glass, **259,** 306
Volcanic rocks, 95

Vorobievite, 204
Vug, 93

W

Water chrysolite, 259
Water sapphire, 258
Wave-length, of light, 55, 57
  of X-rays, 55
Weight of gems, 134
Wesselton grade of diamonds, 124
Westphal balance, 36
Wheel, hardness, 28
Willemite, 270, 314
Williamsite, **274,** 310
Williamson mine, 190
Wiluite, 270
Wood, petrified, 23
  opal, 217
  quartz, 226

X

X-ray analysis, value of, 88
X-ray method, 83, 275
  Bragg, 84
  Laue, 83
  oscillation, 85
  powder, 85
  rotation, 85
X-rays, 49, 183
  wave-length of, 55

Z

Zircon, 79, 104, 143, **212,** 314
  blue, **143,** 215
  heat treatment of, 143
  synthetic, 165
Zoisite, 270, 314